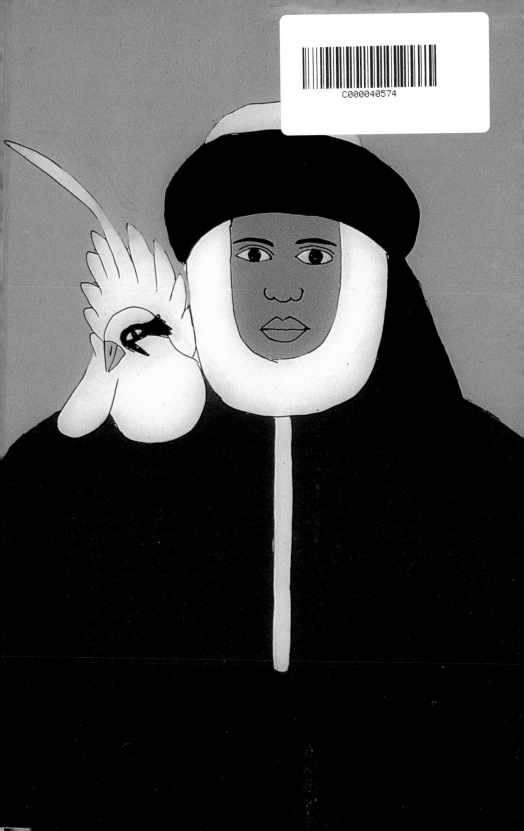

INSIGHT GUIDES

The world's largest collection of visual travel guides

The GAMBIA & SENEGAL

Edited by Philip Sweeney

Updated by Dorothy Stannard

Managing Editor: Roger Williams

Editorial Director: Brian Bell

APA PUBLICATIONS

Part of the Langenscheidt Publishing Group

INSIGHT GUIDES

The Gambia & Senegal

CONTACTING THE EDITORS: Although every effort is made to provide accurate information in this publication, we live in a fast-changing world and would appreciate it if readers would call our attention to any errors or outdated information that may occur by writing to us at Apa Publications,
P.O. Box 7910, London SE1 1WE, England.
Fax: (44) 171-403-0290.
e-mail: insight@apaguide.demon.co.uk.

First Edition 1990
First Edition (updated) 1996
First Edition (revised) 1999

Distributed in the United States by
Langenscheidt Publishers Inc.
46–35 54th Road
Maspeth, NY 11378
Fax: (718) 784 0640

Distributed in the UK & Ireland by
GeoCenter International Ltd
The Viables Centre, Harrow Way
Basingstoke, Hampshire RG22 4BJ
Fax: (44) 1256-817988

Distributed in Australia & New Zealand by
Hema Maps Pty. Ltd
24 Allgas Street, Slacks Creek 4127
Brisbane, Australia
Tel: (61) 7 3290 0322
Fax: (61) 7 3290 0478

Worldwide distribution enquiries:
APA Publications GmbH & Co. Verlag KG
(Singapore branch)
38 Joo Koon Road, Singapore 628990
Tel: 65-8651600
Fax: 65-8616438

Printed in Singapore by
Insight Print Services (Pte) Ltd
38 Joo Koon Road
Singapore 628990
Fax: 65-8616438

Discovery CHANNEL®

This guidebook combines the interests and enthusiasms of two of the world's best known information providers: Insight Guides, whose range of titles has set the standard for visual travel guides since 1970, and Discovery Channel, the world's premier source of nonfiction television programming.

The editors of Insight Guides provide both practical advice and general understanding about a destination's history, culture, institutions and people. Discovery Channel and its Web site, www.discovery.com, help millions of viewers explore their world from the comfort of their own home and also encourage them to explore it firsthand.

The Gambia and Senegal region is a perfect subject for the award-winning Apa Publications formula of presenting the full picture of a destination – the background to its life and traditions – rather than merely offering a tour guide's view of its territory. The colours, sounds and, above all, the culture and philosophy of West Africa's closest neighbours to Europe offer fascinating possibilities for discovery.

A team of specialists was assembled to piece together the mosaic at its most vivid. The original project editor, **Philip Sweeney**, a London-based writer and journalist whose work appeared regularly in several of Britain's national newspapers, visited West Africa frequently, partly to research a book on popular music of the world. He had also previously been commissioned, by *The Observer* newspaper, to visit Senegal and write a profile of the young singing star Youssou N'Dour, who was making news for his work with the rock singer Peter Gabriel.

Sweeney

The majority of the footwork – or, in this case, bush taxi work – was done by **Andy Gravette**, a travel writer who first visited Senegal and the Gambia more than 20 years ago as a special correspondent for the *Sunday Times* of London. Gravette contributes regularly to the Economist Intelligence Unit and produces articles, often supported by his own photography, to a variety of mag-

Gravette

Gueye

*Michael and
Elizabeth Kelly*

Whiteman

Renaudeau

Caswell

azines and periodicals. He is the author of books on Cuba, the French and the Netherlands Antilles.

For an insider's view of Dakar, as well as for the most authoritative accounts of the religious and ethnic composition of the region and of its arts, Sweeney approached the Senegalese television journalist and producer **Amadou Moctar Gueye**.

Gueye studied at the Universities of Dakar and Paris before taking a masters in Mass Communication at the University of Leicester, England, where he polished his English to the level required as presenter of the nightly English language news on Senegalese television. In addition to his television work and his frequent visits on press delegations to Europe and the rest of Africa, Gueye finds time to write books (his latest on *Communications and Politics in Africa*), participates in the running of Sud Communication, a Dakar press agency, and act as correspondent of the London specialist journal *West Africa*.

F ew analyst are better qualified to describe the political structures and conditions of the region than *West Africa*'s editor-in-chief **Kaye Whiteman**. One of London's most experienced and respected commentators on African affairs, Whiteman broadcasts regularly on the BBC and independent television channels as well as BBC World Service radio. A nine-year break from journalism as information officer for the Commission of European Communities in Brussels provided him with invaluable insight into the European perspective of interaction with Africa, not least during his work organising EC delegations throughout the continent. His publications include works on *Minority Rights in Chad* and the Lomé Convention.

If Whiteman has few peers in London on Senegambian politics, **Nim Caswell** is equally pre-eminent as an analyst of the region's economics. Caswell has been working on Africa since 1980, when she abandoned a career as a civil servant in the British Ministry of Agriculture in favour of writing and research. This took her first to Dakar, where she investigated

the downfall of the Senegalese groundnut marketing board, and thence to the BBC radio African Service. Four years as Africa Editor of the Economist Intelligence Unit followed, from where she moved to London's *Financial Times*. Caswell, who lives in north London, is also director of a marketing and consultancy firm specialising in Francophone Africa.

Michael and **Elizabeth Kelly** met Sweeney in Dakar where Michael Kelly was an English language teaching advisor attached to the Senegalese Ministry of Education. Having partaken of the Kelly's hospitality, shared their Land-Rover on trips to St Louis and Banjul and benefited from unerring taste and knowledge of the best places to sample Siné Saloum oysters or *thio farci à la Saint Louisienne*, he knew they were natural choices to guide discerning visitors to the region. Michael Kelly wrote the chapter on Banjul, where he moved from Dakar to advise the Gambian Ministry of Education. Apart from his career in education, Kelly is a published poet and writer of short stories and a translator of African song lyrics from Wolof into English.

Elizabeth Kelly, a qualified teacher, has also held posts in schools throughout the region. A keen cook who has written a book on African cuisine, she contributed the chapter on Senegambian gastronomy as well as painstakingly and meticulously assembling the Travel Tips section on the Gambia.

T he majority of the photographs for the book were supplied by **Michael Renaudeau**, a Paris-based photographer who, either personally or via his agency and publishing company, has been responsible for more than 20 books on countries throughout Africa, the Caribbean and the Far East. Renaudeau's unrivalled archive of photographs from Senegambia was built up over the 20 years he lived in Senegal,

Timeless though the region's beauty may be, events happen and attractions change. This edition of the guide, therefore, has been fully updated on the spot by **Dorothy Stannard**, senior executive editor in Insight Guides' London office.

<u>Preceding pages</u>: primitive artwork; adopting the local look; dressed to thrill on Kotu Beach, the Gambia.

CONTENTS

TRAVEL TIPS

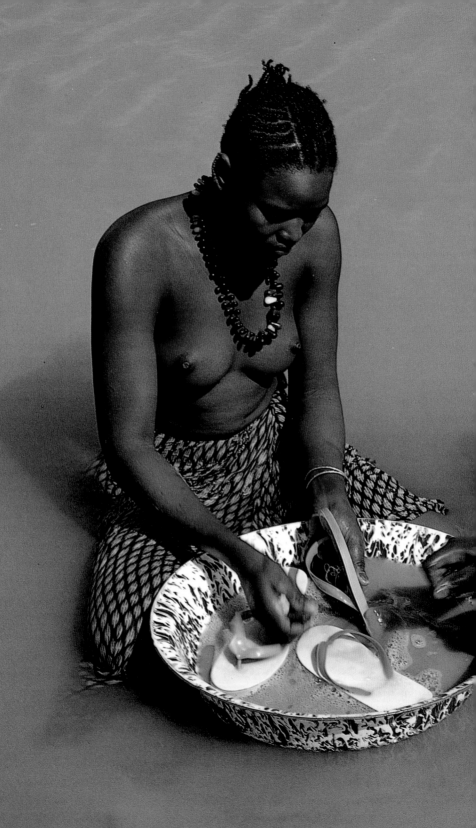

CLOSE – AND DISTANT TOO

You can travel to the Senegambia region by car from Europe – across the Mediterranean, south over the great Sahara and into Black Africa (budget for a month and a couple of good four-wheel-drive vehicles). Or you can fly the distance in six hours and be at a comfortable dining table overlooking a pool by suppertime on the day you leave.

The two methods illustrate the different extremes of the appeal of the region. It is exotic, redolent of the dark age of the slave trade and of the trans-Saharan camel caravans. At the same time, it is a thoroughly practical and convenient holiday destination, easily accessible to holidaymakers who want to see nothing more exciting than a hammock between two palm trees.

Preceding pages: sharing a joke on the bus home; washing sheep in St Louis; washing shoes in the River Senegal; pounding millet. **Left**, function follows form in the Sahel.

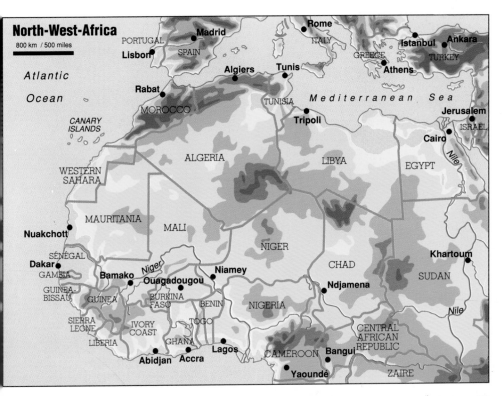

The Senegal Negro, male and female.

Engraved for the Encyclopædia Londinensis, 1818.

J. Chapman, Sc.

Before the Sahara Desert began to creep south and west, the great bulge of West Africa enjoyed a very different climate and landscape from today. Fossilised evidence shows that the land between the Senegal and Casamance rivers was once teeming with wildlife such as antelope and buffalo. Today descendants of those animals are conserved in a National Park near the source of the Gambia River.

Nomadic tribes, attracted by the profusion of game and lush vegetation of the river basins, began to migrate to the region by 800 BC. They established permanent settlements and a neolithic civilisation evolved, supported by a climate and environment conducive to a hunting and gathering lifestyle.

Left to their own devices, the Senegambian people developed their own kind of societies and religions. Sun-worship and belief in natural gods evolved as the people settled into a more established way of life, combining hunting and fishing with the cultivation of crops. A detailed picture of the beliefs and rituals of the ancient tribes is almost lost in the mists of time. We do know, however, that the supreme deity of West Africa at the time was Wulbari, or Nyankopon. This god, who controlled the sun, moon, darkness and blindness, was also known as Anansi.

Human sacrifice: In north Senegambia tribes worshipped Nyamia Ama, the god of rain, storms, lightning – and gold. In the south, people looked to the god Sene who was both kind and cruel. Also the god of rain, thunderstorms and rocks, Sene possessed the power to make the sun bright and to dim the moon.

Represented by a stool surmounted by an iron ball signifying a thunderbolt, the god Guruhi, in southern Senegambia, demanded human sacrifices and was said to torture his victims. His name derived from that of the god of war and of smiths, Gu in the south, Ogun in the north.

Other deities were Shango, the warrior/ magician god, Sagbata the god of disease, Famien of fertility, Akovodun, god of the

dead, and the panther god Agassu. Crocodile gods, tree fetishes, snake worship, river gods and social taboos were common to a network of connected civilisations across Senegambia. Such ancient animist beliefs still influence society today.

Mythology and magic mirrored everyday life and were well developed by around 500 BC when Hanno the Great, a Carthaginian navigator, visited the West African coast. In his *Periplus*, or Circumnavigating Voyage, he related encounters with elephants and hippopotami along the rivers he named "Chertes" (the Senegal) and "Bambotus" (the Gambia).

Less than 20 years after Hanno's visit, Euthymenes, a trader from Marseilles, voyaged around the "bulge" of West Africa, noting the mouths of the two rivers. By this time the Persian King Cambyses had occupied Egypt and, around 470 BC, the Persian Sataspes visited the Senegal River on a mapping expedition.

It was, however, Herodotus, the Ionic Greek historian, who gave the Senegambian region a name, "Garamandes". Tracing a short distance up the estuaries of both rivers, Herodotus noted that the natives practised "silent trade" with tribes which were hostile. Goods were left in a certain place to be exchanged by passing traders from alien tribes. Herodotus also remarked that local people made a wine from the palm tree, a tradition maintained to this day – nearly 2,500 years later.

Following Herodotus's expedition to coastal Senegambia in 445 BC, little was written about the region's exploration until some 300 years later when another Greek, Polyibus, visited Senegal's coast in 146 BC. Further inland, civilised cultures had established large, prosperous settlements such as the one at Jenne-Jeno.

Even by Polyibus's time peoples from the interior of Africa were trading with the coastal Senegalese and Gambian iron workers. Slaves were taken from among the river folk to trade with merchants from the Sahara and further north. Gold, salt and iron became currency along with iron, Phoenician glass beads and copper ornaments. Several of the

Left, early English engraving – the European's idea of the African.

central West African kingdoms were destined to affect the development of Senegambia, particularly as the River Niger rose in the same Futa Djalon mountain range as the Senegal and Gambia Rivers.

Trade in the inhospitable countryside, still covered by dense forest, jungle and bush, demanded the use of river traffic as a means of communication and exchange. Townships like Jenne, recently excavated, show 16 centuries of occupation and trade with isolated settlements on the coastline of Senegal and the Gambia.

Contemporary clay utensils and weapons, burial urns and children's toys discovered in Mali are more advanced than the primitive

tive tribes were forging their identities and, further east, larger groups were founding empires. The strip of Africa south of the Sahara was then known only as Sudan, comprising one region which spread from Egypt to the Senegal River.

It was in the area just east of the arc of the Senegal River that the first major West African civilisation, the Ghana Empire evolved, commanding a large territory of fertile land. Established around the end of the third century AD, it gradually spread west from its capital of Kumbi Saleh in what is now Mali, embracing the country of the Zenega in the north and of the Wolof and Serer peoples in the south. Gold, slaves and ivory were bar-

implements, tumuli graves and few ornaments found in Senegambia. In the millennium before the birth of Christ there was little change in the lives of the tribes between the two rivers.

The people who moved into north Senegambia were known as the Zenega, a branch of a Berber tribe from North Africa. The name Senegal may come from *Zenega*, although no conclusive explanation of the origin of the name is available – another common version is that the word comes from the Wolof *sunu gal*, meaning "our canoe".

Wicker shelters soon developed into more permanently established villages as primi-

tered for salt from the Saharan mines.

Located at a vital crossroads of African trade, the Ghana Empire flourished. Arab travellers described Ghana's king as "the richest man in the world". The Ghana Empire dominated part of Senegambia until the 10th century, during which time another kingdom was established by Soninke, or Tukulor, tribes. From around the 9th century, the Tukulors, who occupied the Senegal River Valley, established the powerful Tekrur Empire.

Early in its evolution, the Ghana Empire was introduced to metal smelting. Iron, in large quantities, was found along the banks of the Gambia River. The discovery of mysterious circles of laterite megaliths associated with an iron smelting civilisation and estimated to have been erected in AD 75 point to an advanced society based between the Gambia and Saloum rivers.

A new faith: Islam reached Senegambia in the 11th century, a cultural revolution that swept over the entire region. Conflict between Muslim Arabs and the Ghana Empire accelerated the spread of the new religion when, in 1076, Abu Bakr, leader of the Almoravid religious order, defeated the Empire of Ghana and allied his forces with those of the newly-founded Islamic Empire of Tekrur.

For almost 300 years the Mali Empire held sway over the leading tribes of Senegambia, to begin with under King Sundiata, and then under his famous grandson, Mansa Musa. Mali was an Islamic empire and once conquered by it the Wolof, Serer and Tukolor tribes were quickly converted to the Muslim faith as well.

Between Cape Verde and the Senegal River, Fulani invaders established a new empire during the 13th century. On the coast another, smaller kingdom emerged at the beginning of the 15th century. Known as the Kingdom of Djolof, it was controlled by the dominant Wolof tribe. Later, this kingdom was divided into Djolof, Walo, Cayor and

The influence of Islam was not readily accepted by native Mandé tribes living in the southern part of Senegambia. For a short while, an Empire known as Songhai, founded by Mandingo and Sussu tribes, controlled the region from the Futa Djalon mountains in the south to the Gambia River. Filling the void between Abu Bakr's Kingdom, which was based east of Senegambia, its land had extended from Niger to the West African coast between the Gambia and Sine Rivers by the year 1235.

<u>Left</u>, European world map, circa 1500. <u>Above</u>, Tuareg slaves.

Baol states. Meanwhile, the Fulani and Tukolor tribes had created a Muslim imamate in the east called Futa Toro.

Gradually, even the resistant Mandé tribes in the south adopted Islam. Seeing the benefits of land and power bestowed on favoured tribes which turned to Islam, the people south of the Gambia River consolidated against the northern tribes under Sunni Ali from 1464, and under Mohammed Askia the Great from 1493.

By this time, however, emissaries from Europe were beginning the exploration which was to have such a dramatic effect on the continent.

Africa
do mappamundi de
Juan de la Cosa
piloto de
Christovaõ colombo
em 1493 desenhado em 1500

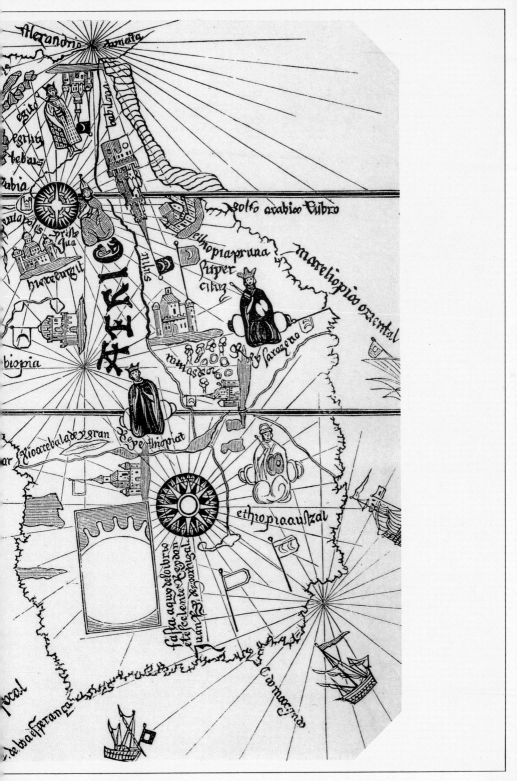

In the ceaseless search for trade and riches in the African continent, numerous early maps had been drawn up by the ancients. The first known chart of the Senegambian coast was drawn up in 141 AD. The Romans, by this time, were establishing themselves in Africa north of the Sahara and had introduced the camel to travel to sub-Saharan regions, expanding their trading routes. In 150 AD Ptolemy mapped their known world showing quite accurately the courses of the Senegal and Gambia rivers and locating a settlement he called Magiora, somewhere on the Senegal. This shows that even as the Romans were pushing Saharan tribes south, townships were growing up along the West African riverbanks.

Both the Phoenicians and the Vikings are thought to have drawn up sea charts of the West African coast in addition to the Romans' mapping of the settlements south of the Sahara. As the religion of Islam spread into Africa from around 622 AD the world's most expert cartographers, the Arabs, documented each conquest and converted settlement.

By 1076 Islam had crept into the area south and west of the Senegal River. With the expansion of trade and education which followed in its wake, detailed charts defined new territories as the faith encroached into pagan Africa. Islamic missionaries, waving a Koran in one hand and a scimitar in the other, were the first outsiders to explore Senegambia.

Imaginative charts: The first serious map of the region was produced in around 1300 by Abraham de Cresques. His cartographic efforts were based more on mariners' tales than on factual evidence and his map was soon superseded by a circular image of the globe made in 1307, the Mappa Mundi. Several of these early maps showing West Africa depicted kings seated on bejewelled thrones, glittering palaces and camel trains of treasure, images that inspired would-be explorers such as the Dieppois who are said to have reached Gorée Island in around 1364.

Indeed, much of the known world's gold did derive from West Africa during that period. As the imaginative illustrations of the cartographers actually materialised and gold began to filter back to Europe from the region south of the Sahara, explorers started to search for routes into the interior from the West African coast.

A leading light, master mariner and financier of ambitious expeditions was Prince Henry the Navigator of Portugal. One of the Portuguese king's champions, Nuno Tristão, reached the mouth of the Senegal River in 1443, and three years afterwards ventured another 200 miles (320 km) further south along the coast.

Another of Prince Henry's mariners, Dinaz Diaz, explored the Senegal River in 1444 and his contemporary Ca'da Mosto noted cotton, rice, exotic animals and the golden jewellery prevalent in the region on his journey up the Gambia River in 1465. He received slaves and gold from a local chief and Ca'da Mosto opened up both major rivers of the Senegambia for exploration and trade (the word Gambia is itself thought to come from *cambio*, meaning exchange in Spanish). It was the practice of barter which drew tribal traders to the coast and attracted merchants from Europe to venture into the West African interior. French traders first sailed up the Gambia River in 1570 and, by 1588, Antonio, Prior of Crato, had won exclusive trading rights throughout Senegambia from Queen Elizabeth I of England.

Black ivory, bitter battles: It was the early Portuguese traders who first developed the idea of sending labourers from Africa to the Americas. The cultivation of sugar cane, which the Arabs had introduced to Southern Europe, had become so important that new plantations were springing up as fast as fresh territory could be found and cleared.

The slave trade from Africa to the West Indies was part of a triangle of trade. Trinkets were shipped from Europe and exchanged for African slaves, who were sold to Caribbean plantation owners, producers of sugar, rum and tobacco destined for the markets of Europe. The business depended on easy access to the sea from harbours and ports on the

Preceding pages: map of Africa by Columbus's pilot, *circa* 1500. Left, Prince Henry the Navigator.

West African coast. Each settlement in the 1600s had its own "factory" or collecting station where slaves would be gathered to wait for the trading ships.

Each coast was named after its produce – the Gold Coast, the Grain Coast, the Teeth Coast (Ivory), the Gum Coast (Gum Arabic) and the Slave Coast. Even tribes were re-named according to their skills. The Kru, for example, were named for their rowing expertise. It is estimated that as many as 10 million slaves were shipped to the New World between 1526 and 1810. Brazil alone received more than three million as a result of Portuguese enterprise.

It was not only the Portuguese, Dutch, in black slavery, preferring to trade in Far Eastern spices, the English and the French had begun regular shipments of slaves from the Senegalese and Gambian coasts. The famous English sea-dog Captain John Hawkins took the first British slave ship to the West Indies in 1562. From that time on, local control of the slave trade alternated between French, Dutch and English entre-preneurs.

In 1617 the first permanent European trading settlement was founded by the Dutch West Indies Company at Gorée. By 1621 the French had dug in on the Senegalese coast at St Louis, and built a fort there. France also built a slave factory on the island of Bocos

English and French who were involved in the lucrative business of trading in "black ivory". It had long been African custom to take and enslave workers from other tribes conquered in battle, and Arab and African marauders had captured and traded in slaves for many centuries.

Although the English were comparatively late in the succession of nations to exploit the riches of Senegambia – the first Portuguese slave ship to leave West Africa for the Ameri-cas sailed as early as 1510 – Elizabethan mariners made up for lost time by organising trading expeditions backed by military force. By the time the Portuguese had lost interest

off the Cape Verde peninsula. The demand for black African slaves to work the Carib-bean sugar plantations was increasing and new slavery posts were set up at navigable points along the coast or on tidal waters of the major rivers.

French expansion was stimulated by the 1633 commissioning by Cardinal Richelieu of the Senegal Company. The Portuguese had built a trading post south of the River Gambia at Gereeja before the mid-17th cen-tury and this had been used by British trad-ers. Once Portuguese traders had established halfway posts at Gereeja and Tankular on the river's south bank they were in a position, by around the mid-1600s, to trade with Sukutu. Situated 250 miles (400 km) up the Gambia River, this Djolof city numbered 4,000 inhabitants in 1507. Gold from the interior, iron from the Gambia, slaves and gum Arabic were bartered by British, French and Portuguese traders.

Florence had been producing gold coinage since 1252, and the Almoravid dinar was the basis of both Spanish and Portuguese gold coins. Several Portuguese trading locations had been established in the region of the Senegal River and the English planned similar posts in the Gambia. At this time West Africa was supplying Europe with more gold than any other source.

bastions in the battles of the slave trade. The first fort on the island was built by the Duke of Courland, Germany, in 1651. For nine years the Duke traded from his island for slaves which he shipped to Tobago in the Caribbean. French privateers seized the island in 1659 but Courland recaptured it in the following year. In 1661 the English named the island after the heir to their throne – James Island (today, a visit to James Island is included in the "Roots" excursion run by Gambian tour companies).

The English were ousted by the Dutch the following year, having hardly had time to build the little fort. But they had made a deal that same year over Gorée Island with the

Charles II of England had heard the legends of "El Dorado", the fabled gold lands of West Africa, and his supporter Prince Rupert set off to explore the Gambian coast in 1652, attacking British Commonwealth shipping until the newly-founded "Royal Adventurers Trading in Africa Company" was established in 1661.

Island forts: The Portuguese first named a tiny island in the Gambia River estuary after a sailor who was buried there. Ilha de San André became one of the most strategic

Left, an Atlantic slave transport, 1844. **Above**, exercising slaves to keep them healthy.

Dutch (and the English kept a contingent at the island fort until the French conquered it in 1695). Again the English replaced the French usurpers in 1713 and held the position until 1719 when the privateer Hywel Davis ransacked the fort.

Six years after the pirate attack, a powder magazine blew Fort James into the river, necessitating another remodelling exercise. Not long afterwards it became redundant as a fort and was abandoned about 50 years later. In the 300 years of European occupation, James Island had changed hands at least 10 times.

Similarly, a tiny, baboon-infested island

ALEX HALEY AND "ROOTS"

One slave taken from the slave compound at Juffure to an American cotton plantation was called Kunte Kinte. Captured from his forest village as a small boy, the Mandinka youth could recall the circumstances of his kidnapping quite vividly. He remembered being taken to Juffure, his last walk on African soil, from the slave compound to the longboat, being hauled on board, his last glimpse of light and breath of fresh river air as he was bundled into the gaping hold, and finally the weeks below deck in stifling conditions with little or no food and water.

Separated from family, tribe and homeland, Kunte Kinte was sold to a plantation owner and put to work on the fields. The boy never forgot his

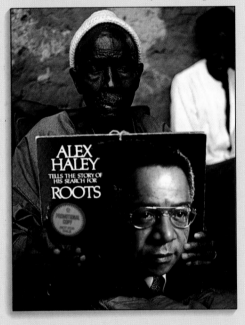

heritage in Africa. Every detail he put to memory and, in his mind retained the thoughts, sounds smells, rituals and traditions of family life back in the Gambia. More importantly, he passed on every detail to his sons, their sons and their sons in turn, until in the 1970s a respected American writer called Alex Haley traced his ancestry back to Kunta Kinte in his book *Roots*.

Reaping critical praise and soaring into the bestseller list, *Roots* earned Haley the Pulitzer Prize and made him a multimillionaire. The book sold one and a half million copies in its first 18 months, and the TV series that inevitably ensued was watched by 130 million people in America alone. In addition, the book became a seminal "black studies" text and Haley was invited to speak at campuses all over the US. The work inspired many black Americans to make pilgrimages to the Gambia, Senegal and Guinea in search of their own African heritage.

One of the book's biggest strengths, and selling points, was the 12 years of painstaking and exhaustive research Haley undertook before writing it. He travelled half a million miles and spent $80,000 tracking down the *griot* (oral historian) who related the story of a Mandinka boy called Kunta Kinte whose spirited resistance to the slave traders had passed into popular legend. He even booked passage on a freighter sailing between West Africa and the States, spending each night in the hold, so that he could better imagine what it was like to 'lie there in chains, in filth, hearing the cries of 139 other men screaming, babbling, praying and dying around you.'

Then, in 1993, 17 years after the book's publication, and a year after Haley's death from a heart attack during a public speaking enagagement in California, the 200-year saga that purported to be a true story was exposed as invention. The evidence against Haley was conclusive, drawn from Haley's own private papers and interviews with scholars and associates. There was no way the Kunte Kinte celebrated at Juffure could have been Toby, the slave owned by the John Waller family in Virginia and the hero of Haley's story. Records showed that Toby had been in America five years before the ship on which he was supposed to have travelled docked in America, and had been dead eight years before he was supposed to have fathered a daughter named Kizzy.

In spite of the expose, the "Roots" tour to Juffure, Albreda and James Island remains one of the most popular excursions for tourists to the Gambia. Its emphasis is on the slave trade in general, but it includes a visit to the Kinte compound at Juffure, helping to perpetuate the Haley myth. Alighting at the jetty, visitors make their way up to the central hut, a small child on every finger. There a woman named Kinte (a common name in the Gambia) is introduced as Kunte Kinte's last remaining descendant and a fading cover of an airline magazine depicting Haley with his long-lost relatives is passed around.

As the guide relates the village's story, small gifts, souvenirs and money change hands. The mood, however, is subdued. While visitors aware of Haley's fall from grace resign themselves to accepting the story's symbolic truth, the villagers barely conceal their bitterness that they haven't benefited in any substantial way from the lucrative Roots industry (and the obvious poverty of the mud and corrugated iron compound suggests their grievance is just). And now that the Roots myth has been exploded, perhaps even the steady stream of tourists, and their 10 Dalassi donations, will eventually dry up. ∎

near to James Island, also in a commanding position in the River Gambia, was fortified in order to protect slave shipping lanes. Dog Island, named after the barking of the baboons, was occupied by the English in 1666 and Fort Charles was established. Although impressive remains of the fortifications exist on James Island, nothing of Fort Charles is now visible on Dog Island.

Across a narrow stretch of the Gambia River from James Island there was another strategic outpost called Albreda by the French. Here they built a little slave trading station on the northern shores of the Gambia River in 1670. By 1681 France's soldiers had fortified the post and it was held until 1857.

base at St Louis in the far north of Senegal. Skirmishes over trade and territory occurred almost monthly during these times until, in 1677, the French Admiral, d'Estrées, drove the Dutch from Senegambia by capturing the Isle of Gorée (or Cape Coast Castle as the English called it).

The British Royal African Company was chartered in 1684 and the Royal Senegal Company was founded by 1696. By this time there were more then 10 main slave trading posts and forts in the Senegambian territory, including St Louis, Gorée, Rufisque, Portudal, Jaol, Albreda, James Island, Juffure and, on the Senegal River, Podor, Matam and Bakel.

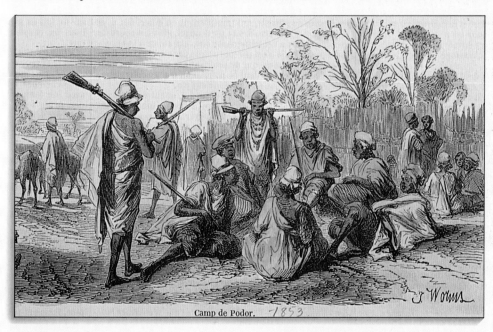

Camp de Podor. 1853

Just behind this French enclave in English territory, an English trading post was built at neighbouring Juffure in 1680. Twice the English forces overran Albreda, but they were only able to defend it against the French for a few months.

Further north, in Senegal, the Swedes had taken the island of Gorée in 1655, the Dutch having retired to Rufisque a few miles away. The Dutch had also constructed a "factory" at Arguin Island north of the Senegal River and the French had, by 1659, fortified their

By the late 1600s, the Portuguese had either been ousted from West Africa or had moved on to fresh trading grounds, and abandoned Portuguese factories were being rebuilt and fortified by the English. Several of these remain as ruins, signifying the extent of river trade in the early 1700s. Gereeja and Tankular on the south bank of the Gambia River, for example, are of particular note. Another fortification is at Tendaba, 62 miles (100 km) upstream from Banjul, and there is another at Berfet.

Slavery's lengthy demise: By 1758 the British had almost ousted the French but, by 1763, the French were back in Gorée. All this

THE WRECK OF THE *MEDUSA*

A tragic shipwreck off the coast of modern-day Mauritania, not far north of Senegal inspired one of the world's most celebrated works of art. Horrific details filtered through to 19th-century France of the loss of the brigantine *Medusa* on its way to Gorée, which had been restored by the Treaty of Paris to the French. In shark-infested waters many French families were drowned by the raging Atlantic waves. The ship had left the mother country in the summer of 1816 with 400 crew and soldiers on board as well as the new Governor of Senegal, going out to take up his post. Its lifeboats

the artist worked on his huge canvas. He was remarkably painstaking, going so far as to build a replica of the raft using details described by the few souls who survived the wreck. Géricault even invited individuals to pose for his sketches on the makeshift platform.

The painting, now in the Louvre, portrays a classical pyramid formation of the living and dead desperately clinging to the disintegrating raft. Because of the graphic depiction of the survivors, the French public were affronted. The storm of criticism paralleled the storm illustrated on the canvas when it was first shown in the "Salon of 1819", in Paris.

A famous artist of the day, Michelet, dubbed Géricault the "Corregio of suffering". Delacroix

were scandalously inadequate: they could cope with barely half the numbers on board.

Some survivors clung to wreckage in the vain hope of rescue away from regular shipping lanes, while 150 people took refuge on a large improvised raft. Only 15 were left alive when a passing ship picked them up weeks later. It was this desperate scene which caught the imagination of an eminent French painter.

Aided by numerous sketches, a few of which are in the Louvre Museum, Paris, and studies of corpses and human limbs made in the Hôpital Beaujon, Théodore Jean-Louis André Géricault created what has become one of France's most treasured exhibits. Between 1818 and 1819,

enthused over the painting as one of the first French Romantic period masterpieces to be exhibited. The giant canvas accompanied a travelling exhibition to England, where it received high acclaim.

Equal in technique, but simpler in subject matter, is Géricault's *Portrait of a Negro*, a vivid and moving portrayal of a young Senegalese. This noted classical study is now on show in the Denon Museum, Chalon-sur-Saône, France. Remaining, however, his most celebrated historical work, *The Raft of the Medusa*, initially named simply *Shipwreck Scene*, gives an insight into the reportage style introduced into French art by the master Géricault. ∎

time, the English had been keeping up a regular trade in slaves to the West Indies and penetrating further into the interior of West Africa. At the Treaty of Paris in 1763 France relinquished its hold on all but the slave factory of Albreda, and French troops were re-stationed north of the Gambia River. Asserting their pre-eminence on the coast, the English eventually controlled Senegal in 1765. The Crown Colony of Senegambia, the first British colony in Africa, was created by 1768.

But St Louis was given over to the French in 1776 and an attack on James Island from Gorée destroyed the entire fort, driving the British to concentrate on the south banks of the Gambia in 1783.

The advent of the 19th century should have been a relief for the indigenous inhabitants of West Africa, as public opinion began to rally around calls for abolition of the slave trade and Britain imposed a ban on slavery throughout its territories in 1807. Instead, the 1800s saw increasing racial and religious strife. The French continued to trade in slaves for another 41 years and, as the British Navy was entrusted with the task of cleaning up the "black ivory" business, they had ample excuse to harass the French along the West African coastline.

Without immense numbers of men, however, it was impossible for the British to prevent the Arabs and tribal chiefs from persisting in the lucrative trade. Although the French had introduced emancipation before the English it was only temporary and slavery returned with a vengeance on the orders of Napoleon in 1802. During the first few years of Britain's anti-slavery policy, more than 100 slave vessels were captured off the Gambian coast, bound either for Cuba or Brazil.

Resettlement townships were set up in the Gambia for slaves captured from the traders. Through this scheme it was discovered that some powerful tribes in the hinterland were selling off entire weaker tribes to traders from the French coast. The trade in slaves appeared to be actually increasing until the British founded an encampment at Banjul (Bathurst) from which to rid the coast of slavers. In 1816 Captain Alexander Grant

entered into a treaty with Kobo's chief for the island of Banjul, renamed St Mary's Island, which was eventually to become the Gambian capital.

From 1821 until 1843 the British territory on the Gambia River was ruled from Sierra Leone. In 1826 the strategic Point of Barra, opposite Bathurst was strengthened by the construction of Fort Bullen. In 1828 Grant negotiated for MacCarthy Island, which was later renamed Georgetown. Plots of land on the north shore were procured from local chiefs and groundnut production was introduced in 1829.

Both sailing and steamships had plied the waters of the four great rivers of Senegal and

the Gambia shipping goods far into the hinterland. Navigable for about 200 miles (320 km), the River Gambia narrowed after MacCarthy Island but still proved to be one of the most important waterways in West Africa. Trading with the far interior was facilitated through this point at the settlement of Georgetown. In Senegal, similar success had been achieved on the Casamance and Senegal Rivers which were also navigable for a considerable distance upstream. However, real exploration, governed not just by the opening up of trade routes, didn't begin in the Senegambia region until well into the 19th century.

Left, Géricault's *Radeau de la Méduse*. **Right**, shackles in the slave-house on Gorée.

"...So geographers, in Afric-maps,
With savage-pictures fill their gaps;
And o'er unhabitable downs
Place elephants for want of towns."
—Jonathan Swift 1667–1745

Long before Swift the satirist penned these words, European sorties into West Africa had opened up lands which lay adjacent to the larger rivers. Portuguese, Italian, French and Dutch expeditions had charted the Senegambia coastline and traced the courses of several major rivers. From the Mappa Mundi of 1307, the Lennox Globe of 1510 and European traders' charts of the early 17th century, the pattern of waterways, deserts, tribal villages and colonisers' settlements slowly evolved.

Few adventurers trekked far into the interior, however – unless, like George Thompson in 1619, it was to chart river banks. Thompson explored as far up the River Gambia as Tenda (Tendaba), around 60 miles (100 km). Just a year after Thompson's trip, Richard Jackson followed the English explorer's maps and succeeded in penetrating deep into the Gambia between 1620 and 1624. In search of legendary riches said to be located near the source of the river, Jackson wrote of his expeditions in his book *The Discovery of the Land of King Solomon* – the first detailed account of life in the Senegambian hinterland.

In Senegal, the French made little effort to venture into the country's interior, even though the Senegal, Siné and Saloum rivers were all comfortably navigable. Arab warriors from the Mauritanian wastes to the north and Moorish aggressors in the east deterred serious exploration. The region also harboured daunting diseases which decimated early settlers attempting to establish bases from which expeditions could be launched. For a century after Jackson's heroic voyage up the Gambia River only a few Europeans ventured further inland than the slave trading stations located near the estuaries of the Senegal and Gambia rivers.

Preceding pages: men of war off the West African Coast. Left, Mungo Park loses another jacket.

In the late 17th century, territorial squabbles between France and Britain deterred any real exploration, but it began in earnest as soon as tension died down. In 1723, the British adventurer Captain Bartholomew Stibbs was attracted to sail further up the Gambia in search of legendary gold mines near its headwaters.

Just 12 years after Stibbs another intrepid explorer, Francis Moore, published an account of his escapades in the Gambia in *Travels in the Inland Part of Africa, 1735*. Then in 1745 a British military expedition constructed one of the earliest up-country fortresses at Podor, Senegal. The British explorer Daniel Houghton made an epic journey up the Gambia River in 1790, crossing the Senegal and reaching the settlement of Simbing before being left to die in the desert by marauding Arabs. The place where he died was visited by the famous explorer, Mungo Park, six years later.

Park in the wilderness: The story of Mungo Park in West Africa is one of bravery and adventure. It typifies all that came to be thought of as stout and British in the Victorian age. With barely any knowledge of the area and equipped with archaic maps, the Scottish doctor took on the daunting task of searching for the source of the vast Niger River. Daniel Houghton (see above) had already sacrificed his life to the quest and it was this fatality which induced the African Association to support Park in his ambitious undertaking.

Park was no novice to the tropics, having been assigned at 21 years of age as medical officer on board the *Worcester* bound for Sumatra on the East Indies trade route from 1792–93. During his stay on the island the young surgeon studied Javan wildlife and its botanical curiosities. On 22 May 1795, having convinced the Association that he was the man for the job, Park boarded a vessel to Bathurst and from there proceeded up the Gambia River to Pisania (Karantaba). Here, 200 miles (320 km) inland, Park, who was still in his early twenties, spent five months learning the Mandingo language. Then, on horseback, and with two helpers at his side, he headed upstream. Today, an obelisk marks the spot where Park left the village in early December.

The story of the "Mambo Jambo" talisman has long been associated with Park's journey through eastern Senegal. Thought to be an idol in the shape of a grotesque snake – similar to the "Rainbow Snake" which is worshipped by tribes further down the West African coast – the talisman was used by the Woolli River people to regulate village disputes by making sacrifices to the image. Park's journals record that he found a mask of the Mambo Jambo spirit somewhere near Tambacounda, towards the confluence of the rivers Gambia and Kouloufou. His story of the rituals associated with the fetish so

was helped back to Pisania by friendly tribespeople.

In Pisania, Park sheltered in a "slave factory" and wrote an account of his first expedition. The book was published in 1799 under the title *Travels in the Interior Districts of Africa* and attracted considerable attention. The same year, the British Government invited Park to lead a party of 45 explorers along the route he'd taken from Pisania. Seven of his party backed out before leaving the Gambian outpost, but Park and the 38 remaining members struggled into the interior. From Bamako, on the Niger River in Mali, Park sent his last missive to the outside world in November 1805. The package con-

confused his listeners back in Britain that the phrase *mumbo jumbo,* meaning hocus pocus or superstitious rigmarole, was introduced to the English lexicon.

Park pressed on eastwards. The following year, 1796, Moorish Arabs imprisoned his company in Upper Senegal. Escaping his captors on 20 July Park reached Ségou in Mali on the Niger River. Eventually he ran out of food and essential supplies in a place called Silla. From here he travelled alone, reaching Kamalia (Kourémalé), south of Bamako in the Kingdom of Malinke, where he was taken ill and came close to dying of a tropical fever. But seven months after this he

tained letters and his journal, giving accounts of native domestic life, and natural history notes.

Pressing ever further up the Niger, Park and his nine surviving companions were ambushed by a band of natives and killed. Only one slave oarsman of the canoe in which the expedition travelled made the journey back to Pisania, where he related the story of the disaster to the Gambian trading station in 1812.

An account of Mungo Park's second journey to the Niger River was published in London shortly afterwards, in 1815, and several years later Park's son died in an attempt to discover the whereabouts of his father's remains. Mungo Park was significant for his persistence, the clarity and abundance of his observations of native life and customs and, above all, for his discovery that, unlike any other West African river, the Niger, which rises in mountains adjacent to the sources of the Gambia and Senegal, does, in fact, flow east.

In Park's footsteps: An unsuccessful attempt to reach the important Saharan trading town of Timbuktu was made by the French explorer René Caillé in around 1816, the same year in which an English expedition managed to reach the town of Bakel. A few years later, between 1819 and 1822, J. Ritchie and

G.F. Lyon made an expedition through Gambia and Senegal in search of the source of the Niger. Following them, a succession of Victorian explorers ventured inland – Dixon Denham, Hugh Clapperton, Walter Oudney and, in 1825, Major Alexander Gordon Laing, whose company reached Timbuktu.

Meanwhile Caillé twice returned to the seaport of St Louis in Senegal to replenish expedition funds from the coffers of the Governor, Baron Roger. It was not until 1827 that Caillé, disguised as an Arab trader,

Left, **Mungo Park crosses the Niger. Above**, **René Caillé en route to Timbuktu.**

eventually reached Timbuktu. By this time naturalists were increasingly visiting West Africa in order to obtain specimens of plants and wildlife. Hardly plentiful in Senegambia, but certainly more widespread during the early 19th century, Africa's greatest beast, the elephant, roamed forest and river areas causing fear among early explorers and exiting wildlife experts.

A hunter named Schmidt, with the support of the French authorities, managed to capture a live elephant. Triumphantly the animal was shipped to Paris and exhibited in the Zoological Park. In 1865 the elephant, which was named "Jumbo", was presented to the London Zoological Gardens – the first African elephant to reach the United Kingdom and the longest-living elephant ever kept in captivity.

A number of ambitious adventurers were still searching for either the source of the Niger, elusive gold mines, or simply the fame attached to making new discoveries right through the 19th century. The German explorer, Heinrich Barth, made excursions in the area between 1849 and 1855; French explorer Henri Duveyrier travelled inland during the 1850s, followed by another German, Gustav Nachtigal from 1869 to 1874. Gerhard Rohlfs pursued a number of ancient trade routes from 1862 to 1878 and Oskar Lenz entered the headwaters of the Senegal River in 1879–80, tracing it down its estuary.

The great adventurer Sir Richard Burton, who visited the Gambia in 1863, gave a lengthy account of his travels in *Wanderings in West Africa from Liverpool to Fernando Po*. He wrote the book under the pseudonym FRGS (Fellow of the Royal Geographical Society). In his account he referred to the region as "the white Man's grave" and an "anti-paradise". Thirty-five years later, Mary Kingsley, in *Travels in West Africa,* commented: "When you have made up your mind to go to West Africa the very best thing you can do is to get it unmade again and go to Scotland instead!"

Whatever the impressions those early explorers had of this part of the African continent, it was their persistence which brought Senegambia to the notice of a wider world. The arrival of river steamers and the construction of railways – the first of which was the Dakar to St Louis line in 1886 – brought an end to the period of discovery.

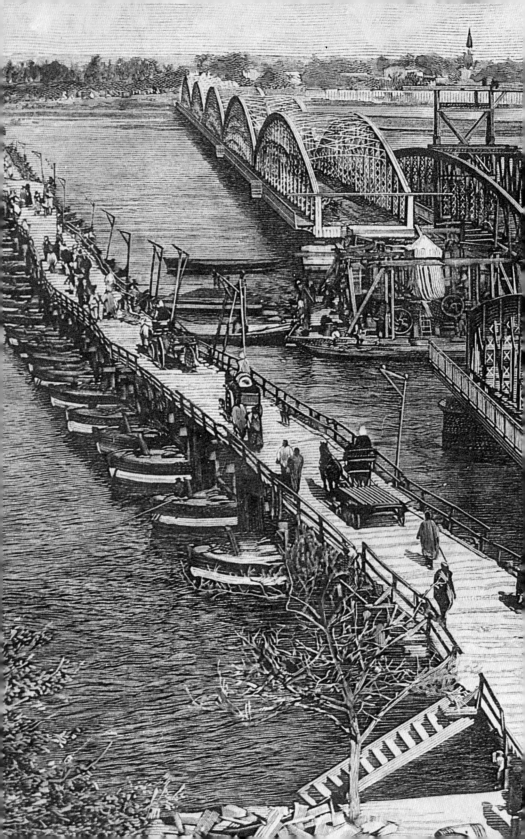

"*Ex Africa semper diquid novi*" wrote Pliny in his encyclopaedic *Natural History*. ("There is always something new coming from Africa.") Colonialism proved the Roman philosopher right. Ancient Rome was the first power to colonise North Africa but it was French and English colonialism in Senegal and the Gambia which underlined Pliny's comment 2,000 years on.

British and French colonists faced similar hurdles in West Africa: either opposition from the native inhabitants or difficulties in administrative development. In Senegal, the story of Governor Louis Faidherbe illustrates the problems and successes of colonialism in West Africa.

Born in Lille, France, in 1818, Louis-Léon-César Faidherbe found himself in 1852 in a country where his exploits would bring him fame. After two years in Senegal the Deputy Director of Engineers was promoted to Major and appointed Governor of the colony. Flouting orders from Paris, Faidherbe took the initiative against opposition from Tukulor chiefs like El Hadj Omar.

Across Senegal, Islamic African leaders such as Samori and Lat Dyor were conducting a *jihad*, or holy war, against the largest colonial presence in Africa. With a strong base in Dakar and a series of strategically placed forts and trading posts across the colony, Faidherbe set about negotiating terms with the tribes.

Marabouts versus the military: Since the advent of Islam the *marabouts*, or religious leaders, had exercised enormous power throughout North and West Africa. In Senegal these leaders stirred up an animosity against the French which had endured since 1798, when the Tidjaniya sect had appeared on the scene from North Africa. Other sects, such as the Mourides and the Khadriya, participated in what were known as the Marabout Wars against the foreign colonialists. The running battles between the *marabouts* and the military spread into the Gambia between 1850 and 1887, although fighting

Preceding pages: building the Faidherbe Bridge, St Louis. **Left**, Faidherbe's statue in St Louis. **Right**, a *signare* and her servants.

there amounted to little more than a series of skirmishes.

The Marabout Wars delayed and hindered exploration of both Senegal and the Gambia after slavery had been abolished in Senegal in 1848. Governor Faidherbe instigated many exploratory ventures into the interior provoking battles with warring tribes and necessitating a series of forts at strategic points throughout the region.

In 1857 Faidherbe founded Dakar and the same year the French relinquished Albreda

to the British. From this time both the French and the English pushed deeper into their respective, barely explored, territories.

Faidherbe had likened the Senegambia region to Canada or India and planned his strategies with this in mind. Saving Napoleon III the expense of another Mexican or Indo-Chinese campaign, the young Governor set his enemies against each other, even getting his arch-rival, Lat Dyor, to fight for the French in 1870.

Over a period of 37 years from 1850, a Pan-Islamic surge encroaching from the north set local tribes and even families against each other. Faidherbe quelled numerous up-

MERMOZ AND THE AVIATORS

The world began to open up to Europeans in a dramatic way with the advent of commercial air travel in the 1930s. Imperial Airways (the forerunner of what would eventually become British Airways) flew south and east to Egypt, East Africa and India. Regular flights to New York from Europe made North America more accessible and, in the late 1920s, airlines even considered flights to South America. But at this stage a direct, non-stop flight from Europe to Brazil remained impossible as early aircraft had a limited range.

But Senegal and the Gambia lie almost exactly half-way between London (or Paris), and Recife (or Rio de Janeiro). Ideal locations for crew and refuel-

company was operating regular flights by airship and Dornier flying boat across the Atlantic from Germany to the United States, but the growing demand for a fast route to South America prompted the construction of an airfield on the site at Jeshwang.

Jeshwang airfield, as this piece of land was called, was Lufthansa's West African base for four years, until the outbreak of World War II. The first Zeppelin stopped over here in 1934 on its inaugural flight from Frankfurt to Brazil. Both airships and Dornier aircraft were employed by the German airline on this route until 1938. (The remains of the old Jeshwang airfield now form part of an industrial park just off the Bakau turn-off on the Banjul–Serekunda road.)

British South American Airways' flying boats

ling stop-overs, both St Louis – Senegal's capital in the 1930s – and Bathurst (now Banjul) in The Gambia, the furthest points west on the African continent, became important air staging posts for the inter-continental flight.

A French aviator, Jean Mermoz, was the first to open air routes from Paris to Senegal, and from there to South America. Aeropostale's depot was established on the narrow spit of land between St Louis and the Atlantic Ocean. Mail was delivered from Guet N'dar's point – now known as the Hydrobase – to within just 2 miles (3 km) of the mailing station.

Lufthansa, the German airline, purchased a piece of land in the Gambia, just outside the capital of Bathurst (now Banjul), in 1932. Already the

established a link to Brazil in the latter part of the 1930s and their aircraft also used the Jeshwang airfield. In 1939, a crash killed 23 people and brought services to a halt. During World War II the British Royal Air Force needed an effective base in West Africa and The Gambia was strategically very suitable. Twenty Sunderland flying boats operated a shipping protection service from Banjul itself throughout the war and the RAF constructed two landing strips at Yundum, 17 miles (27 km) from the capital.

Five years later, the new replacement airport at Yundum, which is today the Gambia's only airport, was visited by President Franklin D. Roosevelt on his way to Brazil. Senegal, by contrast, today has eight airports. ∎

risings incited by the *marabouts* by systematically establishing forts along the Senegal River. The Governor's theories of "assimilation" were adopted by his successor, Admiral Jauréguibéry, who pushed French boundaries as far as Niger by the year 1880.

Faidherbe had ensured his name a place in the history books of African colonialism. Almost as prominent is the place of his fiercest adversary, El Hadj Omar Tall, who returned from a youthful pilgrimage to Mecca fired with a zealous desire to convert his pagan home region to Islam. During his brilliant but brutal 40 year warrior career, he succeeded in forcibly converting a vast tract of Senegal and Mali before Faidherbe finally

to learn that, in the year of his death, 1889, the British negotiated control of the River Gambia. In the same year, the Casamance area, south of the Gambia River, belonging to Portugal, came under Senegalese jurisdiction, thus surrounding British Gambia with French territory.

French expansion in Africa: By 1900 France had extended its colonial power in Africa as far east as Niger, into Dahomey, Chad, the Ivory Coast, Guinea, Upper Volta and north into parts of Mauritania, Algeria and Tunisia (Morocco came later) – a total land area of around 3.29 million sq. miles (8.52 million sq. km and the largest foreign colonial region on the African continent.

crushed him with a coalition of French and African forces.

Louis Faidherbe went on to higher roles in French politics and was instrumental in raising funds for the first railroad in Senegal – from Dakar, the city he founded, to St Louis. Dedicated to the emancipation champion, Victor Schoelcher, Faidherbe's best known book, *Le Senegal, la France dans l'Afrique occidentale* (1889), describes his objective of creating a truly Francophone African state and his work as Governor of Senegal.

Faidherbe would have been disappointed

From the mid-19th century France had granted privileges to its favourite protectorate in Africa. Law decreed that any Senegalese born in the townships of St Louis, Gorée, Rufisque and Dakar automatically became full French citizens. In addition, each region was entitled to locally elected representation in the French parliament.

As part of the "assimilation" process of adopting its Senegalese subjects into French society and politics, the country's first deputy was elected to the French parliament in 1848, serving until 1852. The post became permanent in 1871 but it was not until 1914 that the first African was elected to deputise.

Above, St Louis quay in its heyday.

His name was Blaise Diagne. Born in 1872, he held the post for 20 years, until 1934.

The sliver of land flanking both shores of the Gambia River followed suit. The Gambia had been plagued by civil disturbances and *marabout* uprisings prior to the British and French destruction of the *marabout* fort at Sukuta (Sabiji) near present-day Banjul. At times the country was placed under the jurisdiction of Freetown in the British colony of Sierra Leone.

In 1852, the embryo of the current House of Representatives, the Gambian parliament, was established with both Gambian and white members and Sierra Leone ceased to administer the colony. The British in Gambia had

not had the continuing problem of slavery since its abolition there in 1807, but it was as late as 1895 that the last local leaders and chiefs agreed, with some reluctance, to desist from the practice of keeping slaves.

By the turn of the century, both Britain and France had quelled the native populace sufficiently to establish viable colonies. The French in Senegal had smoothed out most local and racial boundaries, maintaining a strict control through networks of forts and trading stations.

Preoccupation with colonial issues blinded both sides to economic development. It was not until the construction of the first railway,

instigated by Faidherbe, the Governor of Senegal, that commerce began to benefit the region. Trains swiftly covered distances which took road or river traffic much longer. With the completion of the Dakar–St Louis line in 1886 a network of rail routes began to take shape, with major townships linked to the coastal ports.

During the latter half of the 19th century great strides were made in opening up the interior, thanks to the tenacity of successive intrepid explorers backed by military might. Faidherbe was also responsible for an upturn in the region's economy by promoting the groundnut (otherwise known as the peanut) – introduced in the 16th century by the Portuguese, with manioc and maize from Brazil – into a cash crop.

Towards independence: The entire territories of French West Africa were governed from St Louis on the Senegal River until, in 1902, Dakar became the administrative capital on account of its central and coastal location. By 1920 the communes of Dakar, Gorée, St Louis and Rufisque boasted a "colonial council" which consisted not just of local dignitaries and representatives but also tribal chiefs from the interior.

During World War II many Gambians were enlisted to fight for the British, mostly in Burma, while companies of Senegalese infantry swelled the ranks of the French. Just after the war, in 1946, France extended the offer of French citizenship to the colonies, making all French West African states full overseas territories. The same year Léopold Senghor, aged 40, became the first African to sit in the French National Assembly as representative of Senegal. In 1947, and again in 1954, the constitution of the Gambia underwent changes.

Two years later, in 1956, universal suffrage was established in Senegal under the *loi-cadre* reforms aiming at the eventual formation of an independent government. Between General Faidherbe's vision of a wholly French enclave slotted into the map of West Africa and Captain Alexander Grant's earlier attempts to form a liberated coastline, the mould was being created in which two fully independent countries would be formed.

Left, colonial architecture in Thiès. Right, Lat Dyor in full cry.

Senegal never expected to enter independence as a single country. Because Dakar had been the capital of France's West African Federation (*Afrique Occidentale Française*, the AOF), nearly all Senegal's political leaders had favoured maintaining the federation in some form.

On the one hand, Senegal had infant industries that needed the wider hinterland the federation offered; on the other, Dakar itself was a big city designed as the capital of a much wider unit than simply Senegal, and has always seemed top-heavy in relation to the rest of the country. It also housed a large bureaucracy designed for a federation, so although most of the other nationals returned to their territories on the break-up of the federation eager for the new challenges independence would bring, Senegal's main problem in the years of independence was adjusting downwards.

Senegal actually became independent on 4 April 1960 as part of the Mali Federation. This federated the territories of Soudan (now Mali) and Senegal, and was all that was left of the eight-territory AOF after its collapse in 195858. At that time autonomy was largely devolved to the territorial capitals, and Guinea dealt Charles de Gaulle's proposed Franco-African community a body-blow by taking full independence. It was at this time that the nationalist leader (and later despot) of Guinea, Sekou Touré, made his famous speech in front of the visiting de Gaulle.

Touré opted on behalf of his country for independence and poverty over what he considered to be demeaning reliance on France. The subsequent French withdrawal from Guinea was complete, involving the virtual dismantling of the country's infrastructure. The rumour – true or not – that certain officials even took the light bulbs with them was quoted at the time as an example of alleged French pique.

Power struggle: The Mali Federation, named after the ancient African empire, lasted four and a half months before internal stresses

forced a power struggle. This caused the Senegalese to secede from the federation on 20 August, creating two separate republics, Senegal and Mali. Modelled on General de Gaulle's 1958 Constitution of the Fifth Republic in France, it provided for a president, prime minister and a national assembly elected by universal suffrage.

The first President of the Republic, Léopold Senghor, thus came to power in a political crisis. He experienced several more over the first decade of independence, although in

the end his position was consolidated.

In December 1962 he faced a major challenge to his authority from his Prime Minister, Mamadou Dia, in a power struggle in which Senghor dismissed Dia (who claimed the party had sovereignty over the state), and then tried and jailed him for treason. Following the crisis, the constitution was changed in a referendum so that the Prime Ministership was abolished and the president became chief executive with individual powers. An even greater challenge to Senghor's leadership occurred in May 1968 when a combination of student-worker demonstrations (echoing those in Paris of the same month) para-

Preceding pages: flag-portrait of Senghor, Senegal's first president. Left, patriotic majorette, Dakar. Right, the Senegalese national flag.

THE POET WHO REWROTE POLITICS

Among all the African leaders of the independence generation, Léopold Sédar Senghor enjoyed a special position. Others may have equalled and even surpassed his international prestige, or have been more loved by their peoples, but Senghor's place in history came from the way he managed to combine the role of writer and poet with that of practical politician and statesman.

He was also that rare phenomenon, a successful intellectual in politics. This gave him that sense of historical perspective which enabled him to see the need to withdraw from political power in good order and prepare his succession. Senghor (born 1906)

has always taken delight in his mixed ancestry (part Serer, part Mandinka, part Peul, with a name derived from the Portuguese Creole culture of Casamance). It was the perfect expression of his notion of cultural *métissage* (cross-breeding), a recurrent idea in his writing and thinking.

His education, initially with the Holy Fathers in Senegal and, after 1928, as a student of literature at the Sorbonne in Paris, instilled a profound appreciation of French culture. Critics who have singled him out as a black Frenchman have failed to appreciate his basic duality. The philosophical and literary movement *négritude* which he helped to launch in Paris was a reaction to the weight of the French culture he had experienced. And, although an uncompromising theory of the assertion of black African values, *négritude*

still bore the mark of a Parisian literary movement. Much of Senghor's intellectual, literary and even political career revolved around both promoting and redefining *négritude* – an expression which, although he did not invent it, will always be linked to him.

After studying, he stayed in France as a teacher. A supporter of General de Gaulle (in part as reaction to the racism of Hitler and of the Vichy regime), he was taken prisoner of war in 1940. With the Liberation he entered politics, building on the prestige attached to his reputation as the first African to achieve the academic qualification of *agrégation*, qualifying him to teach in a *lycée*. In 1945 he was elected one of the two deputies of Senegal in the French National Assembly, from where it was a short step to ascendancy in Senegal's complex web of party politics. He was also leader of one of two groups of Africans in the assembly in Paris, and was a minister in the 1955 government of Edgar Faure.

When Senegal acheived independence, Senghor became its first president of Senegal. He experienced the full drama of life at the top of the greasy political pole, going through a series of crises before establishing confident supremacy over the Senegalese political scene. The high level of political consciousness among Senegal's diverse and numerous educated élite makes it a particularly difficult country to run, with a volatility that changes from week to week.

Senghor used his own intellectual reputation, and his undoubted access to French political circles, for all they were worth, but he also became a master of Machiavellian manoeuvre, the *politique politicienne* he affected to despise. While the support of the French was important at key moments, he knew he needed to retain the allegiance of the *marabouts*, the leaders of the Islamic brotherhoods dominant in the rural areas of the country. Although for a time he alienated the *marabouts* over problems with groundnut production, he was able to use his Catholic faith to present himself as a neutral force between the different powerful brotherhoods.

Senghor always stressed the importance of culture as the basis of politics, and the vibrancy of Senegal's culture owes much to his patronage – seen, for example, in the first world festival of Black Arts held in Dakar in 1966, arguably Africa's most successful large-scale arts festival. Sometimes his intoxication with ideas made him seem remote, especially when he took up with the "universal civilisation" idea of Father Teilhard de Chardin. His advocacy of *la francophonie* (a colonial language, after all) seemed questionable to some Africans. His rationale was, in part, that it was a way of tying Europe to Africa, fitting in with another concept he advocated – Eur-Africa, two continents tied together in symbolic relationship.

After retiring from politics in 1980 he became the first black member of the French Academy in 1984. His poetry ranges from lyrical evocations of an idealised Africa (*Songs of the Shade*, 1945) to themes of cultural conflict in *Ethiopiques* (1956) ∎

lysed the government. Senghor depended on the armed forces to stay in power (the armed forces stayed more or less solidly behind Senghor as a result of a defence agreement with France and the presence – psychologically important – of a French base in Dakar).

Senghor also drew strength from the endorsement given to his regime by the Islamic brotherhoods, especially the Khalif-General of the Mourides. In 1968 the Mourides mobilised their supporters from the countryside to rally behind Senghor against what was primarily an urban disaffection.

After the turbulence of the 1960s, the 1970s were a period of consolidation for Senghor. But the education sector – the teachers' un-

count of the respect Africans traditionally accord to age.

When, in 1980, he decided to announce his retirement, what had at times appeared to be a highly volatile political situation had become relatively stable. Predictions of a violent demise of the regime proved unfounded, and the mere fact of Senghor's voluntary retirement created a more favourable climate for his chosen successor. This was Abdou Diouf, a technocrat who had served a long apprenticeship of 10 years as Prime Minister, a post which Senghor had reintroduced in 1970 in order to free his time for affairs of state, especially foreign policy (ironically Diouf abolished the prime minis-

ion, the University of Dakar in particular, and even the schools – continued to be a focus for discontent.

Having beaten back organised political opposition either by assimilating or banning other parties, Senghor was strong enough by 1974 to permit one legal opposition party, then two, and finally three while trying to dominate the centre-left by changing the name of the ruling party to Parti Socialiste (PS). The President's advancing years also helped consolidate his supremacy, on ac-

tership himself in 1983 in order to strengthen his own powers).

A new president: In his first two years in power, Diouf enjoyed a real honeymoon. He was helped by Senghor's complete withdrawal from politics, and by the presence at his side of Jean Collin, a French-born Senegalese with vast experience of both administration and politics, who has held the key position of Secretary-General to the government for all the Diouf years.

The favourable start of Diouf's rule also came from his lifting of Senghor's restriction on the number of political parties to three. This permitted Senegal to describe

Left, Léopold Sédar Senghor. **Above**, Dakar's Assemblé Nationale.

itself as a multi-party democracy. By 1985, there were 17 political parties.

The image became tarnished, however, after the 1983 elections, when there were widespread allegations of rigging. In the view of most observers Diouf would have won the election anyway, but he was handicapped by the activities of his own party.

Much of the history of the Diouf years has concerned the President's struggles with the barons within his own party. If Diouf has been able to dominate the party old guard, he still has difficulty adapting himself to the special skills needed to survive in politics.

This was seen again in the elections of 1988. Although his victory was probably

heavy-handed police raids on the campus took place, students had both sufficient liberty and sufficient motive to organise a lengthy protest movement. The strikes of 1988 were sparked by a relatively trivial matter – a disciplinary measure against a student in Thiès – but rapidly escalated into an expression of dissatisfaction with a whole range of issues.

The most basic complaint centred on what President Diouf with some justification described as an economic rather than a political problem. The decline of the economy had increased pressure on the education system. Equipment and books were more and more inadequate or non-existent, and fewer teach-

more honestly won than in 1983, it led to an outburst of violence by disappointed opposition supporters. The frustrations of a worsening economic situation seemed to produce a higher risk of social conflict. Again, the education sector was the most troublesome.

The unrest in the schools and university during the months leading up to the 1988 election is worth examining, as it gives an insight into the political and social feel of the country. In few other African nations does one see such a degree of student politicisation – not least because it would be crushed more brutally elsewhere.

In Dakar University, although a number of

ers were faced with larger classes. At the same time decreasing job prospects were undermining the sense of purpose of the whole system.

The student strikes turned into a general movement of opposition to the government. The leader of the opposition (Parti démocratique sénégalais – PDS), Abdoulaye Wade, was arrested for incitement. It was only after his trial, when he was released with a suspended sentence in May 1988, that tension relaxed. But student unrest worsened again in 1991, and a new strike at Dakar University lasted until February 1992. Meanwhile Abdoulaye Wade pressurised the government into granting the opposition access to the state-owned media; the prime ministership was restored in 1991; and a series of constitutional concessions included a new law limiting the president to a maximum of two terms of office.

Nonetheless elections in February 1993 returned Diouf to the presidency, with 58.4 percent of the votes cast. Regaining the initiative, the government introduced a series of stringent austerity measures to try to reduce the budget deficit. These included cutting public sector workers' pay by 15 percent, and docking one day's pay a month from workers in the private sector. Though these measures were reversed in 1994 fol-

tained violence between guerrilla fighters and the government has caused migration into Gambia and Guinea-Bissau and has had a detrimental effect on the formerly thriving tourist industry there.

The Gambia: In the Gambia, independence came five years later than in Senegal. It was the last British colony in West Africa to attain independence – mainly because it was the smallest and poorest British colony and the British had doubts about its economic viability.

However, the wave of independence that rolled through Africa in 1960 (including especially Senegal) and the independence in the following year of Sierra Leone encour-

lowing devaluation of Senegal's currency, the CFA franc, by 50 percent, they provoked widespread demonstrations, as did the devaluation itself. In August 1994 the 1993/94 academic year at Dakar University was declared invalid because of the disruption caused by student unrest.

Aside from economic problems, the Senegalese government is wrestling with separatist demands by the Diola people in the Casamance area, a region effectively cut off from the rest of Senegal by Gambia. Sus-

Above, President Abdou Diouf inspects the Guards in London.

aged the Gambia to consider breaking its ties with Britain. The option of closer links with Senegal – even leading to a merger – was mooted, but contacts (discreetly encouraged by both the British and French) foundered when it came to working out power-sharing arrangements. Thus the Gambia became an independent sovereign state on 18 February 1965, with Dawda Jawara (a trained veterinary surgeon) as Prime Minister and a "Westminster-model" constitution. As Sir Dawda (he was knighted in 1966), he became President when a republic was proclaimed in 1970. He had been Chief Minister since the success of his ruling PPP (People's Progressive Party) in the first universal franchise elections in 1961.

President Jawara faced his first major crisis on 29 July 1981, when elements in the Field Force, the paramilitary arm of the police (the Gambia until 1981 had no army), attempted a coup, which left 500 dead and was accompanied by ransacking and looting. The coup attempt was quelled with the assistance of Senegalese troops, invited in under a defence and cooperation treaty. But the violence of the event produced a reaction in favour of established authority, and dented Jawara's image.

Although the PPP was able to resume its dominance and continued to win elections,

the shadow of 1981 lingered. In its wake came the formation of the confederation of Senegambia in 1982. For the next three years protocols were agreed on common policies in the field of defence and security, external relations, communication and information. The protocol of defence was particularly significant for the Gambia. It provided for a new Gambian Armed forces, with a small gendarme equipped by France and trained by the Senegalese.

Limited though it was in scope, the confederation made sense in many ways, not least of them economic. It was totally unexpected, therefore, when the short-lived un-

ion was summarily abandoned as "a waste of time and money" by President Diouf in 1989 in response to a critical speech by Jawara.

Following the confederation's dissolution relations between Senegal and the Gambia deteriorated, with disagreements focusing on cross-border smuggling. These culminated in 1993 when Senegal closed its borders with the Gambia, effectively blocking Gambia's trade with neighbouring countries. Though borders subsequently reopened, relations between the two countries remained wary. In the meantime Jawara forged a defence cooperation agreement with Nigeria and a Nigerian national was made head of the Gambia's national gendarmerie and army.

The 1994 coup: In July 1994 another military coup succeeded and President Jawara was ousted from his post after 24 years. The coup was bloodless (tourists in the Gambia at the time are said to have hardly noticed) and apparently welcomed by the Gambians, notwithstanding the extreme economic hardships that came in its wake as the all-important tourism industry collapsed (charter planes on their way to the Gambia at the time of the coup literally turned round in midair). In spite of Jawara's avuncular image, his administration was believed to be riddled with corruption. There are signs that even he was aware of its scale. But his steps to combat it – the announcement in January 1994 of a public complaints commission – had come too late.

The man behind the military takeover was 29-year-old Lieutenant Yaya Jammeh, who quickly pronounced himself head of state. Jammeh claimed the coup had been organised in less than 24 hours and was prompted when soldiers arriving at Yundum airport to welcome president Jawara home from a trip to London had been disarmed, and therefore humiliated, by their Nigerian superiors.

While Western governments denounced the military takeover in line with their policy of not supporting military governments, and more critically withdrew aid, a number of fellow West African states, including Senegal, sent cautious messages of support.

Free democratic elections are promised for July 1996.

Left, Gambia's ex-president Sir Dawda Jawara while still in office. **Right**, Senegalese officials arrive at the holy city of Touba.

A BLEND OF BELIEFS

Of the major religions of Senegal and the Gambia, animism is the oldest and Christianity the newest, but much the most important is Islam, which claims over 90 percent of the population.

Animism is the ancient belief system which considers that all earthly things possess spirits or souls. A tree, an animal, even an inanimate object such as a stone – each fetish contains its own spiritual force. Certain creatures are often endowed with particular significance. In the Kaolak region, for example, the wild lizard is particularly revered; people of the region never harm one of these reptiles, and the crocodile is revered all over Senegambia.

Hand in hand with animism goes ancestor worship. During times of crisis, such as illness or madness, homage is paid to ancestors, usually in the form of an offering or sacrifice.

Strictly speaking, animism as a formal and principal belief has died out except in parts of Casamance, Eastern Senegal and the Gambia. However, a residual attachment often lives on even among Muslims or Christians, underpinning the newer religions. When modern medicine, prayer and the semi-magical remedies of *marabouts* (mystical holy men) fail to cure an illness, people may turn to traditional methods as a last resort. In some cases Christian or Muslim saints become identified with older deities, allowing the two to be worshipped simultaneously.

Among the Lébou of the Cap Vert peninsula, for example, the ritual/ceremony known as *Ndeup* is still held from time to time, though not on set dates. The *Ndeup* is a mystical therapy aiming to extract the evil spirit from a patient. It is held in public in the open, often conducted by women, and involves dancing and drumming.

Christian influences: Arriving with the first Europeans, the Christian religions were for a long time confined to European trading and military settlements. Only relatively late did Christianity begin to spread to the indig-

enous population. In the early 19th century a small French Catholic mission was established on Cap Vert, where the Lébou had declared an independent republic.

Elsewhere, missionaries were fiercely resisted, as Christianity was seen as an attribute of the invading Europeans, while Islam became strongly identified with the resisting kingdoms and their leaders. It was not until Lat Dyor Ngoné Latyr Diop was defeated by the French in 1886 that the Catholic Church established itself on Gorée,

the Little Coast, in St Louis, and in the Gambian townships of Banjul, Georgetown and Basse Santa Su.

Today, Christianity is well established but very much a minority religion, its adherents numbering around five percent of the population. In Senegal, Catholicism is predominant; in the Gambia, with its English influence, the Anglican church is more important. Banjul's little Anglican Cathedral, more like an English village church in size, in no way compares with Dakar's grandiose cathedral.

In a number of churches throughout Senegal and the Gambia, it is possible to attend services adapted linguistically and musically

Preceding pages, Senegalese Republican guards; at the market; street prayers. Left, a provincial church. Right, Muslim prayer beads.

to African practice. Best known for this is the Catholic church at Keur Moussa, near Dakar, where the mass is accompanied by traditional instruments such as the *kora* and *balafon*. So popular has this amalgam of Christian and African culture become that the Keur Moussa services often attract a substantial tourist congregation armed with cassette recorders.

The power of the marabouts: It is more than a millennium since the conquering Almoravids swept down into Senegal from Morocco and Mauritania, bringing a new religion. With its simple rules and direct method of worship, the new faith took root quickly. By the 19th century it was thoroughly iden-

lating society by means of councils of elders, something that still happens at village level to this day. (These councils, similar to those of Ancient Greece, are considered by some ancient historians to have been inherited from Pharaonic Egypt.)

With the advent of Islam, elders began to acquire knowledge of the written word, as embodied in the Koran. In a totally oral society, the knowledge of reading and writing had a power verging on the magical, and the priest-leaders became the *marabouts*. Even today the most famous *marabouts* are held in great awe and consulted by the highest in the land. It is not surprising that, of all the forces in the region, it is the *marabouts*

tified with the political and social structure of the region and the great anti-colonial leaders such as El Hadj Omar Tall and Lat Dyor Ngoné Latyr Diop were also religious leaders.

Although the basic teachings and practices are universal, West and North African Islam has developed certain attributes not found in other Muslim countries. One of these is the existence of *marabouts*, often charismatic figures who are a combination of priest, sage, fortune teller and mystic. The *marabouts* – the word comes from the Arabic *marabutin*, meaning Almoravids – arose out of the ancient Senegambian system of regu-

who are most respected and courted by the government.

The second distinctive feature of Senegambian Islam is the existence of brotherhoods of disciples known as *talibé* who follow individual leaders known as *khalifé*. Entry to a brotherhood may be a hereditary matter (for example, members of the M'Backé families are traditionally Mourides, the Sy are Tidjianes, and so on) or one may join voluntarily. Although there is sometimes a regional aspect to brotherhoods (for instance, the Layènes belong very much to the Cap Vert area), the brotherhoods are multiracial, and anyone may join. Lately a small number of Europeans have joined the Mourides and the Layènes.

There is no formal entry or standard membership fee to a brotherhood. Followers pay whatever tribute, in money or goods, lands and services, to their leadership they can afford. If they have no material wealth, this may mean working unpaid on a *marabout*'s land for a certain period of time. In addition, *talibé* attend the pilgrimages and other ceremonies of their order and observe its special rites and customs. The brotherhoods work together temporally as well as spiritually and members help each other to progress in the material world.

The largest and earliest of the brother-

accepted ultimately as spiritual guide and source of authority. The sub-group, the Baye Fall, are something of a law unto themselves, but compensate for their unconventional appearance and behaviour with their extreme piety and hard work in the service of the order, either in the fields or begging alms in the streets.

Mouridism is noted for placing special emphasis on the importance of work, a characteristic not dissimilar to the Protestant work ethic. Mourides have always been heavily involved in agriculture and the caring for the land. They were largely responsible for the development of the groundnut industry and many of the workers and landowners of

hoods, the Mourides, was founded in the 19th century by Cheikh Amadou Bamba, who, in addition to being a great religious leader, was implacably opposed to French colonial rule. This led to his being deported and exiled on several occasions by the French. The descendants of Bamba, the M'Backé family, have continued to provide the leadership of the brotherhood. There are factions and disagreements over specific items of dogma within the M'Backé family, but the Grand Khalif, Abdou Khadr M'Backé, is

Left, a Baye Fall steward at Touba. **Above**, Magal pilgrims arriving, Touba.

the great Senegalese peanut areas are Mourides. The French encouraged this activity, giving landowners free rein to cultivate large tracts of land in exchange for the trade of exporting the peanut oil. Many poorer Mourides work for minimal recompense on the land of their *marabouts* as part of their religious devotion.

The decline of peanut production and the gradual deterioration of the land means that large numbers of Mourides have been obliged to join the drift to the towns. But they perpetuate their strong social structures and commitment to helping each other wherever they are.

In the streets of Dakar, the great majority of small traders are Mourides, and they are often sponsored and protected by the bigger retailers and wholesalers who also belong to the fraternity. Three times a year (at the end of the Ramadan fast, at *Tabaski*, the "feast of the sheep", and at *Magal*) commercial activity in the Senegalese capital is at a standstill as the Mouride shopkeepers attend to their religious duties.

The great annual pilgrimage of the Mouride Brotherhood, and the greatest pilgrimage in the country, is Magal (meaning "return voyage"). It celebrates the symbolic return of the order's founder, Cheikh Amadou Bamba, to the holy city of Touba, which he

founded in the 1880s. Bamba was exiled by the French colonial administration to the Gabonese island of Mayombé in 1895 and spent his last years also exiled from Touba, in Djourbel.

Magal, like other Islamic feasts, is moveable, falling between the 10th and 11th days of the 11th month of the Muslim calendar. The core of the feast is a night of prayer either in the great mosque or among the followings of individual marabouts.

Hundreds of thousands of pilgrims descend on Touba, travelling by car and bus, on foot or swarming over the special trains. Non-Muslim visitors are permitted to attend, but as there is no accommodation in the town (the nearest hotel is in Djourbel) and as the roads and railways are jammed with traffic, it is not an easy excursion.

All visitors should naturally expect to observe the ban on smoking and drinking in Touba. If they don't, they may well attract the attention of the imposing Mouride stewards, the Baye Fall, with their dreadlocks, colourful patched tunics, clubs and calabashes (used for drinking and collecting coins). The Baye Fall were originally the followers of Cheikh Ibra Fall, one of Amadou Bamba's most dedicated disciples.

Legend has it that Ibra Fall and his followers were excused observance of the traditional Islamic obligation to pray, etc., because of their extraordinary zeal. Recently the movement has regained impetus, attracting numbers of young men, who combine a rather wild appearance with a position of some distance from conventional society. Apart from policing the pilgrims at Magal, groups of Baye Fall work in the fields or walk the streets of towns chanting prayers and begging.

Senegambia's second largest brotherhood, the Tidjianes, was founded by the Algerian Cheikh Ahmed Al Tidjiani in the early 19th century, and brought to prominence by the Senegalese leader El Hadj Malick Sy. Its spiritual headquarters is the town of Tivaouane. Another Northern brotherhood, the Khadriya, founded by the Mauritanian Cheikh Saad Bou, is headquartered in Nimzatt, Mauritania.

The Layènes are a small but very active brotherhood localised in Cap Vert, near Dakar. Their centre is the fishing village of Yoff, near Dakar's international airport. Virtually all of the inhabitants of Yoff adopt the name Laye in addition to their original family name, the word being synonymous with the name of God. Around the Cap Vert peninsula are a number of sites venerated by the Layènes, including a cave in Yoff which is said to be the site of a miracle and a number of stones held to bear the miraculous image of the sect's leader, Seydina Limamou Laye. Distinctive features of the Layènes are their all-white attire and their custom of holding mass marriage ceremonies.

Above, women healers in N'Deup ceremony.
Right, the Mouride leader Cheikh M'Backé.

According to the late Cheikh Anta Diop, the great Senegalese historian and anthropologist, the main groups of people in Senegambia have their origins in Ancient Egypt. To support his theory, Diop draws on a number of disciplines from archaeology to linguistics, and a variety of sources, from African oral traditions to the writings of the Greeks and Arabs.

The half dozen major tribes of Senegambia are subdivided into some 20 distinct ethnic groups. Much intermarriage has taken place over the centuries and it is often difficult for an outsider to discern any difference between, say, a Serer and a Tukulor. For Senegambians, the matter is easier.

Although proud of their common national identity and conscious of the links between the groupings – the tradition of *gamou*, meaning roughly cousinship, stresses the connections between peoples – Senegambians are always aware of each others' backgrounds. A complex set of social and linguistic details, gestures and mannerisms makes it easy for people to recognise each others' ethnic groups quickly and to communicate across the divisions.

Humour is, as always, a great intermediary. A Serer might remind a Tukulor that he used to be his slave in days gone by. Family names and histories are also subjects for fun. When a Seck meets a Gueye, it won't be long before one of them refers to the other's excessive appetite for rice. This is taken in good part – it's better to be greeted warmly with a joke, even at your own expense, than coldly or distantly. Most of the ethnic groups found in Senegal are also found in the Gambia, although certain tribes are especially concentrated in particular regions. The exception to this is the Aku, who live solely in the Gambia.

The Wolof: This large grouping, numbering about 2 million, is found throughout Senegambia, but especially in Senegal (where it comprises 36 percent of the population). The Wolof language has come to be Senegal's main indigenous tongue, spoken by 80 per-

cent of the population. The Wolof are believed to have spread into the central regions of the country between the 12th and 15th centuries, establishing the Djolof Empire. Along with the Mandinka, they were among the earliest and most devout converts to Islam. Virtually all the Wolof are still Muslims today.

The Wolof had a clearly defined hierarchical caste system, which still persists, though obviously in diluted form. At the top were the *geer* (nobles) and *badolo* (ranking some-

where between free peasants and gentry). Lower down the social scale were the artisans, whose crafts were hereditary; this group included blacksmiths, tailors and *griots*, or minstrel-historians. At the bottom came the *jaam*, or slaves.

Theoretically, marriage is forbidden between castes, and it is supposed to be banned even between certain categories of artisans. Although the modern era has seen this prohibition largely relax, one still finds even in the cities family arguments about a proposed marriage with a member of a family of different hereditary position.

In their recent history, the Wolof have

excelled at farming and agriculture, having been instrumental in the development of groundnut cultivation (unfortunately sometimes to the exclusion of other, equally necessary, crops). Unlike in other tribes, it is the men who work the fields, while the women take care of the home, the kitchen and the children.

The Lébou: Sometimes described as a subgroup of the Wolof, the Lébou are concentrated in the Cap Vert region, where they are believed to have arrived from the north around four centuries ago. They are renowned as skilled farmers and fishermen, though in earlier times they had a strong sideline as ship-wreckers and looters.

larly in the River Senegal region but are spread throughout West Africa, where they are also referred to as Fula, Fulani, Foulbé, or Poulo. In the Gambia, they are most numerous in the Upper River district. Their origin is unknown, but one hypothesis traces them back east, to Nubia and Ethiopia and perhaps even further.

The Peuls have traditionally made their living as nomadic cattle herders and their large herds of hump-necked zebu are of immense importance to their culture. Although the cattle are never killed for food, the size of a family's herd marks its social prestige and represents its wealth. Great efforts are therefore made to build up and

As mentioned in the Dakar chapter of this book, the Lébou are unique in operating their own mini-government, which is recognised by the Senegalese government, in the Cap Vert region. This represents the continuation of a tradition founded in the early 19th century, when the French colonial government recognised the legitimacy of a fledging Lébou "republic" before the existence of the city of Dakar.

The Alpularen: This large grouping of light reddish-skinned people is subdivided into two tribes, each numbering between 600,000 and 700,000 members.

The first tribe, the Peuls, are found particu-

conserve herds, and marriages between rich families usually involve the exchange of large numbers of animals in dowry.

The Tukulor: These people, the second wing of the Alpularen, are also major cattle-breeders, but because of desertification increasing numbers of them are having to abandon their inhospitable Sahelian homelands for the cities. The Tukulor were among the earliest converts to Islam, and still remain almost wholly Muslim.

The Sarakholé: These pale-skinned people are the descendants of the 14th-century Ghana Empire, which stretched from present-day Ghana to Senegal and Mali in the east. Their hereditary qualities are military skill, independence and a readiness to travel. Nowadays many Sarakholé have been obliged to emigrate as far as Europe, and they constitute one of the main groups of Senegalese living in France. They have a reputation for resourcefulness and solidarity, sticking close together in their European communities and helping out new arrivals. They are usually profoundly Muslim.

The Serer: The second largest ethnic grouping in Senegambia, the dark-skinned Serer are mainly to be found in the Thiès and Siné-Saloum regions, where they inhabit forested areas and till the land. They and the Diola are the major adherents to Christianity, though

dark-skinned, they grow rice and live in forested areas. Despite threats from other tribes, especially the Mandinka, and from Portuguese and French colonisers, the Diola have survived partly by withdrawing to the forests, to develop a fierce independence. It is not surprising, therefore, that the recent murmurings of anti-Government nationalism in southern Senegal have come chiefly from the Diola.

The Bassari: The third grouping still deeply attached to animism is the small Bassari tribe who live in the region of Senegal's Niokolo Koba National Park. Their traditional thatched hut dwellings and colourful ceremonial attire have made their image a fa-

the traditional animist beliefs still retain a strong hold. Their ceremony of *pangal*, which venerates the souls of ancestors, is one of the most distinctive of animist rituals still practised. The poet-politician Léopold Sédar Senghor, the founding father of modern Senegal, came from this tribe.

The Diola: Also great animists, the Diola comprise a number of subgroups, all of whom inhabit the isolated Casamance region and southern Gambia (where they comprise some 10 percent of the population). Small and

miliar one on postcards and in guidebooks.

The Mandinka: Descendents of the Muslim warriors who swept into the Gambia and Casamance regions after the break-up of the Mali Empire, the Mandinka are still found throughout Guinea, Mali and the Gambia (where they comprise 40 percent of the population). Members of the Mandinka griot musician caste play the unique harp-lute known as the kora which has, in the hands of popular musicians such as Mory Kante, made increasingly common appearances in the concert halls and even the record charts of Europe.

The Aku: The descendants of former slaves from Sierra Leone, the Aku are found exclu-

Left, Malinké woman; Diola man. **Above**, Mauritanian man; Peul woman.

sively in the Gambia. They are an English-speaking tribe.

The Mauritanians: Also known as Moors, these pale-skinned men of Berber stock are distinctive with their finely chiselled features and voluminous pale blue robes. Some cross the border from their homelands in Senegal's northern neighbour herding cattle, sheep and goats. Many others are craftsmen, particularly silversmiths, and traders. Their dominance of the small shop commerce of Dakar led to riots in 1989.

Other peoples: As in most of West Africa, Senegal and the Gambia both have significant, although small, populations of Lebanese, who are invariably involved in com-

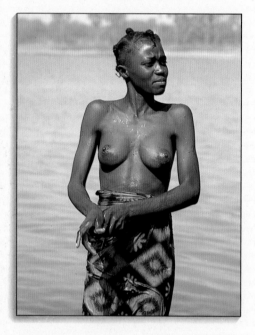

merce large (banking, vehicle distribution) or small (running the ubiquitous *shawarma* restaurants). And, there is a relatively small number of French, although most Europeans tend to be on limited duration contracts.

Ethnic cohesion and strife: Centuries back, the tribal pattern of the territory of Senegambia was one of wars in which one grouping conquered another, ruled, interbred and established complex new social structures before being in turn conquered, driven away or overlapped by a newly dominant tribe. With the advent of Islam, consolidation of peoples and territories into Muslim and non-Muslim blocs occurred. The arrival of Euro-

pean colonisers further united peoples formerly divided into many small groupings.

By the late 20th century, the mix had developed to such an extent that great cohesion and mutual tolerance between the different ethnic groups was the norm. But this order broke down in 1989, resulting in hundreds of deaths, great destruction of property, and serious damage to relations between the two communities.

At the beginning of 1989, Nouakchott, the capital of Senegal's northern neighbour Mauritania, contained many hundreds of Senegalese, mostly working as labourers. At the same time, Senegal's capital contained several thousand Mauritanians, who mostly worked as silversmiths but, more significantly, controlled almost all the little corner shops and stalls selling groceries.

The hard-working Mauritanians, known to the Senegalese as *Naar*, sold small quantities of goods – a single cigarette or a spoon of coffee – and, more significantly, also acted as money-lenders. In this way, they had come to dominate commerce at a street level and to be familiar figures to the Senegalese population at large. Their prosperity in a worsening economic situation had already attracted resentment from the populace when a series of events sparked off full-scale rioting. An argument over land rights on the border between Mauritanian cattle herders and Senegalese farmers resulted in skirmishing which spread to Nouakchott, where Senegalese were attacked by local people. Rumours reaching Dakar of Government-approved attacks on their countrymen provoked young men to take to the streets and attack Mauritanian shops.

Within days, large-scale rioting had torn through Dakar and Nouakchott. At one point, Dakar's main mosque was pressed into service to shelter thousands of Mauritanians seeking refuge from the mobs and awaiting repatriation to the north.

By the time troops restored order in both capitals, hundreds of lives had been lost. In the aftermath, during which Mauritania and Senegal nearly came to war, almost the entire population of Senegalese and Mauritanians were evacuated from each other's countries, while the border remained closed seemingly indefinitely.

Left, Wolof girl. **Right**, Bassari youth.

Jimmy Carter, the former US President, may have got rich on peanuts, but the peasants of Senegambia, for whom the crop has been almost the sole source of revenue since Britain and France started showing an interest in it last century, have very little to show for their labours. For the first thing to know about the economies of Senegal and the Gambia is that they are among the poorest in the world.

The statistics mean less in a country where only a minority can read and write and where very little is counted than they do in the developed West. They can nevertheless give an order of magnitude. Gross National Product – the economists' measure of total national wealth – was estimated at just $370 per head in the Gambia in 1992 and $780 in Senegal.

Stark contrast: To put it crudely, the average US citizen was nearly 80 times better off than his or her Gambian counterpart – in terms not only of food, housing and clothes, but also of health care, education and all the other necessities of life. The tourist, pursued by ragged little boys asking for coins or invited to a standard mud and corrugated iron compound, might well wonder how families get by at all.

It is less easy to comprehend this from the bustling Senegalese capital, with its modern high-rise blocks and traffic jams. "Were it not for the black faces, the vendors with their cola nuts, sweets and tiny twists of peanuts on every corner, the deformed beggars on their wooden trolleys," said one recent visitor to Dakar, "were it not for a certain untidiness, the boulevards could almost be in any French provincial town." Less easy, too, when a minister's wife goes by in her chauffeur-driven Mercedes, richly dressed in embroidered cloth and adorned with gold.

Don't be taken in by such appearances, for this is very emphatically Africa. The ragged urchin may well have a distant cousin who lives in one of the elegant villas surrounding the capital, with all the trimmings of Western

affluence. His father or elder brother may well be in Europe, working as a road sweeper or on a ship, earning a little something to send home.

But, even if he was born in the city, the lad may be called home to a village during the rainy season, to live in a hut made of dried mud and thatch, without water or electricity, to tend cattle or crops. Diversification is the key to survival where there is no social security system, no national health service or Medicare; each influential or wealthy rela-

tive, however distant, is another brick in the wall of insurance against unemployment or death from a simple, curable disease.

Senegambia's natural resources are limited, to say the least: an Atlantic coastline, a climate prone to drought, phosphates and thus-far unexploited iron ore deposits in Senegal, and the possibility – also as yet unexploited – of oil and gas. Senegal, as the former centre of colonial French West Africa and the larger of the two states, has a more developed industry and infrastructure. Both countries remain overwhelmingly dependent on agriculture, and both have suffered acute economic troubles in recent years.

Preceding pages: groundnut conveyor on River Gambia. Left, cement works, Senegal. Right, groundnut sorting, Senegal.

Atlantic coastline: Senegambia's long Atlantic coastline is the one thing distinguishing it from even poorer states such as Mali and Burkina Faso to the east. Witness the fishing community of Ghanatown in southern Gambia, where fishermen from Ghana catch and smoke fish for sale back home. Something like 100,000 fishermen make a living from the waters, mainly using motorised dugouts (the northern fishing communities are a world apart and do not like strangers – beware of venturing onto their picturesque fishing beaches).

Soumbedioune beach in Dakar is the place to see the fruit of their labours – hammerhead sharks, in season; tunny and sea bream; giant

marked the beginning of modern Senegambia. The ships that unload at Dakar port will as likely as not be carrying cargoes for land-locked neighbouring states such as Mali, and much of Gambia's massive import bill represents goods destined for sale in Senegal and beyond.

Some of the trade is official – carried in railway goods wagons, taxed and documented. A vast network of clandestine trade also, however, remains. The Dakar-Bamako "express", that tortuously slow train inland to the Malian capital, resembles nothing so much as a modern-day camel caravan, as fish, fruit, soap and stock cubes are traded in and out of its windows the length of the track.

prawns, lobsters and hideous spider crabs. With the small industrial fleet, these provide a growing proportion of exports. There are agreements too with the European Union, providing tax revenues in return for the right of European boats to fish Senegambian waters. But factory ships from other parts of the world, even from the Far East, still sometimes plunder the oceans, dodging the few patrols and landing their catches clandestinely, far away.

The coast also means trade; it was indeed the arrival of the Europeans and the subsequent establishment of trading posts such as St James' Island, Gorée and St Louis that

Tourism's growth: Winter sun, an hospitable people and beaches so long and empty you could spend all day deciding which patch to sit on are the makings of a tourist's idea of paradise. Tourism is now one of Gambia's main sources of revenue, although development of the industry has not always been smooth. Government loans for hotel construction were not always fully accounted for or repaid, and tour operators creamed off almost the whole of the price paid for holidays. What's more, tourism is vulnerable to political vicissitudes. After the military coup in the Gambia in 1994, revenue from tourism plummeted, causing a devastating knock-on

It may be difficult to believe when you're being mobbed by the persistent young touts of Dakar's open markets, but the peoples of Senegambia are extremely hospitable and lay great store by public and private manners. These are very different from those of the developed West, making contacts in some ways a minefield for the visitor; but don't forget also that your hosts know a great deal more about Western manners and morals than you probably do about theirs.

If you show goodwill but put your foot in it by mistake, any unintended slight will immediately be forgotten. Keep your eyes and ears open, and you will be received with extraordinary generosity. Act arrogantly and the human landscape will freeze over. And never, ever lose your sense of humour – it can get you out of any number of scrapes.

Take a break during your probably exhausting wanders around Dakar or Banjul to watch two – preferably oldish – men greeting each other in the street. They will first shake hands. Then, hands still loosely clasped (emphatically *not* a signal that the pair are homosexual), the formal litany of greeting will begin.

First, a repetition of names, thus:

"Smith."
"Jones."
"Smith."
"Jones."

Then, gazing sightlessly at the horizon, somewhere over each other's shoulders, an interrogation which might be translated very loosely as follows:

"How are you?"
"Fine."
"The family?"
"Fine."
"Everything all right?"
"Thank God."
"How's the wife?"
"Fine."
"Kids?"
"Fine."
"Job going okay?"

"No problems."
"How's your mother?"
… and so on.

Then the roles may switch over, with the respondant posing the same series of questions. With Senegambia's northern ethnic groups, the process may go on for several minutes, and be restarted halfway through the subsequent "proper" conversation. It is a way of reaffirming a relationship, conceived at least partly as one between two family or clan groupings rather than between two isolated individuals. Sociology apart, it has made Senegal's Wolofs, scattered throughout French-speaking Africa, the butt of jokes featuring imaginary inquiries as to the state of health of the family goat or chicken.

The detail of the greetings, which are numerous and complicated, need not concern the casual visitor. What is worth retaining is first, that human – and particularly family – relationships are accorded much more weight in the region than they are in Western Europe or North America. Introduce your elderly parents, for instance, to a Senegambian family and it will be regarded as a great honour.

The drumming and dancing you may see in the streets is probably a baptism to which the whole extended family and neighbourhood is invited. Do not be shy to go and say hello; the odds are that you will be pushed into the circle, amid much laughter and clapping, to execute some few halting steps of Senegambian dance.

Second, drum it into yourself that any contact, however casual, will expect to be greeted before you launch into the matter of conversations. Both friends and business acquaintances will expect to be shaken by the hand, and even the most mispronounced "*Nanga'def*" or "*Kassoumaye*" will give great pleasure – even if it is in the wrong language for the listener.

A woman's place: Senegambian societies present to the traveller an unexpected mix of strength and oppression among women. Much of the legal framework is heavily weighted against them; yet one look at the confident, laughing girls of the towns and villages, or the fierce *madames* of the market place tells another story.

Preceding pages: Glass painting of rich couple with their family *griot*. Left, passing the time of day, St Louis.

It is common for a man to have more than one wife. Marriage can be legally enforced or a looser arrangement without guarantees for the woman concerned. In the towns, it all too often poses problems: of jealousy among women increasingly brought up on Westernised notions of romantic love, and among men who create financial problems for themselves by taking on the social kudos of a second or third wife. Some of the best Senegalese literature, such as Mariama Ba's *Une Si Longue Lettre* or Ousmane Sembene's *Xala* (both available in English), deal with such difficulties.

In the countryside, however, sharing a husband may be the only way to cope with

almost constant pregnancy and childbirth, the demands of farming and family. Remember, too, in looking at the crowds of children (the average number of children per woman is six or seven), that labour is often a family's only asset and that death all too often carries off the young.

Women remain very much members of their own families, even after marriage. Often they retain what Westerners would regard as their maiden name, or use both interchangeably: Gambia's Mary Joof and her Senegalese sister Marie Diouf (the two names are, of course, the same but spelled differently in English and French) will probably

not change their names on marriage, but will sometimes be introduced as Mrs Jallow or Madame Diallo. A woman has little status until married.

In a traditional milieu, and sometimes also in sophisticated society, the wife's family will normally be paid a bride price to compensate for her departure. Marriages are organised by the two families, although only rarely against the wishes of the couple. In the countryside, girls are often married off as young as 12 or 13 (and can be "promised" as young as seven). In spite of the influence of Islam, promiscuity is prevalent and early marriage is often seen as the only way to avoid premarital sex and pregnancy.

The vast majority of Senegambians may be Muslims, but almost no women cover their faces and only Beydane women from across the border in Mauritania are kept indoors. Practices vary between country and town, and from north to south, but across the area the women have a good deal of economic independence from their husbands: they farm, travel and trade on their own, and carry considerable weight in the household. A Senegambian man will think more than once before crossing his mother, and even the most cosmopolitan Wolof male will profess himself helpless before his wife's or lover's sexual wiles.

All this makes travelling in Senegambia a real pleasure for a single woman and far less hassle than, say, in the Mediterranean countries. As far as clothing is concerned, there are no taboos about arms or shoulders, and bare breasts are considered far less indecent than in the West – though no Senegambian could begin to understand why anyone should wish to lie out half-naked in the sun. Almost all local women wear headscarves, though this is not expected of the visitor. It is, however, frowned on for women to expose their legs above the knee – mini-skirts are out – and only young boys would normally wear shorts in public. Otherwise, more or less anything goes.

Most Senegambian men, at least in the towns, enjoy a pretty active sex life and a woman moving around on her own can expect to be propositioned every now and then. This is almost never meant aggressively, and is best brushed off as a joke; invent a husband along the lines of boxer Frank Bruno, if you haven't got one already, or suggest some other time when the sun is not quite so hot. Either way, expect some very direct questioning about your family status: "Are you married?" or "where is your husband?"

Rude encounters: Finally, remember that, however charming most people will be, the occasional Senegambian can be rude. Southern ethnic groups – and particularly the Diola of parts of Gambia and Senegal's Casamance region – are exceptionally easy-going and have manners that resonate well with those of Europe. The Wolof, the dominant group in northern Senegal, have more aggressive manners and a more raucous sense of humour. They also tolerate a certain amount of institutionalised bad behaviour – for in-

mirer of your wristwatch or to the housewife offering you yet more of her best cooking.

There are many beggars on the streets, often damaged by tuberculosis, polio or leprosy. These have their place in Muslim society, which sets great store on alms-giving (Aminata Sow Fall's delightful novel *La Grève des Battus* suggests devastating results if the beggars went on strike). Give them your small change if you feel like it.

But be wary of the over-persistent stranger. Dakar also has its share of more or less sophisticated con-men, who will spin you a yarn about having had their wallets picked on the way from the airport. It has street vendors who will pester you mercilessly to

stance, from members of the *griot* musicians' and praise-singers' caste.

Perhaps because of the long economic crisis, a sort of half-institutionalised begging has become common in Dakar, and is much decried by older Senegalese. It is possible that people may come up to you asking for money or to take your possessions, to which the response is a laughing "It's not mine" ("*C'est pas pour moi*") or "Next time" ("*La prochaine fois*"). A direct "No" would be rude, whether to an over enthusiastic ad-

purchase tacky or overpriced wares. And it has pickpockets and thieves – though stealing is heavily censured and incurs a heavy prison sentence. A thief caught in a market may even be beaten to death by the crowd.

Outside Dakar's tourist haunts and highways, the odds are that any contacts will be made from genuine friendship and hospitality. The young boy who offers to show you around Banjul's market may be hoping for a present, but he is also out for a more interesting afternoon than he would have otherwise; and he will know of others who have even been invited to Europe by tourists they have befriended on the way.

Left, short back, sides and top. **Above**, plaiting hair, an intricate work of art.

distinct Gambian cuisine. The overlap of ethnic groups in both Senegal and the Gambia means that many of the dishes and drinks mentioned previously are enjoyed in the Gambia as well as Senegal, albeit with a Gambian name.

Benachin, a Wolof dish (bena = one, chin or kin = pot, i.e. a one-pot meal – Gambians say the Senegalese serve their rice and sauce separately) resembles *cheb-ou-jen* but is often made with meat instead of fish (Senegalese *cheb-ou-yap*). *Domoda*, made best by the Mandinkas who grow most of the groundnuts, is similar to the widespread West African dish *mafé*. *Sisay yassa* is the same as *chicken yassa* (chicken marinaded in lime

is the *nyama-nyama* or *amuse-gueules* (finger food, sometimes known as "small chop"), sold and eaten at all times of the day. Examples to be tried are *akara balls* (*accra* in Senegal) and *oleleh* (Gambia only), both made from black-eyed beans (*nyébé*), *pastels* (small hot pastry fritters stuffed with spiced fish) and fish balls (*boulettes*), both from Senegal, fish cakes from the Gambia (a larger version of pastels), *fataya* (meat-filled pasties of Lebanese origin) and, of course, roasted groundnuts, prepared daily and which should be bought hot and loose, not languishing in a plastic bag left over from the day before.

Traditionally, neither Gambians nor Sen-

juice and onions and then grilled). Yet all three are completely Gambian dishes.

Red palm oil goes into *plasas* (a corruption of Sierra Leonean "palaver sauce", itself coming from the Portuguese "*palavra*"), a stew made with smoked fish and greens and eaten by the Akus. Fish is fresh and plentiful and should be enjoyed but beware the oysters harvested from the creek mangroves which have not had the advantage of sea-washing, as these can cause hepatitis.

A feature of both Senegal and the Gambia

Left, Dakar bistro, exterior. **Above**, fish, the national dish.

egalese eat prepared desserts. The meal is rounded off with a piece of pineapple or pawpaw (*papaye*), a fresh orange cut into quarters or one of the many delicious fruits found locally, including mangoes, watermelons, melons, guavas, passion fruit, grapefruit, limes, bananas or soursop (*corrosol* in French – a large green-skinned fruit with black "prickles" but with a delicious scented white flesh).

Cooking and eating in both Senegal and the Gambia are based on the tradition of hospitality. Meals are copious, geared to feeding a large family and always having enough for the unexpected guest. Food is served on a large flat tray, rice underneath and vegetables arranged over the top, with careful attention to final presentation. (It must appeal to the senses of sight and smell as well as to taste.) This is placed on a mat on the floor and the family sits grouped round, helping themselves from the central dish.

Traditionally, eating is done with the right hand, so a bowl of water is provided before and after the meal for handwashing. A little rice is rolled up in the fingers, squeezed into a ball and popped into the mouth. If you feel you cannot manage this, a spoon will be provided. Succulent pieces of fish, meat or vegetables are broken off by the hostess and tossed in front of the visitor because stretch-

jen, *domoda* and *mafé*, chicken *yassa*, groundnut soup and stuffed mullet (in Senegal only) are sometimes offered. But even then, a certain freshness can be lacking, which may be due to overcooking and keeping warm or perhaps to the fact that it is usually men who cook in hotels rather than the housewives who are experienced in cooking on a large scale at ceremonial family gatherings. The gourmet visitor will have to seek out the smaller bars and restaurants or be lucky enough to be invited to a Gambian or Senegalese home for lunch.

A few recipes: The following two recipes are in African-style quantities, suitable for a large family:

ing is not good manners.

French influence in Senegal, though relatively unobtrusive in the cooking, has left the Senegalese with a taste for fresh French bread, dressed salads and *hors-d'oeuvres*. British culinary practices have fortunately not affected Gambian cuisine but have regrettably left their mark on some modern hotel kitchens. These have a tendency to serve unimaginative meat dishes in bland sauces, chips with everything and fiddly unseasoned garnishes.

Regrettably also, not enough traditional Gambian or Senegalese dishes find their way on to hotel menus. *Benachin* and *cheb-ou-*

Chicken Yassa
  2 chickens
  6 limes
  6 large onions
  ground red pepper
  salt/ground black pepper
  bayleaf
  oil for frying
Cut chickens into eight large pieces. Squeeze juice from the limes, and mix with salt, peppers and bayleaf. Pour over the chicken pieces. Slice onions finely, spread over chickens and mix in well together with two spoons of oil. Leave for minimum two hours (or overnight) to marinade.

Later: drain chicken pieces and grill lightly, preferably over charcoal or wood. Heat the oil in a frying pan. Drain onions and sauté gently in the oil till soft. Add the marinade and cook for five minutes. Then add chicken pieces and one glass water. Check seasoning. Cover and simmer for 45 minutes. Serve with rice.

Benachin/Cheb-ou-jen (thie-bou-dienne)

- 3.5 lbs (1.5 kgs) thiof or other white fish cut in steaks
- 4 oz (125g) tomato puree
- 12 oz (400g) cooking oil
- 2 hot red peppers
- 4 oz (125g) dried fish (if possible)
- 8 oz (250g) carrots

2 cloves garlic
parsley, salt, black pepper, bayleaf
1 small piece yète (optional)
3.5 lbs (1.5 kgs) rice (pref. small grain)

Chop half a red pepper, spring onions, garlic and parsley and pound together (or blend) with a pinch of salt to make a paste. Stuff a small amount into a slit made in each fish steak. Slice onions and fry gently in oil, add dried fish, then the stuffed fish slices and fry until golden. Remove fish, add tomato puree diluted in three litres water and bring to the boil. Add prepared vegetables and the fish pieces. Season to taste, float the remaining pepper on top, bring back to the boil and simmer, covered, for 20 minutes. Remove

- 1 small cabbage, cut in quarters
- 10 oz (300g) cassava root, peeled and cut in pieces
- 10 oz (300g) sweet potatoes, peeled and cut in half
- 6 oz (200g) pumpkin, peeled and cut in chunks
- 10 oz (300g) aubergines, unpeeled, cut in halves
- 6 oz (200g) turnips, peeled and cut in chunks
- 3 large onions

Left, buffet by the pool. **Above**, beach restaurant in St Louis.

the fish pieces, then the vegetables as they become cooked. The cassava will take the longest. Place in a dish, pour some of the sauce over them and keep warm until all have been cooked. When all the fish and vegetables have been removed, put aside a little of the sauce, then pour the rice into the remaining liquid (there should be approximately twice the amount of liquid to rice) and cook until absorbed. No liquid should remain.

Turn rice on to a large platter with the fish and vegetables attractively arranged on top. Serve with lemon quarters and place the extra juice in a jug.

As fast as the popularity of soccer spread in Europe, so it did in its former colonies and, today, both Senegalese and Gambians are enthusiastic players, often competing internationally. Youngsters can be seen on any open patch of ground or on the beaches playing barefoot. Regular inter-West African matches are held at the Parc des Sports in Dakar, and the Box Bar Stadium or the new Friendship Stadium, built by the Chinese, in Banjul. Football attracts large crowds and tickets are not expensive.

Wrestling rules: The traditional national sport of both countries is wrestling. Dating back to the days of the Mali Kingdom in the 11th century, the sport was once reserved for those of royal lineage. Later on, it became important to all classes. Skill in wrestling could enhance the standing of a chief and at the same time elevate a man of relatively humble birth to a position of power and prestige. Now most villages have a cleared area of ground where the sport is practised – usually on Saturday or Sunday afternoons. Though traditionally held after the harvest when villages had sufficient food to offer hospitality to visiting teams, matches are now held most weekends. It is well worthwhile attending (some hotels offer wrestling as a half-day excursion, but it is easy to go independently), as much for the liveliness of the audience as the action in the ring. Spectators, including many women, shout, cheer, whistle, and hurl abuse while praise singers commend the combatants' skill with songs and drums, and young girls sell snacks for tense onlookers to chew on. The sport also offers a fascinating glimpse into the Senegambians' belief in magic. A wrestler's strength is believed to derive from *nyamo*, a spiritual power which is unleashed by danger. In order to increase their *nyamo* wrestlers adorn themselves with amulets and anoint themselves with magic potions concocted by their *marabouts*.

Teeing off: Most of the popular Western participant sports are represented in the two

countries, but often only as a service to visitors. On the outskirts of Dakar, on the Route de Camberène there is a nine-hole golf course and Club Méditerranée at Cap Skirring has its own mini-golf course. In the Gambia, golf is played on the 18-hole course of the Banjul Golf Club in Fajara.

Tennis players are much better catered for, although most courts are attached to hotels or resort complexes. There are two tennis clubs in Dakar; the Tennis Club Dakarois at Les Marinas, Hotel de N'Gor and the Union

Tennis Club; the University along West Corniche Road also has tennis facilities. Almost every beach hotel of more than 20 rooms in Senegal and the Gambia provides tennis courts for residents or guests.

Watersports: It is in watersports that West Africans excel. Gambians and Senegalese are born swimmers. Just watch the local children diving off rocks, jetties or boats and playing in the Atlantic surf. Most swimming pools are reserved for residents but, since both countries have miles of attractive coasts, Senegalese and Gambian families make long treks to spend the day on the beach. Apart from some specifically designated "safe"

Preceding pages: a wrestling bout in progress. **Left,** wrestler taking "magic potion". **Right,** calisthenics on a Senegalese beach.

THE DAKAR RALLY

Each Christmas Day, competitors converge from more than a dozen countries to participate in a motorsport event notorious for its danger and excitement. The "Dakar", as the Paris to Dakar rally is known, tests the stamina and endurance of man and machine in a 21-day trek through eight countries and over 6,370 miles (10,200 km) of daunting terrain.

Since a small group of adventurous Frenchmen started it in 1978 as a means of escaping from the northern European winter, the Dakar has gone on to attract the biggest names in rally driving and sponsors from every walk of life. Cigarette and clothing companies' decals, along with those of hi-

accidents on the rally, including six fatalities, caused the Pope to criticise the safety standards of the event. The Dakar is a notoriously difficult event. There is no chance for the drivers to familiarise themselves with the course beforehand, and the co-driver (navigator) has to be able to read the road book at 130mph.

The route of the Rally snakes via Barcelona to Tunis, down into the Fezzan region of Libya, where Colonel Gadhaffi offers free fuel for the vehicles and permits the (generally banned) consumption of alcohol by participants in the race. From Ghadames on the Libyan-Tunisian border, the track winds across Libya to Sebha and down to Termit. From the oasis town of Agadez in the Aïr Mountains of Niger, a now straggling line of battered machines makes it way to Niamey, the

fi and watch manufacturers, adorn the 250 cars, 170 motorcycles and 70 support trucks which nowadays make up the field. For manufacturers such as Peugeot, which has a major export market in Africa, the publicity generated by success in the rally is immensely important. Their vehicles' frequent high placings have contributed to Peugeot's reputation for toughness and reliability.

Among the numerous controversial mishaps which have dogged the rally's short history have been the temporary loss and expensive rescue of Mark Thatcher, the accident-prone son of Britain's ex-prime minister, while he was participating. In 1986, the originator of the event, Thierry Sabine, died when the helicopter in which he was travelling crashed in the desert. In 1988, the number of

capital of Niger, and thence to Gao and Timbuktu in Mali. Along the way, restaurateurs hike up their prices and traders set out their wares to take advantage of the festival atmosphere that accompanies the annual visit of Les Dakeurs.

From Timbuktu the race hots up – as if the rising temperatures are not hot enough. The route is downhill, south, through the Sahel to Bamako, capital of Mali. The race has only three days to get to its final destination, Dakar. By this time the field has usually narrowed to around half the original number of vehicles. Champagne, the victor's trophy and a laurel wreath await the winners. Prizes go to both motorcyclists and cars, and all who compete the course get the accolade of "Dakeurs", survivors of the world's most harrowing rally. ∎

beaches, strong currents and the undertow can be a hazard.

Pointe Bernard, in Dakar, has a famous swimming pool overlooking the beach. The Lido on Route de la Corniche, L'Ocean, Domaine de Ouarer and Sub-nu-Gab are other popular pools. In the Gambia, Cape St Mary and Barra Point are both good, safe beaches and the Atlantic Hotel in Banjul has a fine pool, as do all of the major tourist hotels on the coast.

Sporting activities at most resort hotels are well organised and often centre on the pool or beach. A favourite in Senegal but unknown in the Gambia is the traditional French game of *boules*, almost obligatory for holi-

the main hotels along the coast, with the best choice available from the Atlantic Hotel in Banjul. St Louis and Dakar are fast becoming popular among yachtsmen, and more yachts have been stopping off in the Gambia in recent years, the favourite moorings being at Denton Bridge.

Rod and line: The waters off the Senegambian coast are some of the richest in the world, with a large and varied range of fish. Sports fishing in both countries is a favourite pastime. Boats can be hired or trips arranged to follow the great game fish such as marlin, barracuda, sailfish, bonito, swordfish and capitaine. See the Angling Centre in Dakar, or the Sports Fishing Centre on Gorée Island

daymakers at Senegal's beachside hotels. Popular in both countries are beach games such as volleyball and table tennis. Some hotels even have squash courts.

In resort areas one can hire a variety of watersports equipment for skin diving, water skiing, sailing, boardsailing and para-sailing. In Dakar equipment can be rented at L'Océan, Le Lagoon, Les Marinas, Cercle de la Voile and at the Plage de Hann. In the Gambia equipment can be hired at most of

Left, Jacky Ickx negotiates a splash during the Dakar Rally. <u>Above</u>, Dakar stadium with a wrestling match under way.

for rentals in Senegal.

In the Gambia, Sportsfishing Ltd operates both from the shore and in the river. Based at Denton Bridge, the company runs barracuda trawling half-day excursions and a full-day "all species" trip (see *Travel Tips* for further details).

In Senegal, similar facilities are offered through a number of tour operators. Around Dakar Les Almadies (Club Mediterranée), offers deep sea fishing facilities daily. Club Mediterranée at Cap Skirring and the Hotel de Paris in Kaolack arrange regular trips, as does the Domaine de Nianing and the nearby Centre Touristique de la Petite Côte. In

Casamance, at the Hotel-village de la Pointe St George, special river and sea angling excursions are organised. Most fishing trips depend on enough people – generally four or five – being present before being viable.

Horse riding is unusual in the Gambia, where there are few horses. In Senegal, however, the sport is followed avidly. At L'Hacienda near Dakar there is a riding school; other stables are located at Palm Beach, Hotel Saly and at Club Adiana. In Mbour, the Domaine de Nianing has horse riding facilities, as does the Ranch de Doli hunting lodge out in the Djourbel Region. At Camp Retba, near the lake of the same name, a riding school offers treks along the dunes.

On the hunt: This is popular in Senegal but few hunting trips are organised in the Gambia. Some hotels in Senegal specifically cater for hunting parties; Les Paletuviers has established a hunting camp in the Siné-Saloum region. Nearby is another hunting centre, known as Medine Djicoye, and the Gîte d'Etape at Richard Toll provides for hunting enthusiasts.

There is a camp at the reserve of Maka Diama for hunters and, in the Casamance region, the camping centre of Khobe, near Kolda, offers hunting facilities. At the Hotel de la Poste in St Louis, at Le Relais Fleuri hotel in Badioure, and at L'Hacienda just outside Dakar hunting parties can be arranged. On the steamship cruises, which ply the Senegal River, hunting excursions form part of the cruising activities. Firearm permits, which are mandatory for those not hunting with a licensed guide, are best applied for in advance.

The Water and Forests Bureau in Dakar issues hunting permits to those with insurance, firearm certificate, regulation permit papers and dues. Permits come in three categories. The Small Game Permit is issued for one day's shoot taking not more than 15 stone partridges, guinea-fowl, bustards, francolins or hare. The Medium Game Permit includes the small game but also the shooting of one of each of the following: gazelle, oribi, waterbuck, cob, warthog or two great bustards. A Big Game licence is issued only through authorised hunting guides. The hunting season runs from mid-December until the end of April.

<u>Right</u>, canoe race, St Louis.

119

for a great variety of animals and birdlife. Some of the animals are difficult to see because of the dense undergrowth in these regions but, where the bush meets the river, wildlife spotters can sometimes catch a glimpse of the wild forest boar. Around five ft (1.5 metres) in length, this is a particularly mean animal and it can do severe damage with its curved tusks.

In the hinterland small deer and the occasional waterbuck can be seen at the water's edge, the best place for wildlife watching. The African finfoot, like a large darter, takes its Latin name, *Podica Senegalensis*, from its native country.

A curious crested bird, often found near streams have created islands. Most are completely overgrown with dense vegetation and tall trees. Usually the islands are ringed by mangrove trees and practically inaccessible, but breaks in the foliage created by mudflats can be used as a landing for canoes. Skirting the islands by boat one can observe a great deal of wildlife, including olive baboon colonies, families of green-coated vervet monkeys with their white "bibs", red-jacketed Patas monkeys, and the rarer red colobus monkeys.

Wildfowl in great flocks rise from their perches in the upper branches of the mangroves as one approaches the islands. Often seen slumbering on a mudbank, the croco-

water, is the hoopoe, or its less common cousin, the green wood hoopoe. Glossy ibis nest in the gnarled branches of mangrove and one might catch a glimpse of the rabbit-sized water chevrotan, a little deer even smaller than the tiny duiker which also come to the riverbanks for fresh water. Here, francolins sun themselves, waders tiptoe across mud banks and one might see a rail stalking between reed beds.

Inland, where the rivers snake through *bolongs* or built-up river banks, meandering

Left, pelicans in Djoudj, Senegal. **Above**, a crocodile in the Gambia River.

dile is becoming less common in the lower reaches of the rivers. There are three species of crocodile in this part of West Africa. The most common is the Nile crocodile which can reach 15-16 ft (5 metres) in length. The West African Dwarf and the Bottlenose crocodiles are rarely seen, or more correctly, rarely identified.

Few hippopotamus inhabit the region, although some have been seen far up the Gambia River and in parts of the Parc National du Niokola Koba. Most river banks have their snake population and numbers of monitor lizards. Both the lizards, which can grow to 4 ft (1.2 metres) long, and pythons, are good swimmers and can often be seen crossing from bank to bank.

Inland from the river banks, where the jungle is thick, small deer may be seen. The Duiker and Oribi are typical forest mammals. Another inhabitant of the dense undergrowth is the warthog, which is becoming increasingly rare because of relentless hunting. This is also baboon territory and troops of them can sometimes be observed as they cross roads between one forest shelter and the next.

The variety of birdlife in high forest includes hawks and eagles. Diligent ornithologists may spot the harrier, kite, lizard buzzard, harrier eagle or goshawk. In between

forest and river the West African river eagle might be seen, or the osprey.

Parks and reserves: Situated within a day's flight from Europe, Parc National du Niokolo Koba in southeast Senegal is the nearest place to Europe where one can view the continent's larger animals in their natural habitat. This extensive reserve is not only the major game park of Senegambia, but also the only one in the region to rival the great reserves of East Africa.

The park's lions are among the largest known and the magnificent Derby Eland is the world's largest antelope. Both are easily seen on guided safaris in the park, as are

buffalo, gazelle and black antelope. Leopards are rare in Niokolo Koba but their traditional food, bushbuck, roan antelope, waterbuck, cob and the little duiker are found in abundance. A variety of apes can be spotted, and also hippopotamus, crocodile and warthog. More than 300 species of bird have been logged, 70 species of animal and at least 60 of fish.

Senegal contains six more national parks, if one includes the Lac de Guiers, famed for its waders, Scoter duck, rail and teal. Djoudj is famous for its pelicans, flamingo, crowned cranes, wagtails and storks. The Parc de la Langue de Barbarie is noted for two things: the thousands of birds which migrate from Europe during the winter, and its turtle breeding grounds. The Parc du Delta du Saloum is known for the seasonal abundance of migratory birds and the seabirds that use the wide estuary waters.

The Parc de la Basse-Casamance attracts visitors for a wide variety of wildlife, including the stately Derby eland, the Buffon Cob and several kinds of monkeys; there are about a dozen wildlife-watching lodges in the Casamance region. The national park of the Ile de la Madeleine was established to protect its large colony of seabirds from disturbance by amateur archaeologists visiting the site.

In the Gambia there is only one nature reserve open to visitors, at Abuko, not far from Lamin, but many regions of forest and river have been designated protected areas. These include Bijilo Forest on the coast (next to Kololi Beach Club), and five other fenced-off areas up-country: Salaji, Nyambai, Kabafita, Furuya and Gambia's largest reserve, the Kiang West.

Park areas in the Gambia are warden-protected and closed to visitors. UNESCO's World Heritage scheme has listed both the Djoudj National Park and the Niokolo Koba Parks as areas of world importance. Senegal became party to the World Heritage Convention in 1976 and the Gambia joined in 1987. The "Banjul Declaration", issued by the ex-President of Gambia, Sir D.K. Jawara, in 1977 for the protection of the country's flora and fauna has become a guideline for both Gambians and visitors to the country.

<u>**Above**</u>, **rehabilitated chimpanzees, Gambia.**
<u>**Right**</u>, **a mighty baobab.**

THE BAOBAB TREE

The most prominent feature of the West African landscape, the baobab tree, dominates the savannah of Senegambia. Not a giant compared to the kapok, which can grow to over 160 ft (50 metres) in height, the baobab rarely exceeds 70 ft (21 metres). Its barrel-like, grotesque trunk, however, often acquires a girth of more than 30 ft (nine metres). The angular branches of the baobab look more like roots – giving rise to the Senegalese tale that the devil must have uprooted the baobab and plunged it back into the earth upside-down.

eaten either fresh or dried. When powdered they are known as *alo*, a preparation which is traditionally used for curing rheumatic ailments and inflammations. The acidic fruit can be made into a refreshing drink; the pulp has long been known as a remedy for various ailments, particularly ones relating to circulation, and the gourd-like shell is used as a container.

Musical instruments are fashioned from the bark, which can also serve as packing paper and be woven into rope or even cloth. In this region, where malaria is rife, the bark is also believed to have quinine-like properties and the seeds, which are rich in phosphates, are used in the manufacture of fertiliser and soap.

Wandering nomads have found a temporary

This is not the only myth to be associated with the baobab. Because of its ability to store water in an immense trunk, it has magical properties in the eyes of desert dwellers. The pulpy nature of its large yellow fruit has earned it the name "monkey bread tree" among Africans. Few villages in Senegambia are without an aged baobab and some are estimated to be more than 1,000 years old. Superstition surrounds the tree because, like humans, the baobab gets smaller rather than bigger as it gets older – unlike any other tree.

The baobab has no shortage of practical uses. The sweet-smelling, white flowers provide decoration in times of festival. The leaves are

home in the hollow trunks of venerable baobabs. When dead, the tree is a source of precious firewood or materials with which to construct canoes or fishing floats because of its light, spongy consistency. In places it is therefore known as the "cork tree".

The baobab features in countless folk tales and myths. It has also given its name to many hotels and restaurants, and to one of Senegal's most early "roots" music groups. The strongest use of all for the baobab has been as a burial place. In certain communities, members of the griot minstrel class could not be interred beside other castes and the massive hollow trunks came to be their traditional mausoleums. ∎

Bogué

F'

One of the first things to hit you about the Gambia is its quaintness. Whether you arrive by air at the little Yundum Airport with its open-air concrete tables for baggage collection, or by ferry over the river from Senegal, everything seems small, homely and rather jolly. There is little sign of extreme poverty – though virtually none of wealth either. The people are for the most part friendly and relaxed, certainly by comparison with the citizens of Dakar, who have all the stresses and strains of an overcrowded city life.

Particularly if you have come from Senegal, you will notice the British colonial legacy everywhere. The navy-blue police uniforms, the Silk Cut cigarette logos and the street vendors' tattered sunshades, the Express Fish and Chips shop in Banjul with its bougainvillea-covered wooden frontage – all these remind you constantly where much of the country's newer mode of life came from. Beneath this veneer, of course, the older culture of the region continues unaffected; the mosques, the markets and the unhurried social life could be on either side of the border with the Gambia's big neighbour.

Although most tourists spend little time there, it is in the dowdy little capital of Banjul that the colonial influence is most noticeable. The balding parade ground in the centre of town still serves as an occasional cricket pitch. Lunching in the Braustuble restaurant near the Law Court, you may sit at the next table to a pin-stripe suited, gowned Gambian barrister who could just as well have emerged from the Old Bailey.

Twenty minutes' drive away on the Atlantic coast, the big hotel complexes belong to a newer, more international world, with their swimming pools, water sports and evening entertainments. But they too have their own personalities.

The different nationalities who patronise them may influence their style. Germans and Scandinavians were among the earliest holidaymakers to discover the Gambia along with the British, and the French are now beginning to come down for an interesting break while visiting Senegal. Whether you want company or solitude, there's plenty of room on the pale sandy beaches and in the Atlantic rollers to make the Gambian Coast a great holiday spot.

And finally there's the river, the long snaking watercourse whose shape is the shape of the country itself. A trip by Land Rover or boat, or a combination of the two, will provide fascinating glimpses of the rich bird and animal life, and of the traditional bush village way of life too. For a small country, the Gambia has a lot to offer.

Preceding pages: hanging out the washing on Gorée Island; canoes and spectators in St Louis; Bassari initiation ceremony costumes. **Left**, River Gambia, key to the country.

BANJUL

Banjul, still known on signposts up-country as Bathurst, is the Gambia's capital. Estimates of its population hover around 45,000, and as Banjul is on **St Mary's Island**, surrounded by open sea, the mouth of the River Gambia, Oyster Creek and a network of mangrove creeks, it is hard to see how it can grow much more. The only bridge connecting it with the mainland is Denton Bridge, built in 1986 to replace the old Denton Bridge and to mark the Gambia's 21st anniversary as an independent country.

Wealthy Gambians and expatriates tend to live and play west of Banjul, on the more spacious mainland at **Bakau**, **Fajara**, **Kotu Beach** and **Kololi**, flanking the Atlantic Ocean. Less affluent Gambians and migrants from neighbouring countries have converged on **Serekunda** (9 miles/15 km from Banjul), the most densely populated town in the Gambia, with a population of around 103,000, and the hub of the country's transport network. Serekunda has more of the heaving bustle one associates with a Third World city. Its labyrinthine market is more intensely African than Albert Market in Banjul, and its bars a little more louche.

Banjul remains the seat of government, the headquarters of banking and commerce. To the casual observer, the city can seem depressed, shabby, small and dusty, and riddled with potholes once past the relatively grand entrance leading into Independence Drive. But equally immediately it gives an impression of relaxed liveliness. Everywhere people are on the move. They crowd about their business, trading, hoping to sell or to make a bargain, visiting. The most stationary looking sewing-machine operator or barrow boy will have moved on to a fresh pitch 20 minutes after you first sight him.

Banjul's ethnic mix is as diverse as that of the rest of the country: Aku, Fula, Diola, Mandinka, Sarakholé, Serer, Wolof. Some are immediately recognisable by caste or feature, clothing, facial scarification, but others are less obvious. There are Moors from Mauritania, Lebanese, Yoruba, Guineans, Guinea-Bissauans, Malians, and a wide variety of Europeans working in aid organisations, tourism or simply retired. Tourists are usually distinguishable from local expatriates by their clothing, colouring and deportment.

Banjul's charms emerge easily from the dust and disrepair. The roads are in need of remaking but the slower, careful pace of locomotion they require, even in rare pedestrian-free sections, leaves time to notice much more than the tired state of the paintwork. The marvellous light picks out courtyards, arches, lattices, verandahs, flowering trees, standpipes and cooking pots and local clothing styles and headdresses, especially in the back streets.

The tendency is to look for distinctive monuments, public landmarks, but Banjul's attraction is more intimate. As everyone will tell you, the real wealth of the Gambia is its people – the attractiveness of domestic living, of people going self-containedly about their affairs, of the amazingly enduring good nature and welcome on all sides.

To reach Banjul from the main hotel strip, either take a tourist taxi, which is expensive (the driver will usually wait on your return) or walk to the nearest bus-stop and pick up a bush taxi, which will cost just a few dalassi. Some tour companies also offer introductory tours of Banjul, often combining a look round the town with a visit to the crocodile pool at Kachikally and a visit to a batik factory in Bakau.

Colonial architecture: Banjul possesses a number of interesting historical, cultural, social and gastronomic features. **State House** and its adjoining cluster of government offices (The Quadrangle contains the Ministry of Tourism) can be glimpsed across the rather moulting expanse of **MacCarthy Square** with its iron fence, mini-bandstand, cricket pitches, and occasional traders' stalls frequently moved on by the police, but rapidly returning.

The tiny **Anglican Cathedral** in **Independence Drive**, by MacCarthy Square, is demure and appealing. Also nearby is the beautifully kept **National Museum**, devoted to African culture and the history of colonialism. The **Catholic Cathedral** on the corners of Picton Street and Hagan Street is larger and more opulent-looking than its Anglican counterpart and its interior is also of interest architecturally.

The new **Great Mosque**, on Box Bar Road, is rather uncompromisingly new-looking, for all its splendour. It is one of the few mosques in the Gambia large enough to accommodate a special section for female worshippers, who in most smaller mosques are confined to the verandah.

The lasting joys of Banjul, architecturally, are the surviving bungalows and storyed-buildings in what the museum calls "Creole style", with balconies, shutters, dormer windows and steep roofs. Often on pillars raised above the ground, usually with weathered corrugated roofs above wooden upper floors,

they might better be called Krio-style or Aku-style houses.

Banjul is a low-lying city as well as a small one. Modern buildings are rather anonymous and undistinguished. There is not much of the panache of Dakar's public buildings and villas. Even the buttressed pyramidal building of the **Banque Internationale de Commerce et Industrie** in **Wellington Street** cuddles so closely to its neighbours that it has no chance to shine and startle as its cousins do in Ziguinchor and Kaolack in Senegal.

The vibrant focus of market life in Banjul spreads behind the new façade put up by Chinese constructors along **Russell Street** for the famous, colourful, inexhaustible **Albert Market**. This was destroyed by fire in 1988 and the new frontage promises a lasting elegance which the makeshift lanes of local and imported produce behind successfully dispute. Clothes and beads and kola nuts, tresses to plait into hair and skin lighteners, tea and fruit, and many other things can be found. The market has

been going strong since the middle of the 19th century and it takes more than total combustion to stop it.

Round the corner, in Buckle Street, is the **Methodist Bookshop**, where you can buy a variety of locally produced publications giving an insight into Gambian culture, as well as imported books and magazines. This is also the best place to come for maps.

The Lebanese cloth stalls along **Russell Street**, **Cameron Street** and **Wellington Street**, are full of bolts and rolls and odds and ends of gloriously varied lengths of cloth which ride marvellously on African skins but need great discrimination to suit European ones. As visitors quickly notice, the Gambians place enormous store on being well-dressed, and a woman's wardrobe is considered a major household expense. Excellent cloth for men's lightweight suits, summer shirts and shorts can also be bought inexpensively. Local tailors wait to run up clothes for a third of European prices with great competence. Bargaining is essential.

The President's residence, Banjul.

The Gambian cloth and clothes sellers concentrate on tie-dyed dresses and shirts, hand-painted T-shirts and "bush hats", which are seldom worn except by Europeans. The National Library has a fetching red and white *ashwebi* (matching outfit) for its staff, and one sees the occasional non-Gambian African or Afro-American in local tie-dye robes.

Watering holes: Thirsty or hungry after sightseeing and shopping? The popular nourishment places for visitors are the Braustuble restaurant-bar in Leman Street, the African Heritage on the first floor of the arcaded building just beyond the CFAO supermarket in Wellington Street and the Atlantic Hotel on Marina Parade.

The **Braustuble** is German-Lebanese run and has an inside restaurant and bar, air-conditioned in season, and an outside area with scrubbed tables and benches under thatch covers and a circular bar. There are also examples on the walls of the stylishly grotesque, mannered, engraved wood pictures of Tonton, as he signs himself, whose work

is also prominent at Le Relais restaurant at M'Bour in Senegal.

The **African Heritage** is imaginative and attractive. It has a long first-floor pillared balcony, with one side open above the stalls and activity of **Wellington Street**, the road leading to the docks. It is run by a Danish-African couple who mix running the restaurant with selling art objects. The clothes, jewels, carvings and pictures on sale are individual, which is reflected in their prices.

Specialist visitors often photograph the art at the African Heritage, as it is the most permanent and accessible collection in Banjul. The centre also offers views over the estuary beyond the Shell petrol station, which are sometimes populated by dolphins jumping in pairs or families and always by ferries ploughing to and from **Barra**.

Alternatively, the **Atlantic Hotel**, on Marina Parade, is an attractive place to have lunch. The old Atlantic hotel, the forerunner of this one, was the first hotel in the Gambia. Its architecture is striking and in spite of signs of lack of

A family compound in Banjul.

maintenance (though a facelift is promised) it remains the favoured location for civic and expat functions. The hotel also has a notable bird garden, established in 1990, where some 150 different species have been recorded, including the Senegal kingfisher, the red-cheeked cordon-bleu, the shikra and the red-billed hornbill. One advantage it has over the hotels along Kotu Beach is its superior location for watersports.

For the more adventurous traveller in need of lunch, just off the beaten track in **Cameron Street** are two Lebanese *shawarma* houses, where hamburgers and Lebanese pitta-bread sandwiches stuffed with spicy mixtures are cheaply available. Further off the beaten track, are *tangana* or chop bars or casual eating tables at odd corners (in Albert Market, for example) where *benachin* or *domoda* are very cheap.

Established visitors, and residents, can plug themselves into informal "bowling" networks for delicious and varied eating. "Bowling" is a local system by which a cook, normally a Gambian woman, supplies bowls of food at agreed times on agreed dates at agreed prices to an agreed place. For example, a friendly Lebanese store can turn into a temporary dining room over a bowl of hot curried stew and rice and roasted groundnuts, for less than £1, with lots of spicy gossip and commentaries on current affairs, business and scandal tossed in. After lunch, investigate the backstreets, off **Lasso Wharf** and **Box Bar Road**. Banjul is small but, like Mrs Blain's haberdashery store off Albion Place, it is chock full of vivid surprises. Choose a taxi-driver who is in no hurry. Perceptions always need training to appreciate the nuances of a new place, but Banjul is worth the extra effort.

Magical mudflats: The mudflat area on the outskirts of Banjul, on the **Bond Road,** can be magical at high and low tide. Hulks, wrecks, little ships, plants sprouting through the islets of abandoned vessels, wading birds, pelicans, herons, plovers, gulls, emerge, depending on tide, out of shining water or glistening dark mud.

Below, locally made furniture. Right, waiting for the Barra ferry.

THE GAMBIA COAST

The Gambia's coast fits most people's image of paradise. For some 40 miles (64 km) white coral sands and feathery coconut palms curve towards a sea of peacock blue. The waters are warmed to a comfortable tepid by the warm Guinea Current, while the shore, one of the most westerly in Africa, is cooled by northeast trade winds.

Early mariners, deterred by the huge Atlantic rollers which can make matchwood of small craft, sought out river mouths and backwaters in which to retreat from autumn squalls. With an estuary over 3 miles (5 km) in width, the Gambia River provided a sheltering arm for a series of trading posts, and soon evolved into one of Africa's most important waterways.

Orientation: Almost all the 65,000 tourists that visit the Gambia annually are bound for its beaches. After landing at Yundum airport, they are transported by coach to the strip of coast stretching south of the mouth of the River Gambia. Many never even visit Banjul, and few do more than glimpse Serekunda, the most populous town, on their journey to and from the airport. The beaches begin immediately west of Banjul, the first stretching for almost 5 miles (8 km) before curving off at Cape Point. Great scallops of silver-sanded beach extend as far as the eye can see, edged by lagoons, mangroves or village compounds and broken here and there by creeks and small waterways. Picturesque additions to the scene are occasional fishing boats being hauled over the sands and big-horned white Zebu cattle slowly making their way down to the water's edge to lick the salt from the rocks.

But it is at Fajara that the fabulous Kotu Beach begins, flanked by a string of low-lying luxury hotels and villas, and stretching as far as Kololi (where the beach bars peter out and a *"plage sauvage"* disappears into the horizon). Kotu is the most populated beach, though even here the sands are far from crowded. Holidaymakers are joined by traders touting woodcarvings, handsomely dressed women selling fruit and hair-plaiting services (bargain ruthlessly) and, at certain times of the day, Gambia's top athletes, who generally prefer to train on the clean-washed beaches than the dirt track of Banjul's stadium. All the big hotels have commandeered small patches of beach for their guests (though the beach as a whole is public) and employ security guards to chase away over-persistent touts. The hotels also monitor swimming conditions, which are hazardous when the sea is rough – on no account swim when the red flag is flying.

From Bakau to Kololi: After the salt flats encircling Banjul, and wide **Denton Bridge** across **Oyster Creek**, the district of **Bakau** is a broad, built-up area behind several attractive, cliff-bound bays. Translated as "big place", Bakau has a tight network of residential compounds, a supermarket, the **Gamtel** communications centre and local markets on the landward side of **Atlantic Boulevard**, and hotels, élite residences and

fishing beaches on the seaward side.

While Bakau is the location of the British and American Embassies, the **New Town** houses an industrial centre, and the Chinese-built stadium.

Out on **Cape Point** is the four-star **Sunwing Hotel** and the two-star **Amies Beach Hotel**. Further south along the Bakau strand is tiny **St Peter's Church** overlooking the village fishing bay. Past the marketplace and Romana's on the left are the beach-top **African Village** and **Tropic Gardens** with traditional thatched bungalow rooms. Next door to the Tropic Gardens is the **Atlantic Guest House** on the very top of Bakau cliffs.

Take a stroll down Atlantic Boulevard, past batik stalls (The Factory in Bakau is the place to see batik in the making), women selling peanuts, boys vending kola nuts and beautiful displays of hand-carved African masks, or hire a bicycle to tour the town and visit the sacred crocodile pool at **Kachikally**, located in the centre of Bakau's huddled native compounds. This small, weed-clogged pool (actually much deeper than

it looks) contains around 70 crocodiles (the brown crocs are female, the olive-green ones males). There is no perimeter fence, and the knowledgeable guide encourages visitors to touch the creatures as they sun themselves on the banks (if you do, avoid their heads, which are sensitive). The water in the pool is considered curative, and barren women come to douse themselves in the little brick enclosure next to it. Any child born after such ritual bathing is invariably given the name Kachikally. As well as barren woman, the pool draws others in need of its fortifying powers, including wrestlers and politicians. A word of warning: the crocodiles seem docile out of the pool, but will undoubtedly attack anyone who falls into their watery home.

Close by is **Bakau craft market**, where you can buy the usual range of wood carvings, batik clothes and tablecloths, and jewellery.

Past Bakau, the beach curves to a rocky point, **Fajara**, a pleasant residential area (where Atlantic and Pipeline

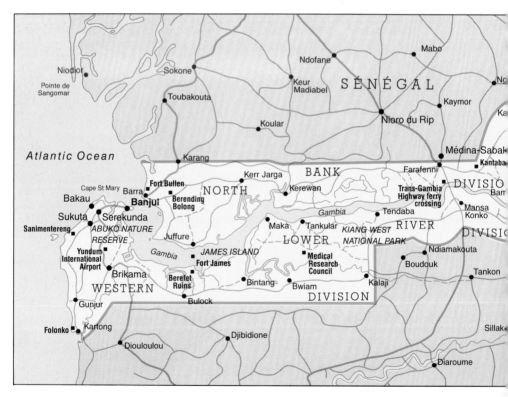

roads meet) favoured by foreign diplomats. The presidential residence is located on Fajara Point as is the **Fajara Hotel** and the **Fajara Golf and Country Club** (temporary membership to the club is available at very reasonable cost; caddies and equipment for the 18-hole golf course can be hired). The Fajara Club is charming and dowdy, or depressing and dowdy, depending on your viewpoint. The bar and entrance hall feature glass cases of sports trophies and photographs of RAF aircraft and their crews on visits to the Gambia. The atmosphere is a mixture of old colonial club house and village hall. It is worth bearing in mind as a change from the bars of the international hotels.

A more stylish possibility is the hotel-restaurant **Francisco's**, situated on the corner of Atlantic and Pipeline roads, whose lushly tropical terrace is a great place to dine.

The grounds of the golf club offer a short cut to the start of **Kotu Beach** and **Bungalow Beach**, **Bokutu** and **Kombo Beach** hotels, the latter part of the French chain Novotel. On the way, you will pass the large **Fajara craft market**, one of the best places to buy souvenirs, with reasonable prices and a wide range of goods. Flanking the beach are Il Mondo's beach bar, which offers fishing trips, and just behind Bokutu Hotel a small nature trail inhabited by monkeys. The cluster of hotels and beach bars here have attracted their own small craft market, and are served by the usual Gamtel office, supermarkets and clutch of cigarette vendors-cum money changers.

Between Kotu Beach and **Kotu Point** is the **Kotu Stream**, a trickle in the dry season, a torrent in the rains (should you become stranded on one side while walking along the beach, an enterprising local will probably appear to ferry you across for a small fee).

From the junction of the road leading to Kombo Beach and Bungalow Beach hotels, a long road running between scrub and pasture leads to the plush **Kairaba Hotel**, the country's only hotel of 5-star standard (visit the wonder-

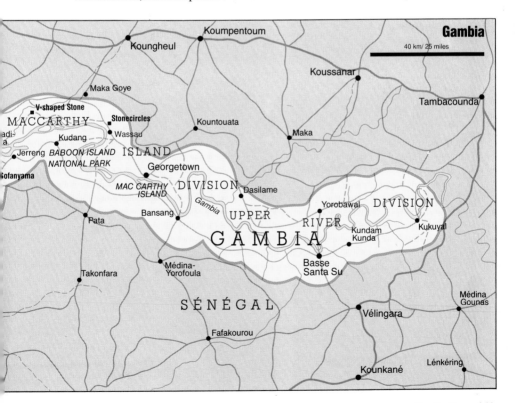

ful Somerset Maugham-style bar for cocktails), and the **Senegambia Hotel**. Dotted around the hotels are several good restaurants, including Valbonne, an upmarket Italian, Al Basha, a highly-rated Lebanese, and Dolphin, a popular English bar and restaurant.

A dirt track leads down past the hotels to **Kololi Beach Club**, an attractive time-share complex, whose **Brasserie** restaurant is open to non-residents. Next to this is the German-sponsored **Bijilo Beach Forest Reserve**, where for a small admission charge you can follow figure-of-eight trails, perhaps spotting monkeys and giant hornbills along the way. The Bijilo area offers not only the myriad birdlife of virgin Gambian forest, but a host of seabird varieties and flocks of variegated waders.

Rounding the great, sandy curve which is the extension of Bijilo and its beach you will reach **Bald Cape**, opposite the **Bijilo Islands**. From this vantage, look along the massive sweep of fine coral sand with only the fishing boats of **Brufut**, scattered palm-thatched shel-

ters and a green line of cocoa palms interrupting the blue of the sea and the blue of the sky. A little further south is **Salitor Point**.

Bush and beach parties are among the most popular excursions on offer at most tourist hotels and through the main tour operators. West African Tours, Black and White Tours and Gamtours all provide four-or six-wheel trucks and Land Rovers which take parties through the typical wooded bushland lying behind the coast. As a full day's excursion the Bush and Beach trip includes a morning's drive into grass and savanna land, possibly visiting palm-wine tappers' encampments (where a tapper will obligingly shin up a palm tree to show you how the sap is harvested), a market garden venture and maybe a school, culminating in a drive along the beach and a beach barbecue. In the afternoon, the tour, which does not keep to a rigid itinerary, usually stops off at a fishing village to see catches – often including turtle and shark – being hauled in.

The fishing villages offer one of the

Left, fresh shark tonight. Below, the beach at Fajara.

MANGROVE: THE FRIENDLESS TREE

John Steinbeck wrote: "No-one likes the mangrove." He was right: the ungainly tree with its roots buried deep in stinking mud, its gaunt branches and leathery leaves, has few sympathisers among the human population but is attended by a veritable zoo, aquarium and aviary of wildlife. However, not only do the mangrove swamps provide shelter for a wide range of creatures, but man also feeds, either directly or indirectly, off the curious tree.

Extending for almost 80 miles (130 km) up the Gambia River, the mangrove is a tropical evergreen which clings to salty tidal mud flats spurned by other life. Over 2,000 miles (5,000 km) of the Gambia's coastline and inland waterways are covered and the area is growing because of the mangrove's habit of "creating" land. Small lagoons and creeks along the coast, often in places where the sea breaks over the coastal sandbar, are typical habitats of the dense vegetation and stilt-like root systems of the mangrove.

There are four varieties of the tree: the red, most common on the west coast of Africa; the black, or honey, mangrove; the white; and the button mangrove. Each is salt-loving and among the few plants which can cope with water of a high salinity. The mangrove may grow to 80 ft (24 metres) in height and prefers regions with high rainfall. The trees grow in clumps between the low and high water marks and produce a particularly large quantity of vegetation and dead matter which decays into a very nutritious mire.

The roots, characteristically angled out of the mud, breathe in their oxygen requirement and almost leapfrog across the new banks of litter formed as the trees mature. The red mangrove sheds more than three tons of leaves per acre per year. In this way the mangrove adds to the coastal land and its special seed design and germination habits ensure that the "colony" grows.

Producing more than 300 seeds per year, the mangrove is a quick coloniser. The quill-like seeds germinate while still on the tree from the large, yellow, fleshy blooms. Between six and 12 inches long (15 cm), the germinating seed falls into the water surrounding the mother tree and inverts gradually because of its buoyancy. The sprouts touch land and the tiny plant takes hold and roots.

Should the seed be caught in a current, it will drift, alive, for up to a year until it is washed against suitable soil or further mud flats. Roots and debris along the coast break the force of the ocean waves and the seagrass, which grows in profusion beneath the stilt-lined waters, collects more vegetable matter increasing the banks on which the mangrove are embedded.

From the seaward side man takes his canoes into the backwaters and creeks of the mangrove's mysterious domain. One knows neither when one is on new dry land nor a mile out in the Atlantic; the forest of semi-floating, knee-deep trunks and thick, green canopy all looks the same. On this side of the mangrove reaches, the fishermen take an astounding variety of marine produce from shrimps and lobster to sea bass, electric eel, catfish and yellowtail snapper. Snook, tarpon and other game fish can be hooked in the mangrove margins. It is also an ideal location for the hunter: a myriad species of duck and wildfowl either roost in or migrate through this part of the Gambia's coast and river estuary. To the landward, man harvests oysters and mussels, crabs and other crustaceans. The mangrove wood also makes excellent firewood for charcoal and it can be fashioned into carved implements and used as building material. However, indiscriminate felling has, in some areas of the West African coast, dangerously depleted the mangrove and upset the ecological balance. This is not yet the case in Senegal, or in the Gambia.

Indirectly, the mangrove helps the human population by creating a "buffer zone" between the relentlessly buffeting waves of the Atlantic and the vulnerable, sandy-rocked shoreline. The plant also acts as a filter as it breaks down a good deal of waste which otherwise would pollute the shoreline. Finally, as the tree-line marches into the sea creating more land area, the rich soil behind it is eagerly tilled by local farmers. Unlovable maybe, but very useful. ∎

Among the mangroves.

purported to trace the author's ancestry from the tiny village, through the days of the slave trade, to modern America. Juffure and a reconstructed slave compound are a short walk from the ruins of another slaving post, **Albreda**.

Little in Albreda now remains from those harsh days except the ruins of the main building. The "freedom flagpole" has long since disappeared, but guides will point out where it stood in the middle of Albreda's compound. By reaching the old flagpole without being felled by bullets, a slave, it was said, would be granted his freedom. Poignant graffiti on the ancient walls read "Remember our tears." Nearby is the even older, Portuguese site of the trading post of **San Domingo**.

Out in the river is another British trading station dating from 1651. Fort James, on **James Island** is now a ruined shell inhabited by lizards, rats and snakes and held together by the roots of baobab trees. Facing the French outpost of Albreda across the waters, the fort ensured clear passage down the river for British and American slave ships until the mid-18th century.

After slavery in the British colonies was abolished in 1807, naval ships based at James Island intercepted more than 100 French and Portuguese slave vessels off the Gambian coast. A couple of cannon, thick stone and brick walls and parts of the dungeons (in which up to 140 slaves were impounded) are all that is left of the once-impressive fort. Even the island itself is gradually sinking. However, it is a poignant site. The beaches of the islands are littered by tiny beads, said to belong to female slaves who lost them in their struggles against the slave traders.

Motor launch excursions, like those offered by *Joven Antonia*, brought to West Africa from the Canary Islands, regularly take visitors on a half-day tour of the more interesting sites, allowing time to wander in Fort James's overgrown ruins, and to listen to tales of the slave days from village elders in Juffure. The trips usually include a buffet lunch on board, plus mid-morning and after-

The signature that made Juffure's name.

noon refreshment and, if you are lucky, the chance to see dolphins swimming in the estuary.

Apart from James Island, **Dog Island** and **Pelican Island** both have historical backgrounds. Leased in 1816 by Lieutenant Colonel Alexander Grant from the King of Kombo for the princely sum of £75 (US$133) a year, Dog Island was a source of the stone which was used in the building of many of Banjul's early construction.

Wrestlers and crocodiles: It was probably off Dog Island or James Island that the boundaries of the Gambia were first established. As no settled frontier divided British Gambia from French Senegal, it was agreed that the extent of land each side of the Gambia River which would define the country would be decided by the firing range of a gunboat lying in the mainstream of the river. It can be deduced that, in the 1890s, gunboats had a firing range of around 10 miles, the average width of the country each side of the river.

A shot fired inland from Dog Island would probably have landed somewhere near another interesting site. **Berending** is a small settlement north of Dog Island. A sacred crocodile pool in Berending attracts visitors who care to make the detour off the road from Barra to Senegal. Gambian wrestlers and pilgrims bathe in the pool in the hope of superiority in the ring or the healing of their ailments.

A number of similar sacred pools exist along the banks of the river, mostly dried up or shallowly filled with damp mud in which a surprisingly large number of crocodiles wallow. All of them have a reputation for magical healing qualities and draw pilgrims, many of whom walk for several days to reach a particular sacred pool.

Pot-holed and covered with red laterite dust, which gets into every nook and cranny, the road east runs through deep brush. Scrub, thorn trees, baobabs and silk cotton trees dot the dry landscape on the landward side. On the river banks, mangrove swamp and winding *bolongs*, or backwaters, form an impenetrable jumble. Buzzards, crows, pin-tailed

weavers and Wydah birds add life to the vista and small clumps of thatched roofs indicate the presence of village compounds.

From hamlets of conical-topped *rondavels*, or huts, surrounded by walled vegetable gardens, children peer out to watch the few vehicles which use this route. Often they will chase the Land-Rovers – the most common vehicles as four-wheel drive is essential on this road – and play in the dust churned up by the cars' struggles over pot-holes and gullies.

Often the only sight of adult life is women drawing clay pots of water from the village well. Saudi Arabia's Islamic Fund has provided many new hand pumps for isolated villages and one can see even the smallest of children pumping frantically in order to fill the long stone water trough from which goats will drink. Buckets of water for domestic use are filled from a spout or a similar trough. Where there is no running water, women often bring their washing to the well head and brightly coloured gar- **James Island.**

162

ments washed and left to dry in the sun form patchworks which are irresistible to the photographer.

The men of the villages are generally out working the fields (as opposed to the vegetable gardens, which are worked by women), extending or repairing their compounds or simply indoors sheltering from the sun's heat. On Fridays lines of men can be seen in their best robes walking to the nearest mosque.

As one drives through the flat countryside, clumps of green trees against the iron-red landscape reveal the whereabouts of villages and agricultural plots. Local produce is sold or bartered by the roadside, onions and radishes, oranges, bananas, cassava and yam laid out neatly. In some areas it is the produce of the palm – oil, wine and palm nuts – that dominate the makeshift roadside stalls. In other regions mounds of groundnuts, shelled and unshelled, and bottles of groundnut oil are for sale. Old groundnut sacks are have all manner of ingenious applications, including in some cases clothing.

Vegetables raised in this arid soil require constant watering, as do the Zebu cattle, the few pigs and the ubiquitous goats. The frequent trips backwards and forwards from allotments to wells are kept up even under the midday sun. As the two can be some distance apart, young girls with water pots balanced on their heads work in relays.

Transcontinental crossings: A ferry crosses the bolong at **Kerewan** where the road is a couple of miles from the river. After several little settlements like **Kinte Kunda** and **Saba**, a detour can be made to the larger village of **Salikene**, surrounded by mangrove. A visit to the rice fields is an interesting way to see how the crop is grown, harvested, winnowed and ground in much the same way as it was in the distant past.

Herons, storks, cattle egrets and other wading birds can often be seen in the water-filled paddy fields. After Salikene the settlements become more isolated and, for about 25 miles (40 km), the bumpy road runs across flat countryside to the town of **Farafenni**. Although

Tilling the land.

THE SENEGAMBIAN STONE CIRCLES

Between 150 and 300 miles (240 and 480 km) up the Gambia River, across the northern border into Senegal and south as far as Guinea, lies a collection of ancient monuments which remain one of Africa's greatest riddles. An anthropological and archaeological enigma surrounds the rings of massive standing stones scattered across the barren countryside.

Experts assume that the laterite megaliths indicate the earlier existence of a sophisticated African culture. Their formation, say experts, could point the way towards the discovery of an early empire whose only known remaining evidence is the stone circles. The circles are remarkably reminiscent of other megalithic tumuli such as those in Brittanny in France, which are generally held to be disposed in such a way as to indicate a connection with the sun, and therefore sun-worship. The peoples who live in the region nowadays hold the stones to be the work of an unidentified "earlier" civilization.

An ancient civilisation responsible for the

mysterious burial grounds may have existed before that of the "Ghana" Empire (not to be confused with modern Ghana). A royal city, named Cantor by the Arab chronicler El-Bakri in AD 1067, was thought to lie near the sites of the stone circles and its discovery could open up a new chapter in African history.

Some experts believe that the obelisks were erected as they now stand. Early skeletons have been found buried in the centre of some circles, as well as tools, pottery and miscellaneous ornaments.

Around 40 sites are dotted along the north bank of the Gambia River between **Kau-Ur** and **Wassau**. Thought to have originally been covered by laterite earth mounds, the standing stones sometimes include oddities such as the strange "lyre" or "V" stone at **Ker Batch**. Archaeologists think the megaliths were made and erected over 1,000 years ago and have now weathered down to a smooth, knobbly rust-red surface, like solid iron ore.

Most sites contain around 10 to 20 stone circles, whose circumferences vary. Some stones have flat or concave tops and tourist guides have been encouraging visitors to place small stones on top of the standing stones in order to "make a wish", which confuses the original order of the stones. Typical of sites abused in this way is **Wassau**, where the first of the Government rest houses and caretaker centres was erected. Several small buildings and a little display room at the end of a bumpy track are the forerunners of more sophisticated museum and reception buildings planned for the future.

Very little has really been done to unearth the origins of these "mystery sites", equalled only in sub-Saharan Africa by the ruins of Kumbi Saleh, the capital of the Ghana Empire, or those of ancient Zimbabwe. A so-called curse on those disturbing the sacred sites is related by local leaders. As early as 1931, a Captain Doke, an expedition leader called Ozanne, and the archaeologist Parker, all mysteriously died shortly after excavating some of the stone circle sites.

However, the team led by F.A. Evans, director of the Anglo-Gambian stone circles expedition in 1964–65, has so far escaped the legendary curse. One of the earliest victims was Richard Jobson, who came across the sites in the 1620s and wrote his account in *The Discovery of the Land of King Solomon* in 1633. Don't be put off by ancient spells – the stone circles are one of the wonders of the earth's "darkest" continent. ∎

Stone sentinels guard their secrets.

Farafenni is almost five miles (eight km) inland from the Gambia River, it is the north bank's centre for transcontinental traffic.

Traffic from Senegal travels down the Trans-Gambian Highway to Casamance and the south, crossing the river on the two flat-bottomed ferries. Lorries and cars queue for places on the diesel-powered craft while *pirogues* and dugout canoes offer alternative transport. Many travellers, tired of the rough condition of the north bank road, cross to the better kept south bank route for the remaining 50 or so miles (80 km) to **Georgetown**.

Although the north bank road cuts off a great loop in the river, it is worth a detour into this curve of the river to see **Elephant Island** and its resident families of monkeys. Its name is all that remains of the few elephants which lived in the Gambia until around the 1920s. A canoe trip around the island can disturb the occasional crocodile and flocks of heron from the dense undergrowth covering the island.

To get an idea of the full extent of the birdlife hereabouts ask the canoe's owner to take you to the south bank rice fields. Watch out for snakes – particularly green mambas – on the raised dirt tracks into the rice fields. Canoes can be hired at **Bambali**, where one can also rejoin the track leading to the main north bank road.

Just off the route to the next township is the historic village of **Kantaba** where the last wars of the Badibu took place. There was once a small fortress here, built by the British in the 1840s. **Balangar** is the next village on the route before the important groundnut centre of **Kau-Ur**. In this area the first of the mysterious stone circles can be seen, many of which dot the countryside north of the river and into adjacent Senegalese territory.

The road arcs around a swampy region at the headwaters of a large creek called **Nainija Bolong**, passing more stone circle sites such as **N'Jai Kunda**, **Ker Batch**, with its famous "lyre stone", and **Ker Jabel**.

Waiting for the ferry.

After passing through a number of small villages, the road heads back to the river at **Wassau**, site of the country's largest concentration of stone circles. A ferry links **Kuntaur** via a trail to the south bank highway but the north bank route cuts across another bend in the river before **Georgetown**.

A diversion at Kuntaur is **Baboon Island National Park**. This 5-mile (8-km) long group of islands is home to hippopotami and crocodiles, as well as a sizeable bird population. The species for which the island is famous, however, is the Olive Baboon. There is also a small population of chimpanzees, which are released here after "rehabilitation" at the Ape Rehabilitation Centre in Abuko Reserve, near Banjul. The main island and several smaller islets cover almost 1,500 acres (600 hectares) along this wide bend in the river.

Visitors are not encouraged on Baboon Island as the primates, which come originally from zoos and circuses in Europe, can easily be disturbed. The project's director, Stella Brewer, occa-sionally invite specialist wildlife parties to inspect the progress of the orphaned animals.

For visitors arriving by yacht or *pirogue*, a warden might join the craft from Baboon Island in order to pilot the boat near to where about 20 chimp-anzees congregate. If one is lucky, there is a chance to photograph the apes in their natural habitat – impossible any-where else in the Gambia. With time to spare, one might arrange a *pirogue* tour around the island from the village of **Kuntaur**. The boatman will usually point out one of the river's more famous obstacles just off the river bank near the village, the wreck of the steamer *Lady Denham*.

Back on the eastbound road, after the thriving, brick-built village of Kuntaur, and the dust track leading off to **Wassau**'s stone circles, a long straight, laterite road cuts off a wide bend in the river. In this bend lies the giant island of **Kai Hai**. Locals tell stories of a "dragon" which is supposed to haunt Kai Hai Island, and the number of villagers it is said to have devoured.

Visiting the island by canoe is an eerie experience. Overgrown foliage casts a permanent shadow over the few paths through its forest. However, approach-ing Kai Hai from the west reveals a part of the jungle that has been cleared and there is evidence that at one time rice was grown on the "haunted" island. Opposite, on the south bank, is a small landing stage from where one can take a short track to the Georgetown road.

Baboons and barbecues: The north bank road joins the river again at **Lamin Koto**. This village has been an impor-tant tourist facility since the creation of **Janjang-Bureh Camp** (book accom-modation in advance: see *Travel Tips* for details), an idyllically sited camp surrounded by forest and bordered by the river. Opened in 1988, Janjang-Bureh consists of *rondavels* in the local style set in a clearing on the riverbank. Each circular mud-brick and whitewash *rondavel* is adapted from the traditional African village hut with thatched roof, verandah and basic amenities (shower and WC).

Stella Brewer with gorilla Julia.

The camp acts as a base for wildlife excursions into the nearby rice fields, forests and creeks. The camp has a cookhouse equipped with a traditional clay oven, an outdoor restaurant/bar and a mooring for yachts and the villagers' canoes. River excursions from Janjang-Bureh are an exciting way to see parts of the bush not accessible by truck or large sailing craft. One sees much more wildlife from a dugout canoe paddling silently into waterside forest than from a noisy truck or Land Rover.

Lamin Koto's 50 or so villagers are now benefiting from tourist visits to this part of the river. Not only do locals act as guides, oarsmen on the small fleet of dugouts, and staff the camp itself, but the entire village regularly turns out in the camp compound to entertain visitors (for which they are recompensed by the German organisers). A real African evening with authentic food and dancing, unlike those put on at the coastal resort hotels, is presented at Janjang-Bureh. Strangely masked figures, characters dressed in leaves who whirl around like dervishes, and dancers disguised as animals or wielding lethal-looking weapons.

Prior to the evening dances, visits are encouraged to the village itself. The locally brewed alcoholic beverages should be approached with some caution. However, the rice and vegetable dishes are delicious. Carvings and other handicrafts at Lamin Koto are well worth bargaining for – both more original and cheaper than those at craft centres near the coast.

The camp is just a short walk from the jetty for the motorised ferry to **MacCarthy Island**. On the other side of the camp, along a rough trail, are the village rice fields. These paddies and the surrounding forest offer an astounding variety of birdlife. A morning expedition before breakfast, as the sun rises, is an unforgettable experience.

Local guides lead small parties through the forest. A good guide to west Africa's birdlife, a pair of binoculars and a camera are essential accessories. From time to time, paradoxically, as the

A typical river village.

hushed "crocodile" of bird spotters tip-toes through the swampy rice fields, a cacophony of rattling cans, shouting children and drum-banging women breaks the dawn silence. Every bird for miles is either petrified with fear or frightened into heading for the distant hills – the village bird scarers are shoo-ing the buffalo weavers from their pre-cious rice crops!

Janjang-Bureh is the most easterly organised camp site, although simple accommodation can be found at **Basse Santa Su**.

Mungo Park's memorial: A short truck ride east takes the traveller along a trail to the Mungo Park memorial obelisk at **Karantaba Tenda**. However, the riv-erside location of the concrete obelisk makes it easier to reach by boat. The stone marks the spot where the explorer Mungo Park disembarked in 1804, on his fateful second expedition to find the source of the Niger River. The birth-place of ex-President Sir D.K. Jawara is a short drive west at **Barajali** village. The historic Georgetown on MacCarthy

Island is also a few minutes across the river from Lamin.

Georgetown, built on the mile-wide MacCarthy Island, is an attractive set-tlement with an interesting past and several relics from its slavery days. It is a trading centre for the eastern section of the country and there are several markets in the town. Two ancient forts now stand in ruins and nearby is an old slave house. Further out of the town a Government rest house has been pro-vided for visitors.

Founded in 1823, the town has all the architectural hallmarks of colonialism. Wooden houses with iron roofs are slowly falling apart and one of the town's main features is the Armitage High School, located on the edge of town. In the main street the police station sports three iron posts which once offered free-dom to those slaves who managed to grasp them. The capital town of **Mac-Carthy Island Division** has a pretty building set back from the main road. This is the Divisional Commissioner's house and office. A mosque stands in **Pretty in red.**

168

the middle of the residential quarter of the town, which has only one principal shop.

A ferry links MacCarthy Island with both the north and south bank roads, which rapidly deteriorate from this point onward, although the south road has undergone considerable improvement. Most travellers up-country select the south bank road from Georgetown to **Basse Santa Su**. The north bank road, however, has several more points of historic and natural significance for those prepared to persevere.

The bumpy track runs through real bush and a guide is advisable – plus a four-wheel drive vehicle and cushions. From Georgetown the road hugs the unseen border with Senegal, returning to the riverside at **Karantaba Tenda**.

After Karantaba the countryside continues with sandy plains and reed swamps which surround the many bolongs. The swamps, which fill when the river floods its banks, are known locally as *banto faros*. At **Yorobawal**, a side road connects by ferry to the town of Basse Santa Su. Almost all travellers will gratefully take the detour after 50 dusty miles (80 km) of pot-holed track from Georgetown.

Another decaying colonial town, **Basse** is now no more than a large village with a few ageing Victorian buildings, a school founded in the late 1920s and two cinemas. Basse is a main depot for the area's peanut trade and a cotton industry has been established here. One huge market dominates the town and roadside stalls sell all manner of goods. After enduring the north bank track in the dusty heat, the first place to make for is the little bar/café adjacent to the marketplace.

Back on the main route to **Fatoto**, the most easterly town in the Gambia, the place to watch out for next is **Sutukoba**, 40 miles (64 km) further upstream. This is the ancient site of a large settlement and trading town which thrived during the early 15th century. It lies on the edge of the Djolof Empire's territory and its old name means Great Sutuko.

Excavations are planned in this his-

Coming home from school.

toric area, north of which are the two hamlets of **Gunjur Kuta** and **Gunjur Koto** – one old and one comparatively new – located on the border with Senegal and noted for the traces found there of early civilisation. Fifteen miles (24 km) further on, the road rejoins the River Gambia at the ferry of Fatoto. To reach the Senegalese border, the traveller would need to cover the last 10 miles (16 km) by canoe.

The site of the border is at the **Falls of Barrakunda**. The road now crosses the river at the ferry and returns westwards along the south bank back to Basse Santa Su. One diversion off the road from the river crossing of Fatoto is the ghost town of **Perai Tenda**, where abandoned shops and colonial trading posts testify to the prosperity of early riverside trading towns.

The South Bank Route: Visitors preparing for the 240-mile (385- km) journey from Banjul to Basse Santa Su, should make contact with the government rest houses and safari camps before leaving. Most tour operators will provide infor-mation on the up-country accommoda-tion contacts. West African Tours, Black and White and The Gambia River Experience cover the route to Basse with different stopover combinations.

By the well-surfaced south bank road, it is possible to cover the distance from Banjul to Georgetown in less than five hours, but only at a most exhausting pace. By boat, the journey takes a lei-surely three days.

The initial section of the road out of Banjul and through Serekunda (bumpy and badly maintained) passes the **Abuko Wildlife Reserve** on the right. The re-serve, which is open to the public, com-prises around 250 acres of tropical jun-gle devoted to West Africa's smaller mammals. Chimpanzees born in Euro-pean zoos are brought here for rehabili-tation before their release on Baboon Island near Georgetown. Early morning or late afternoon are the best times to visit the park.

Close to Abuko Reserve is the village of Lamin and **Lamin Lodge**, a charm-ing, higgledy-piggledy restaurant-bar **A river cruise.**

inka, which is the name given to the region's largest town.

There is often a police check on the Soma road. The police station is almost opposite the town's massive market on the left side of the road. A little caution should be exercised in Soma as the highway crossroads offers good pickings to the less honest of both Gambia and Senegal.

Pottery and kola nuts: The road now follows a great curve in the Gambia River, skirting mangrove swamp in the region of Elephant Island and cutting through rice growing areas. In places rice fields stretch for miles like great, flat marshes with clumps of palm and solitary baobab trees. Before the bridge over the **Sofanyama Bolong**, a new overnight camp is planned, offering accommodation in 20 *rondavels* along the same lines as Tendaba Camp. Run jointly by a German couple and the Gambian Tourist Board. The camp is located just off the main road before the village of **Pakaliba**.

All along this part of the route ven-

dors display ceramics, cane furniture and other local products. If you are on an organised tour, the guide might suggest that the group purchase some kola nuts before visiting a local compound – the nuts are a gift symbolising sincerity and goodwill.

From some parts of the road, the river and its many islands may be glimpsed. The islands have exotic names – **Dankuku**, **Pappa**, **Deer**, **Baboon**, **Bird Island** and **Kai Hai**. Before MacCarthy Island comes into view the road runs through an area of red, rocky terrain and passes a National Rice Project on the left. A monument to the Chinese, who first introduced the rice system and the mechanical pumping devices to the region, stands, overgrown, on the left side of the road just before reaching the first of Georgetown's two ferries. Sadly, due to neglect, the efforts of the Chinese during the 1950s and 1960s have been undermined. The pumping machinery which they installed and which feeds river water to the rice fields is now in very poor repair.

The ferry from the south bank to MacCarthy Island is manually operated by means of a hawser stretched across the channel. All visitors to Georgetown join the ferryman in helping to haul on the heavy metal cable. On the other side of MacCarthy Island, the ferry which takes passengers and vehicles to the north bank is motorised.

Most travellers detour from the main road to cross over to Georgetown to stock up with water and food at the town's one store. Continuing east from the junction with the Georgetown road, the hilly countryside is wilder than before, with scrub and bush. A little further on is the river and the ferry crossing at **Bansang**, an important market town where one can buy the pottery for which the region is famous.

From tiny clay pots incised, painted or carved, to giant earthenware water containers, the potter's art here has a distinctive quality and the reds of the laterite hills around are echoed in the colours of the pots. Particularly prized is the pottery from the villages of **Sotuma** and **Aldhungari.**

The 19th-century trading houses are the last major buildings on the wide streets of Basse. From here, eastwards, the road turns into a dirt track leading to Fatoto. The big covered market in Basse is well worth a visit, although it is mainly for the sale of livestock and foodstuffs and there is little that can be classed as souvenirs. Buildings include the large peanut warehouse on the riverside, where groundnuts are loaded on to barges, a few turn-of-the-century buildings, two cinemas, a church school and the Apollo Two hotel.

As one leaves Basse Santa Su and the comfort of a metalled road, the largest village before the town of Fatoto, **Garowal**, is on the left side. Fatoto itself is not more than 20 miles (32 km) from Basse but the trip is rough and dusty. The town has a groundnut collection factory and a ferry and it lies just six miles (10 km) from a major road which leads 40 miles (64 km) to **Tambacounda** in Senegal.

Right, cooling off at the coast.

If the Gambia's capital seems like a small provincial town in England transported to West Africa, Senegal's first city is much like a large French one which has drifted south a continent. Dakar's turn-of-the-century municipal architecture and marble war memorial would not look out of place in Clermont-Ferrand or Marseilles. You can sip a proper *espresso* on the terrace of a café watching the Renaults and Citroens, slightly more battered than European ones perhaps, driving by.

The French influence in the field of catering and hotel-keeping, combined with the size of the country, means that there are a reasonable number of pleasant, medium size hotels to accommodate tourists who wish to tour rather than to stay in one place. Older establishments such as the Hotel de la Poste in St Louis or the Hotel Aubert in Ziguinchor offer excellent value coupled with great atmosphere.

Modern luxury complexes in the international style are not lacking, of course. Club Mediterranée's hotels at the Pointe des Almadies and Cap Skirring and the brand-new resort of Saly Portudal offer beach and leisure facilities to rival anything in Africa. If you are looking for complete relaxation, it is possible to book a package to one of these and not move outside its landscaped, well-equipped premises at all during your two-week holiday.

If you want to investigate the country, however, Senegal is notable for the great variety of its landscape, all within range during a 10-day tour. At the northern border near the picturesque old colonial capital of St Louis, the dry sandy wastes of the Sahel stretch up round the edge of the Sahara to the Atlas mountains, Morocco and the Mediterranean. In the south, the lush green mangrove creeks and forests of Casamance herald the mysterious depths of Central Africa beyond.

In between lie hundreds of miles of sandy Atlantic beaches, the bird-thronged delta of the Sine-Saloum, the great religious centres of Touba and Tivaouane, the bustling avenues and nightclubs of Dakar and hundreds of simple villages where a stop will bring crowds of giggling children and, if you choose to introduce yourself, a glass of tea and a chat under a tree with the older generation.

Though it has pressing problems—the encroachment of the desert in the northeast, the overcrowding and unemployment of Dakar – Senegal remains a peaceful and friendly country, and its rich scenery, flora and fauna are highly accessible.

Not for nothing is the Wolof word *Teranga* much used in the naming of hotels and other facilities—it means Welcome.

Preceding pages: in the dry north; forest initiation ceremony; Dakar sunset. Left, mounted drummer of the Republican Guard.

THE DAKAR REGION

Dakar, Senegal's capital city, is a meeting point of African and European civilisations and a staging post on the route between tradition and modernity. And yet its creation, and the European occupation of the area of Cap Vert where it now stands, occurred late in the region's history. The first Europeans to arrive were the Portuguese, who landed on the Pointe des Almadies in 1444 but did not settle.

The native inhabitants of the region, who would have in all probability sailed out to meet the strangers in their expertly handled canoes, were Lébou tribesmen. There are a number of theories about the origins of the Lébou. One has it that the name comes from a Greek word meaning "black", and that the Lébou originated among the early black kingdoms of Ancient Egypt, where they came into contact with the Greeks who named them.

Another is that they came from much nearer, from the region of the River Senegal, and their migration southwards was punctuated by unsuccessful attempts to settle in other kingdoms along the way. Whatever the principal explanation, it seems clear that a number of waves of settlement occurred and that the Lébou are a composite of groups originating from other races. Lébou surnames are closely linked with the villages they come from: the M'Bengues and the Sambs are from **Ngor**, the N'Doyes and the Gueyes are from **Ouakam**, and so on.

The Lébou were among the first populations on the continent to set up a system of government akin to a modern republic. This happened early in the 19th century, when the state so constituted was recognised as sovereign by the French Crown.

The Dakar region therefore has managed to retain a high level of independence from protectorate or colonial status. The mini-government of the Lébou still exists and is recognised by the modern state of Senegal. Elections are held to nominate the *Serigne Ndakaru*, or head of state, and the representatives of the 12 Lébou constituencies known as *pinthie*.

France's power base: Of course, the original Lébou have long since been outnumbered as new inhabitants of all races moved to the growing capital. Dakar, with its sheltered deep sea port, took over from the island of **Gorée**, formerly a much more important colonial outpost, in the 1850s as the volume of trade and modern communications such as the trains began to make the little island impractical.

As the French began to build up Dakar, the city gradually grew to represent French power and influence over the whole of West Africa. Thus, the architectural legacy of colonisation is particularly impressive here.

This is not to say that Dakar, like St Louis, retains its colonial atmosphere largely intact. Dakar is now a large modern city. Although at the turn of the century its population was still under 20,000, its post-World War II boom

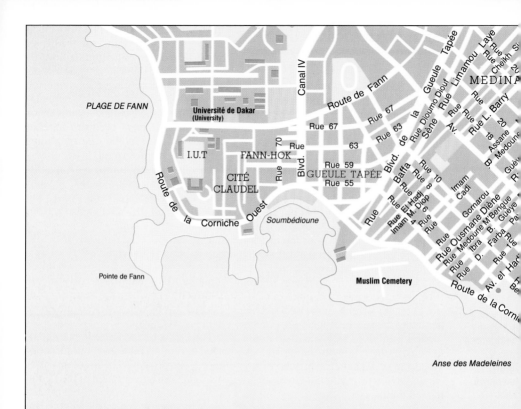

PLAGE DE FANN

Université de Dakar
(University)

I.U.T

FANN-HOK

CITÉ
CLAUDEL

Route de la

Corniche Ouest

Soumbédioune

Pointe de Fann

Canal IV

Route de Fann

Rue 67

Rue 67

Rue 70

Rue

63

Rue 59

Rue 55

GUEULE TAPÉE

Blvd. de la Gueule Tapée

Rue Dioumo Diouf

Sène

Av.

Rue

Rue Limamou Laye

Rue

Rue Cheikh Si

MEDINA

Rue L. Barry

Assane

Medoune

Guèy

Baffa

Rue 10

Rue 8

Rue 6

Rue 4

Imam
Cadi

Imam

Gornarou

Rue El Hadj

Imam M. Diop

Rue Ousmane Diène

Rue Medoune M'Bengue

Rue Ibra B.

Rue D. Farba

B. Guèye

Rue D.

Rue 11

Pa

Av. el Had

Be

Muslim Cemetery

Route de la Corni

Anse des Madeleines

Atlantic Ocean

Dakar

800 m/ 0,5 miles

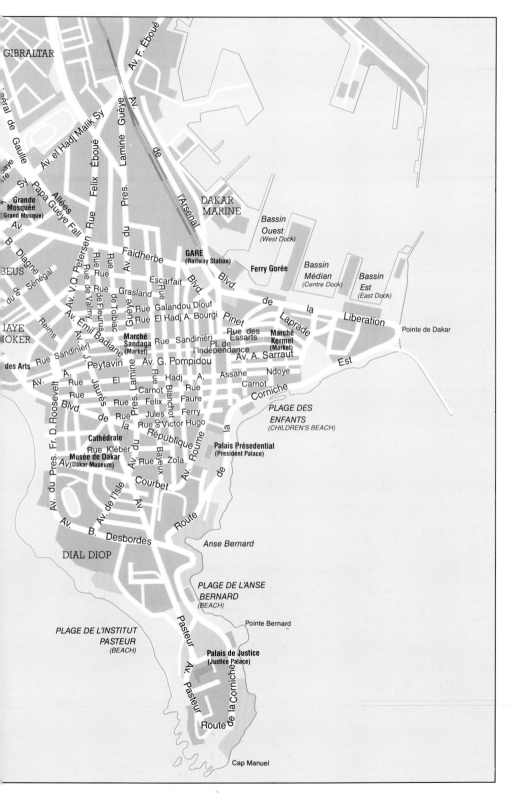

GIBRALTAR

Av. F. Éboué

Av. Lamine Guèye

Av. el Hadj Malik Sy

Av. el Hadj Malik Sy

néral de Gaulle

Allées Papa Guèye Fall

Rue Félix Éboué

Rue Lamine Guèye

de l'Arsenal

Pres.

du

SY

Grande Mosquée
(Grand Mosque)

Av.

B. Diagne

Sénégal

de

du

BEUS

IAYE
IOKER

des Arts

Reims

Rue Sandiniéri

A.

Av. J.

Rue de Valmy

Rue de Fleurus

Rue de Tolbiac

Rue V.Q. Petersen

Av. Émil Badiane

Peytavin

Jaurès

El

Rue

Rue

Blvd.

de

la

Av. du Pres. Fr. D. Roosevelt

Blvd.

Cathédrale

Rue Kléber

Musée de Dakar
(Dakar Museum)

Av.

Av. de l'Isle

Av.

B. Desbordes

Courbet

Bayeux

Rue

Av. du

Av. Roume

Route

DIAL DIOP

Faidherbe

Av.

Grasland

Rue

Escarfait

Rue

Galandou Diouf

El Hadj A. Bourgi

Blvd.

**Marché
Sandaga**
(Market)

Rue Sandiniéri

Av. G. Pompidou

Hadj

Carnot

Felix

Jules

Rue de Victor Hugo

Bayeux

Zola

Rue

Blanchot

A.

Rue

Faure

Ferry

Pl. de
l'Indépendance

Assane

Carnot

Ndoye

Av. A. Sarraut

Pinet

Rue des
Essarts

**Marché
Kermel**
(Market)

Blvd.

DAKAR
MARINE

GARE
(Railway Station)

Ferry Gorée

**Bassin
Ouest**
(West Dock)

**Bassin
Médian**
(Centre Dock)

**Bassin
Est**
(East Dock)

de

la

Liberation

Laprade

Est

Corniche

**PLAGE DES
ENFANTS**
(CHILDREN'S BEACH)

Pointe de Dakar

Palais Présedential
(President Palace)

de

la

Anse Bernard

**PLAGE DE L'ANSE
BERNARD**
(BEACH)

Pointe Bernard

**PLAGE DE L'INSTITUT
PASTEUR**
(BEACH)

Pasteur

Av. Pasteur

Route

de la Corniche

Palais de Justice
(Justice Palace)

Cap Manuel

République

Pres. Lamine

increased the figure to 300,000 by 1960 and almost a million by 1980. Overcrowding, as in most other African capitals, is becoming a problem as unemployed country people steadily migrate into the city.

The origin of the name Dakar is unclear. The favourite theory is that it comes from the Wolof word *daxaar*, the name given to the tamarind tree. It is said that early Europeans mistook the word, which they heard from the local people, for the name of the original settlement. It is also possible, however, that another word meaning "refuge" is the root, and that the Lébou used the term to refer to the terrain they settled after their lengthy migration from the north.

Central Dakar: The obvious place to begin a tour of Dakar is in the large oblong **Place de L'Indépendance**, which has been the central point of the city ever since it was a village 150 years ago. Most of the banks and airline offices are located in or near this square. Contrasting with modern multi-storey blocks such as the Hotel Indépendance in one corner and the Sofitel in another are traditional French structures such as the marble War Memorial, the Chamber of Commerce and the Foreign Ministry (in colonial times a lawcourt).

To the east of the Place de L'Indépendance, the leaf-shaded **Avenue Albert Sarraut** leads down towards the sea at the **Pointe de Dakar**. The end of the Avenue is marked by the tall ochre and brown bank building designed by the celebrated architect Goudiaby. Beside it, set back from the avenue, is the large modern Novotel, which enjoys panoramic views over the sea to the island of Gorée.

In the late afternoon the Avenue Sarraut buzzes with life as housewives do their shopping at the supermarkets or at the circular **Marché Kermel** a block to the north. The cool, dark bar of the **Hotel de la Croix du Sud** or the pleasant little French-run **Brasserie Sarraut** a little further along are good places to stop for refreshment.

To the north of the Place de L'Indé-

Sandanga market preparing for a shower.

pendance, the **Avenue Georges Pompidou** (formerly the Avenue Ponty, and sometimes still referred to by this name) runs up to the crossroads by the big neo-Sudanese style **Sandanga Market**. Formerly the heart of the French colonial shopping and business district, the Avenue Pompidou is rather run down nowadays. It is still a hive of activity, however, with street vendors selling everything from kola nuts to digital watches, beggars, the occasional hustler or pickpocket, and many shops and cafés.

Around the Avenue Pompidou, mainly to the south, is a grid pattern of side streets containing many pleasant stuccoed colonial buildings with balconies or interior courtyards, bougainvillea draped over the walls and so on. Good examples of faded colonial buildings with great charm are the **Hotel St Louis** in the **Rue Felix-Faure**, and the **Auberge Rouge**, on the **Rue Blanchot**, both of which have good, modestly priced restaurants – although neither is luxurious.

At the end of the afternoon, many Dakarois take a stroll along the Avenue Pompidou window-shopping, stopping to chat with acquaintances or have a drink in one of the French-style café-bars with terraces opening on to the pavement. The **Avenue du President Lamine Gueye**, which leads from Sandanga Market to the **Place Soweto** is similarly used, and on this street one may also find kneeling worshippers spilling over from the small mosque on the corner of the **Rue El Hadj Assane N'Diaye**.

Continuing west past the Sandanga Market junction, the Avenue Pompidou becomes the **Avenue André Peytavin**, and passes a large compound containing two-storey colonial buildings with wide shaded balconies running all the way round the four sides of the first floor. These are now occupied by various Government departments. The avenue ends at the cliff-edge overlooking the wide bay of the **Anse des Madeleines**. Turning right, one enters the long sweeping **Route de la Corniche Ouest** which leads to the University

quarter and **Soumbédioune Beach**. Turning left, one enters the **Boulevard de la République** which runs back, not quite parallel with the Avenue Pompidou, towards the east of the peninsula near the Place de L'Indépendance. The Boulevard contains the Théâtre National Daniel Sorano, which is Senegal's major centre for the performing art. Here, music and drama are presented throughout the year.

Opposite the theatre is the white block housing the national radio and television company (ORTS) which is not open to the public.

Further east along the boulevard is the Roman Catholic **Cathédrale du Souvenir Africain**. An imposing edifice holding 2,000 worshippers, the cathedral has within its precincts a large garden and an elementary school. It was built in 1929 in a mixture of styles, with two towers reminiscent of minarets, a great pseudo-Byzantine dome and a massive monumental façade. Continuing down the Boulevard de la République one comes upon the great wrought

iron gates of the Presidential Palace on the Avenue Roume at the end of the boulevard. The gates are guarded by the red-uniformed Presidential Guards, who do not object to being photographed. The palace itself is a majestic white mansion, green-tiled and built in 1907, set in a lovely garden with the ocean as a backdrop.

The Plateau and South: Having walked the above circuit of the **Plateau** – the central and oldest part of Dakar – you will have noted that walking is quite practical around the area and that this part of the city, laid out simply to a grid pattern, is easy to get to know. Almost opposite the Presidential Palace is a massive 10-storey block housing a considerable number of Government functions. This edifice, known universally as *le building*, commands a wonderful view of the peninsula and the surrounding sea from its roof terrace, and it is possible to obtain permission to go up to take advantage of this fact.

To the north, the Avenue Roume rejoins the Place de L'Independance. Proceeding south from the Presidential Palace, however, you first pass the main hospital and following west as the road becomes the **Avenue Courbet**, you enter the Place Soweto (formerly Place Tascher). Overlooking this large circular place is the modern building of the National Assembly and beside it the Dakar Museum, in neo-Sudanese style, which houses the **Institut Fondamental d'Afrique Noire** (IFAN).

Facing the museum is the **Avenue Pasteur** which passes the Le Dantec Hospital, the Institut Pasteur and the British Embassy as it heads south towards the tip of **Cape Manuel** with its powerful lighthouse (which may be visited for another splendid view).

Returning north towards the Place de L'Indépendance by the seafront route, you travel along the winding **Route de la Corniche Est**. This road, welcoming enough during the day, can be a lonely route at night and it is wiser not to walk it alone. Passing **Pointe Bernard** and the little bay of **Anse Bernard** with its good beach, you continue along the rocky ocean-front, looking across at the

Flower seller, Kermel Market.

island of Gorée, to the futuristic low concrete buildings of the **Lagon 1** and **Lagon 2** hotels, with their excellent restaurants.

To the north of the Place de L'Indépendance, through the **Rue Canard**, which is also known as Allées Robert Delmas, shaded by its tall trees, one passes the 1914 colonial **Town Hall** and the **Post Office** before arriving by the port on the **Boulevard de la Libération**. To the left is the magnificent colonial railway station with its vaulted brick façade ornamented by coloured tiles and its great canopied interior. To the right, the boulevard goes past the docks to the end of **Dakar Point**, with its half-finished sea-wall protruding into the Atlantic.

The port of Dakar is the largest and best equipped between Morocco in the north and the Ivory Coast in the south. It was the first major port in West Africa and an automatic stop-over for ships on the way south from Europe. Past its extensive oil, groundnut and fish depots, its great cranes, and continuing along the path of the railway lines, you come to the **Gare Routière** (or bus, coach and communal taxi station), a seething mass of travellers, drivers, vehicles in various states of dilapidation, and a thousand vendors with trays of drinks, oranges, cigarettes and virtually everything else a traveller might require on their journey.

Further out still is the big port-side industrial zone and an adjacent district of HLMs, the French-system mass low-rent housing units. Immediately northwest of the Plateau district, on the **Allées Papa Gueye Fall**, is the **Grande Mosque** of Dakar. Built in 1964 with financial assistance from King Hassan of Morocco, the building is inspired by the Mohammed V mosque in Rabat and in the Maghreb style. It is possible to climb its tall minaret every day except Friday, when the mosque is open only to Muslims for prayer.

The Medina and the markets: In the lee of the Grande Mosque, to its northwest, lies the "African quarter", as it once was, of the **Medina**. This tightly-packed district of low plaster houses set in a square grid of streets was built in the 1920s to house the survivors of the plague epidemic of 1914–15. By day a bustle of vendors and craftsmen in little workshops, the Medina at night buzzes with Dakarois walking the darkened streets to meet, talk and visit the little blue or red-lit *dibiterie* cafés or rudimentary bar/discos.

Two blocks from the Grande Mosque is the great concrete **Iba Mar Diop** stadium, where various sports take place, including African wrestling which packs in the crowds every weekend and on some evenings. Further out of town up the **Avenue Blaise Diagne**, opposite the Medissa School complex, is the **Tilène Market**, the least Europeanised of Dakar's markets. Here it is possible to buy charms, *gris-gris*, magic potions to ensure success in love or bring about a rival's downfall. Browsing among the stalls, you will find monkey paws, ground antelope horns, wings of owls and much more besides.

The other two markets of Dakar are somewhat less exotic, but essential to

Old and new, Dakar.

visit nonetheless. The **Sandanga Market**, located on the crossroads at the top of the Avenue Pompidou, is the city's largest market, a warren of cloth sellers and tailors, fishwives cutting up great silver-scaled *thiofs*, stalls selling cassettes (many pirated or bootlegged from the radio) and shoe shops. Some of the best buys here include leather work, ready-made or made to measure, pottery, rush and basket-work and *boubous* or the cloth lengths to make them (known as *pagnes*).

Dakar's third market, the **Kermel Market**, situated in a beautiful circular building off the Avenue Sarraut, is the most "de-Africanised" of the three. It is heavily frequented by expatriate Europeans. Its speciality is flowers – a gloriously colourful profusion, offered by women whose dress and demeanour are often scarcely less colourful. It is also reasonably good for craft objects, although its prices will probably be slightly higher than elsewhere.

Until 1989, a special feature of Dakar was its resident population of Moorish craftsmen (from Mauritania), distinctive in their distinctive bluebell coloured all-enveloping robes. Skilled silversmiths, many of them congregated in tiny stall/workshops in a number of locations, particularly the **Cour des Maures**, near the Sandanga Market on the Avenue Blaise Diagne. Following the racial violence in Senegal and Mauritania between their African and Moorish populations, however, many Mauritanians were repatriated north to their country of origin.

West of the Medina, reached from the Plateau via the long curve of the Corniche Ouest, with its joggers (and occasionally muggers) is the fishermen's village of **Soumbédioune**. Every evening the beach fills at five o'clock with the returning boats and the housewives come to buy the day's catch for their evening *thie-bou-dienne*. Between the beach and the large Muslim cemetery with its hundreds of simple stone graves all pointing in the same direction (towards Mecca) is the **Soumbédioune Craft Village**.

Checking out the latest sounds.

192

This complex, of up to 100 stands where carvers, leatherworkers, weavers and tailors work and sell their wares, was created in 1961 and is well worth visiting. From Soumbédioune it is also possible to take a *pirogue* over the short stretch of sea to the little islands known as the **Ile de la Madeleine** and the **Ile des Serpents**. The latter, an uninhabited island, is visible from any point on the Corniche Ouest. It acquired its name (the Isle of Snakes) as a result of a mishearing.

It was used to detain for a period of exile a French soldier called Sarpan convicted of a misdemeanour. Because his name rhymed with "serpent" in French, the island became identified with snakes, although none live on it. There are, however, a lot of interesting plants, flowers and, above all, migratory birds.

Towards the Far East: Beyond Soumbédioune is the residential suburb of **Fann-Hok**, and behind that, the extensive campus of the **University Cheikh Anta Diop** of Dakar. The institution

was named after the eminent Senegalese professor whose researches into the antecedents and early social and political structures of African peoples were of such profound influence. Flanking the coastline in front of the University are the elegant modern villas belonging to the country's social, business and political élite.

Further out of town than the University is the **Mermoz** district, named after the famous French aviator who flew the Atlantic from Senegal in the 1920s, and then **Ouakam**, now incorporated into Dakar's urban sprawl. A French military base here maintains a modest but not negligible force of around 1,000 men. Emerging into open country now, one passes **Les Mamelles**, the narrow steep hills which overlook Dakar, one of which has a powerful lighthouse (open to visitors) on its peak.

Continuing further, one arrives at the **Pointe des Almadies**, the most easterly point on the African continent. A large plot near the point is occupied by Club Mediterranée's complex, which con-

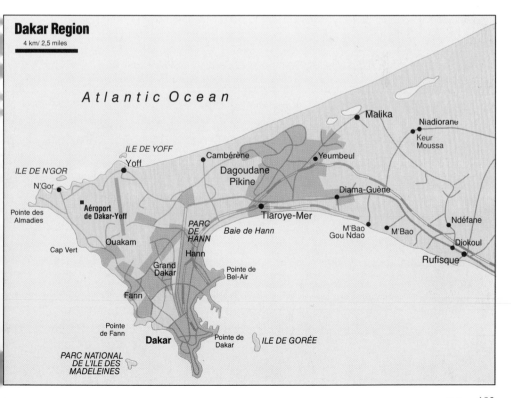

Dakar Region
4 km/ 2,5 miles

Atlantic Ocean

tains two restaurants, a large swimming pool, nightclub, theatre and the usual beach and sports facilities. Just outside the complex, a little oyster farm supplies two or three simple beach-front seafood restaurants. It is still possible to see remains of some of the wrecked ships which came to grief over the years rounding the reefed point.

Next to the Pointe des Almadies is the traditional Lébou fishing village of **N'Gor**, with its maze of houses, sandy beach with a little mosque and nearby naval station. It is possible to be taken in a *pirogue* from the beach to the little island of N'Gor, a mile offshore (negotiate at the quay). Near the village, by an extremely fine sandy beach equipped with all facilities, is the Meridien hotel complex.

Continuing northeast from N'Gor, the road skirts the airport before arriving at the Lébou fishing village of **Yoff**, situated opposite the **Dakar International Conference Centre**, with its bold modern triangular buildings. Yoff, the spiritual centre of the Layène Muslim broth-

erhood, is well worth a visit, especially on Friday afternoon when the sect's members, who comprise the entire population of the village, wear their distinctive white robes for Friday prayer. The occasional Ndeup ceremonies (*see chapter on Religion*) are also fascinating to witness but unpredictable when it comes to timing.

On the road back towards Dakar from Yoff, you enter the sprawling new housing area of the **Patte d'Oie** (Goose's Foot) before rejoining the northern suburbs of Dakar.

Along the northern coast of the peninsula are a number of new suburbs and districts which have sprung up to cater for the overspill from the burgeoning city. **Pikine**, up the road from Patte d'Oie, is the most telling example of the rapid demographic changes which have occurred. This new town, which grew out of the sand in the late 1960s, contains half a million people and is still growing.

Around the area of Pikine was the 19th-century frontier of the Lébou's ter-

Club Mediterranée, Pointe des Almadies.

ritory, where they had built a boundary wall of sand and clay to repel invaders. In between Patte d'Oie and Pikine are the poorer working class districts of **Parcelles Assainies** and Guédiawaye. Further north, the traditional Lébou village of **Camberène** is now surrounded by an assortment of new housing projects, the **Golf Sud**, **Golf Nord** and Hamo, financed by a mixture of public and private funds.

Cause for concern: Along the northern coastline, continuing from just outside Dakar all the way up to St Louis in the north, is a series of natural depressions, highly fertile because of their water retention, which provide much of the fruit and vegetables for the markets of Dakar. The rate of encroachment of Dakar's population is causing concern as to the long-term future of the **Niayes**, which are increasingly under pressure. In the area of **Sangalkam**, with its experimental agriculture institute, many of the small farms are owned by wealthy Dakarois.

Following the southern shore of the Cap Vert peninsula out of Dakar on the **Route de Rufisque**, you will pass the **Point of Bel Air** and the village/suburb of **Hann**, with its long sweep of beach and its forested Zoological Park.

The road continues, bordered with coconut palms (wayside boys still offer you freshly-cut coconut slashed open at the top so that you can drink the milk) but also now with industrial installations. After 15 minutes the village of **M'Bao** is reached and a little further on two more Lébou fishing villages, **Bargny** and **Yen**.

The first major town outside Dakar on this coast is **Rufisque**, the former colonial port and settlement. In the 19th century, this town was an important centre for peanut-processing and it was one of the four *communes*, along with Gorée, Dakar and St Louis, which were the earliest entities represented in the French National Assembly. Today, its colonial town hall and a number of other old buildings remain, but its financial survival depends largely on one business: its cement factory.

<u>Below</u>, leave your shoes on the beach. <u>Right</u>, have them shined for the city.

been acquired by rich expatriates such as Mark Gilbey, of the gin fortune, and the Aga Khan. This has lead to fears that Gorée would become a semi-deserted luxury retreat, but as yet there are no signs of things becoming so extreme.

In addition to the tourists who come over on day-trips, the island's educational establishments – three schools, infant, elementary and secondary, the so-called **Université des Mutants** – and the two museums, as well as the basic services (including post office, clinic, police station) provide jobs for the inhabitants. A number of civil servants from Dakar are also lodged on Gorée, in some cases in former administrative buildings. Ex-guards from the prison (now moved) which used to be housed in the Fort d'Estrées, and their families, continue to comprise a part of the population.

The arrival of the launch from Dakar is always an important event. The midmorning boat will be bringing back Gorée housewives gone to the mainland to do their shopping. Tourists will be met by island children and youths offering, usually politely and unpersistently, to show them around. A number of private yachts may be moored inside the shelter of the mole, and usually the beach will be well-used.

Walking up from the beach into the central area around the **Place du Gouvernement**, one is immediately struck by the visual beauty and the tranquillity. There are no cars on Gorée and most of the streets and paths are covered with sand, or sometimes paved with blocks of basalt from the island. Baobab and palaver trees shade the public areas and colourful bougainvillea drapes the terracotta walls and sprouts through collapsed roofs.

A fortunate gentleman: The most visible, and most luxurious, restaurant on the island is the **Hostellerie du Chevalier de Boufflers** with its charming terrace overlooking the beach and the landing jetty. The establishment has two simple bedrooms which, as they are the only two hotel rooms on the island, are extremely difficult to book. (The former

Beautiful old house renovated.

Relais de l'Espadon, the island's other, larger, hotel, closed down in 1981 and has failed to re-open since, in spite of constant rumours that restoration has been made possible and is under way.)

A drink or meal either on the terrace of the Hostellerie or in its cosy dining room, draped with fishing nets and hung with a mixture of African carvings and fishing objects, is highly recommended. The French owners produce excellent versions of local seafood (the seabass known as *thiof*, lobsters, crayfish, prawns, clams and other rarer shellfish and crustaceans) cooked in the French manner. One should also know a little about the figure after whom the hotel is named.

Jean-Stanislas de Boufflers became Governor of Senegal in 1785, and moved his residence from St Louis, which he didn't like, to Gorée. A poet and aesthete, Member of the Academie Française, he was also an appreciator of feminine beauty, and among the *signares* of Gorée found ample scope to indulge the latter taste.

The *signares* (a corruption of the Portuguese *senhora*) were women of half-European, half-African parentage who acquired great wealth and power on Gorée (as they did in St Louis too) via liaisons with the European merchants, administrators and military men. These relationships were recognised as in effect temporary marriages which ended when the men returned to Europe. After scooping up the sand of their beloved's footsteps and a brief period of mourning, the abandoned women would seek a new "husband".

The richest *signares*, such as Anne Pépin (de Boufflers' mistress), Victoria Alberis and Cathy Louette, had large houses, and substantial entourages of slaves and women servants. It was the job of these servants to parade after their employers carrying their jewellery on display. The 18th century saw a period of lavish entertainment and considerable elegance among the small community on Gorée, with balls and banquets diverting the exiled Europeans, who were nonetheless making large sums of money from trade.

Victoria Alberis's house, with its prow-like end balcony still stands on the corner of the Rue Malavois and the Rue St Germain, where it now houses the **Historical Museum** of the **Institut Fondamental d'Afrique Noire**. The museum houses a collection of African prehistoric remains, rooms devoted to the great African empires, the European trading period and assorted other exhibits including a collection of African musical instruments.

Education and relaxation: A second museum, the **Musée de la Mer** (of the sea), situated a block away from the Hostellerie du Chevalier de Boufflers, offers a collection of 750 species of preserved fish and 700 molluscs and crustaceans, harvested from the coast of Senegal. The major attraction for most people, however, is the **Maison des Esclaves** (the House of Slaves), a beautiful piece of architecture (containing a famous double-crescent stairway) which masks its acute cruelty of purpose.

The curator of the House of Slaves, the energetic and fascinating Joseph

Warm stone and twilight at the end of the day.

N'Diaye, shows visitors the chains and shackles, the small ground-floor cells in which the slaves were locked up at night while waiting to be shipped to America, and the first-floor apartments, spacious and balconied, where the masters lived. He will explain how the women and children cooked and cleaned for the master while the men were made to quarry and break the yellow marble and basalt which were used to replace the native Bambara's wood and thatch dwellings with stone houses.

There are a number of other buildings of great architectural interest which demonstrate the typical configuration of the former slave-dealers' houses; the **Douga Dieng** house, which is to house a documentation centre on the Black Diaspora; the former **Angrand House**, in whose ruins open-air theatre is occasionally performed. All these buildings share the typical strong defensive exterior, interior courtyard with verandahed first-floor European quarters, and ground-floor cells for the slaves.

Other monuments of Gorée are the **mosque**, one of the oldest stone mosques in the country, the pretty early 19th-century **Church of St Charles Borromeo** and the earliest building in the island, the **Portuguese Church**, which dates from 1482. At either end of the island are military fortifications. At the south, on the hill which dominates the island, are the remains of the **Castel**, while at the north the old **Fort D'Estrées**, also known as the **North Battery**, awaits its conversion to an annexe of the Historical Museum.

Probably the most enjoyable way to see Gorée, though, is to stroll at random through the streets, so rich in lovely if decaying houses and in atmosphere. If you know a resident, or get to know one during your stay, you may be invited into their home for a leisurely tea session. If not, you may stop at one of the little cafés along the beach and the seafront promenade of the **Quai des Boucaniers** for a drink or a meal. **Thiam's**, run by a former waiter at the Hostellerie du Chevalier de Boufflers, is good and very cheap.

The Victoria Alberis house, Gorée.

Less problematic are likely to be the handmade leather goods, gold and silver jewellery wrought in the roadside booths by Malian and Mauritanian craftsmen, and bronze castings.

Ocean rollers: From Thiès, one can reach the beautiful beaches north of Dakar by joining the coastal road at the point where Kayar is sign-posted. The Atlantic coast consists of long, straight beaches of white and golden sands, drifting dunes topped with hummocks of sea-grass and ocean rollers which would look at home on postcards of California. As one travels away from the Cap Vert peninsula, there are a number of points of interest before the Atlantic Coast beaches. It is wise to have a guide when visiting these sights, particularly if one wants to understand the background to some of the historic sites.

Sebikotane is the location of the famous William Ponty School, which has trained a number of the country's statesmen. Its imposing edifice rubs shoulders with some magnificent examples of mid-19th century architecture. Nearby

is **Ranch Filfill**, a Lebanese enclave created in the middle of this dry, desert-like area and planted with exotic tropical plants and flowers.

A diversion off the road, to the north, leads to **Keur Moussa**, a monastery best visited on a Sunday because of the special masses sung each week to the accompaniment of traditional Senegalese instruments.

To the north of the peninsula is a string of large lakes, **Youi**, **Malika**, **Mbeubeusse** and **Lac Retba**. Between the lakes and the coast large areas of afforestation have been created. **Lac Retba** is significant as it was on this lake that the famous aviator, Jean Mermoz, who created the first airmail service to South America in 1930, landed his seaplanes before Yoff airport was established.

Near the lake is the settlement of **Bambylor**, close by the tourist camp on the coastal dunes. Run by a group of Peuls, the camp, known as **Ndiaga Peul**, is set in delightful surroundings with an endless white beach fringed by cocoa

palms. The accommodation is rather basic, but the scenery and the succulent seafood make up for the spartan conditions. A crossroads is reached at the village of **Mbayak** where one can either return to Dakar, divert down to Rufisque or continue up the coast to the main attraction north of Dakar, **Kayar**.

Kayar and canoes: A "canoe", on the formerly French West African coast, means a *pirogue*, a long, narrow, double-prowed dugout which plies the rivers and creeks. They are generally carved in one piece from the buoyant wood of the baobab tree. The larger *pirogues,* drawn up on the beaches as one travels along the coastal road north of Dakar, are carvel-built. Almost every beach and bay from Cap Vert to St Louis sports fleets of these colourfully decorated boats lining the high-water mark.

The boats are the product of generations of craftsmanship and design. Constructed from an easily carved red wood similar to teak, the main frame consists of planks warped to a flat centre board which defines the *pirogue's* narrow,

high-sided profile. In length, the traditional *pirogue* can vary from two to 20 metres and its width generally accommodates side-by-side paddlers with a central well for net and catch. At each end of the craft a curious prow gives the *pirogue* its knife-like shape and the entire construction is fashioned by a team working with hand adzes and finished by bringing up to smooth surface ready for paintwork.

To watch the laborious work of the boatbuilders on the Senegal coast is like watching the progress of a hand-built car. Working under an awning of woven palm thatch, the foreman directs the precise measurements and guides each adze stroke until the form is perfect. Often broken glass is used to prepare the surface for its final coat of paint.

Blues, black, patriotic greens, yellows and reds are applied in layers to a stylised pattern. The craft may be dedicated to saints, either Christian or Muslim. Crescents, stars, diamonds, hearts and flowers exquisitely painted, bedeck *pirogues* with names such as *Malik Sy*

On the beach at Kayar.

or *Mahmood Gadafi*. Sometimes inscribed in Arabic and with intricate scrollwork, the proud beak of a bowsprit is often adorned with a Senegalese flag.

From the beaches of Kayar, hundreds of these *pirogues* brave the ocean far out from the coast in order to follow the shoals of migrating fish such as sea bass, tunny, hake, swordfish, barracuda and shark. On shore, in the maze of smoke-houses and cabins, net huts and food booths there are taxidermists who specialise in preparing shark's heads and sailfish trophies for collectors of sporting souvenirs.

Huge drying frames and long fish-smoking huts are crammed onto the shore at Kayar with little alleyways in between. On the beach, as soon as the fishermen return with their catches, the prime fish are sold off fresh from the *pirogues*. Brightly dressed women with enamel bowls on their heads haggle for squid, octopus, red mullet and choice cuts from the larger fish. Everyone on the beach is busy and each appears to have his own role in the process from the netting of the fish to the loading of large, gaily-painted lorries.

There is a hierarchy among the fishermen and the catch is carefully portioned out down to the last entrail. Even the small boys who organised the palm log rollers on which the great fishing boats are manoeuvered to and from the water are paid in fish. Between July and October, the population of Kayar more than doubles when fishing becomes a full-scale industry. A good percentage of the catch is sent for sale abroad.

The best time to visit Kayar beach is a couple of hours before sunset in order to watch the last catches of the day being brought in and the hundreds of fires being lit along the wide beach. The most popular accommodation on the Kayar coast is the **Auberge des Cocotiers**, where the variety of fish dishes defies the imagination.

Essential stopover: To reach the next main seaside village, **M'boro**, one should return to the crossroads at Mbayak taking the road which passes between the lake and the shore. M'boro

Having a corking time by the sea.

lies about 30 miles (50 km) north of Kayar and is also a fishing centre. Near the village of M'boro, the **Rose Lake**, or **Lac Rose**, is a spectacle not to be missed. The lake, which inspired Sir Michael Tippett's final work, *The Rose Lake*, has its own peculiar movement in the form of the thousands of birds which throng its opaque pink mineral waters. Flamingo, spoonbill, pelican, heron, tern, waders of all kinds and a variety of seabirds congregate on the placid waters, making this an essential wildlife photographer's stopover when touring the West African coast.

Although one could travel even further up the coast to the more isolated villages of **Fas Boye** and **Lompoul**, these remote villages are only reached by long diversions off the main Dakar to St Louis highway. The recommended tourist circuit is to take the road from M'boro, east and inland to the religious centre of **Tivaouane**, the capital of the Tidjiane sect. This strict religious order was brought to Senegal by Malik Sy and its leaders still reside at Tivaouane. The main feast of the Tidjiane sect is *Gamou*.

North of Tivaouane, the minor towns of **Mekhé** and **Kébémer** provide stopping points on the main road to St Louis, and finally the larger town, **Louga**, is notable as a major depot for the collection and processing of groundnuts, but for little else.

Folklore festival: There are a number of traditional feasts and celebrations in this region. Entertainment managers of hotels and tourist complexes have added their own, Hollywood-style variations and costumes. This makes it difficult for the visitor to ascertain how much of the spectacle presented is authentic and how much is choreographed for tourists.

One of the more popular dances performed traditionally during the month of May is known as *syniaka*. The dance is performed by girls who are coming of age in the villages of the Thiès region. In early times, the ritual of week-long seclusion also included the practice of female circumcision. Today, the formidable surgery has been all but stamped out, but the ceremony at the culmination of *Syniaka* remains a favourite tourist attraction.

Towards the beginning of June, the rituals of female fertility and witchdoctors' forecasts for newly-born children are celebrated with exhortations to gods and with colourful dances. This period is known as *Kunyalen* and preceeds the *Fil*, another ceremony observed during June–July.

Fil involves songs, poems and stories, coincidentally offered up just before the annual rainy season. The dances and incantations of *Fil* usually predict good crops and a healthy future for the village. Women feature as the main performers in most of the rituals of the Thiès region and another of their ceremonies, *Ebunaay*, is enacted only by women and includes the exotic and erotic dances known as *bugereb*. These rites generally last for about a week and culminate with the selection of the village's beauty queen. Today, on the stages of tourist hotels, these once important, long-drawn-out ceremonies are condensed into performances which can take as little as 20 minutes.

Left, collecting salt in the Pink Lake. Right, playing in the cotton.

The Hotel de la Poste, while typical of the colonial architecture of St Louis, is not, however, the most luxurious hotel in the city. The **Mame Coumba Bang** which has 40 air-conditioned rooms, is the most modern hotel. It is furnished in classical French style and has a popular restaurant, an intimate bar and the city's only swimming pool. **La Résidence** is a comfortable, family hotel much like the Hotel de la Poste but smaller, with only 30 air-conditioned rooms, a traditionally decorated restaurant and bar frequented by office workers.

Built on a grid pattern, St Louis is easily seen on foot. At one time, no building was allowed to be higher than the **Grande Mosque**, just along the **Quai Roume** from the Hotel de la Poste. Located on the **Avenue du General Villiers**, at the north of N'Dar Island, the Grande Mosque is a spectacular structure set in the grounds of an ancient fortified mansion. Right at the end of the island is the **Public Works** building and **Radio St Louis**.

It takes a couple of hours to walk around the main island comfortably, especially if one stops to admire the fine architectural details of some of the larger buildings, the iron fretwork balconies, wooden shutters and elegant arcades and colonnades. Many of the streets bear the names of famous French writers and were laid out around 1873.

Crossing over the Pont Servatius one is immediately in the main marketplace. Wolof tribesmen wearing loose, embroidered shirts guide their fabulously decked out wives around the maze of booths and Peul women commandeer odd corners of the bazaar where they can set out their dried fish or red and green chillies.

Turning south from the market along **Avenue Lamothe**, running down the centre of Guet N'Dar, one comes to a very different part of St Louis. The white walls and red-tiled roofs give way to a more randomly constructed sector, only a few metres from the elegant 18th-century quarter and its tree-lined avenues. Here the Wolof fishermen have set up their village. Amidst their huts

Faidherbe Bridge in the mist.

and *pirogues*, one can observe nets being mended or drying, smoke-houses, fish being dried on racks and a constant bustle of people. The river side of the narrow spit is covered with a patchwork of vegetable gardens. It is worth remembering that the inhabitants of the fishing village, while peaceful and law-abiding, do not always take kindly to strangers peering curiously at their extremely basic accommodation and visitors may not be made to feel particularly welcome.

Pressing on briskly through the village, a kilometre south of the market is the strange and impressive **fisherman's cemetery** where rough tombs covered with fishing nets lend a weird and uncanny air to the vista of sea, sand and low huts. At the southernmost point of the spit is the **Hydrobase**, once the location of the famous French airman Jean Mermoz's airmail service. The buildings here have now fallen into disrepair and the whole area has an aura of decay. The huge sand dunes running along the shore attract picnic and bathing parties.

As the Hydrobase and the beach are quite a distance from the centre you may decide you want to hire a carriage for the journey. Opposite the fishermen's quarter is the **College Blanchot** and the **Research Centre** on the tip of N'Dar Island. A little further on, the **West Quay** of N'Dar runs the length of the island up to Servatius Bridge. The large building behind West Quay is the city hospital.

Daily trains run from Dakar to St Louis, taking about seven hours to cover the 165 miles (265 km). Carriages are usually packed and therefore it is wise to arrive at the station well before the train departs in order to secure a seat. There are weekly flights between Dakar and St Louis.

Outside St Louis: There are two major excursions which may be made from St Louis. Both of these are described more fully in the **Senegal River Region** chapter. The first is the riverboat *Bou el Mogdad,* which makes weekly trips up the Senegal River between November and May, leaving from the quayside at St Louis. The second is to the world famous bird sanctuary of the Parc National des Oiseaux du Djoudj, which is 38 miles (60 km) from St Louis by road. Djoudj, which is the third most important bird sanctuary in the world, is recommended if wildlife is a major part of your interest in West Africa.

South from St Louis is the **Langue de Barbarie** (Barbary Tongue) coast. Consisting of a long spit of sand dunes and exposed, flat islets, this peninsula is also a national nature reserve protecting hundreds of sea turtles which have adopted the lonely coastline as a nesting ground. The presence of these turtle colonies makes the park of the Langue de Barbarie an internationally important reserve.

The sandy coastline also attracts birdwatchers for the variety of migratory wildfowl which come here both from Europe and southern Africa. Just 100 metres wide and 15 miles (24 km) long, the Langue de Barbarie covers about 4,200 acres (1,700 hectares).

The two villages of **Patou** and

St Louis' Catholic cathedral.

Gandiol are generally included in the itinerary of *pirogue* tours to this small reserve in the early morning. These trips are not run to a set schedule and must be arranged with individual *pirogue* owners. Occasionally parties of ornithologists advertise on noticeboards in St Louis hotels for passengers to join their pre-arranged visits to the reserve. Nouvelles Frontières, Jet Tours and Air Afrique also organise excursions to the Langue de Barbarie.

The year's finale: Most spectacular of all the festivals in Senegal are the St Louis *Fanals*. Likened by some to the carnivals of the Americas, the *Fanals* take place between 21 December and 1 January. They date from colonial times when the predominant religion of St Louis was Roman Catholicism. Christmas Eve Mass was an important social occasion where ladies born of mixed race competed with each other to display the most sumptuous gowns and the richest jewellery.

Every year the gowns became more extravagant. The rich half-castes, often mistresses of the merchant élite, employed pages to support their trains and carry lighted lanterns in their path. While the ladies attended the service, the lantern carriers held their own competition outside the church to see whose paper lantern was most artistically constructed. Coloured paper, cloth and tinsel were fashioned into fabulous shapes lit from inside by candles.

Today the *Fanals* are real works of art sponsored by local businessmen and paraded through the streets of St Louis in a whirl of excitement and a carnival air. Paper and cardboard, silver foil, gilt, tinsel and coloured cloth are used to create spectacular designs. Ships, aeroplanes, buildings and monuments, masks – even replicas of mosques – are displayed in a great procession. A prize and the honour of best exhibit is awarded to the company responsible for the most attractive lantern.

Visitors flock to St Louis to witness this spectacle, which is as vibrant as many of the carnivals of the Caribbean or Brazil.

Pirogue by old trading houses.

THE SENEGAL RIVER REGION

More than 1,000 miles (1,600km) in length, the Senegal River is still less than half the length of the Niger, which is West Africa's longest river. Rising in the Fouta Djalon mountains in Guinea, the river creates a large curve embracing both the Gambia and Senegal itself, of which it forms the northern boundary. Its wide arc flows around great plains of near-desert, such as the Fouta and the Ferlo.

Unlike Senegal's other major rivers, the Ferlo, Siné, Saloum and Casamance, the Senegal flows constantly throughout the year. However, during the October–May dry season, it is quite shallow and the shrinking waters reveal a riverbed covered with large mudbanks and sandbars. These obstacles to navigating craft make the river especially treacherous, as they move during the heavy rainy season and their whereabouts cannot be accurately plotted.

Several government schemes are in hand to control the flow of the river and improve conditions, not only for boats but also for the farmers who rely on the river waters for cultivation. Vast fields of millet, rice, maize, sorghum, tobacco, sweet potatoes and vegetables, such as onions and tomatoes, are grown along the fertile plain of the Senegal.

As very little of the pasture on the river banks is rich enough to support grazing, many of the villagers live from fishing in the teeming waters. However the river bursts its banks every rainy season creating some fertile areas and, close to the coast, new irrigation schemes have made large-scale rice cultivation possible.

In 1947 the Delta Irrigation Scheme was opened at the head of the river increasing rice production to its present level. Another interesting product from the Senegal River Region, which used to support thousands of workers, is gum arabic, drived from the acacia tree. Though the industry is not as active as it used to be, large quantities of gum arabic are still harvested for use in the textile and pharmaceutical industries.

Up a lazy river: Meandering through a huge region of arid and unproductive land, the River Senegal and its banks support thousands of people. Apart from the numerous villages which survive from cultivating millet, the entire length of the Senegal supports a great number of fisherfolk. The river is tidal for almost the first 300 miles (500km) of its length. Fishing is not restricted to such freshwater catches as carp, catfish, eel and bass, as the saline waters of lakes, marshes and creeks formed by the Senegal produce fish like snook, sea bass, lady fish, wrasse and even some of the larger marine fish. Spears, rods, all types of net and even basketwork traps are employed, as are all manner of dugout canoes, from one-man skiffs to six or eight-paddle craft.

Larger boats are constructed from traditionally designed planks, shaped into double-prowed fishing boats similar to those used on the ocean. Along the riverbanks, these craft can be seen at various stages in their construction, under palm-thatch shelters that protect the carpenters and boatwrights from the sun's heat.

Larger boats also ply the waters of the river which are navigable as far as Kayes in Mali. However, this is only possible in the high water season and really large craft can only navigate as far as **Podor**, 180 miles (280km) from the sea. Cruise boats sometimes make expeditions up-river as far as **Richard Toll** and occasionally Podor.

Flamingoes galore: Senegal's third smallest national park is located far in the north of the country, tucked under the Senegal River 40 miles (60km) from St Louis. The park, established on an island created by the Gorom Stream, is known as the **Parc National des Oiseaux du Djoudj**. Created in 1971, the park extends over 150,000 acres (60,000 hectares) and is one of Senegal's two World Heritage sites registered with UNESCO.

Djoudj, the world's ninth most important ornithological site, attracts thousands of birdwatchers each year. Winter is the time to see the park; then the marshy region becomes a seething mass of migratory fowl. The park is open from 1 November to 30 April and closes each day at noon. This means a very early start is required if one is taking a *pirogue* excursion to Djoudj from St Louis or driving the 90-minute ride to the reserve.

Most organised itineraries include a visit to **Tigue Lake,** which marks the boundary between Djoudj bird sanctuary in the north and the Maka Diama hunting reserve. The entire area between the crook of the Senegal River and the St Louis to Rosso road is known as the Djoudj basin.

More than 3 million birds are said to populate the Djoudj basin at any one time. Statistics read like a birdwatcher's paradise – more than 500,000 migratory ducks of varying species are estimated to visit the lakes and marshes during the winter season and over 12,000 white pelicans flock to the region. In addition, many thousands of brilliant pink greater flamingoes feed on the rich source of **Riverbank activity.**

shrimp and crustaceans found here, and spoonbill, a great variety of heron, stork and bustard can be observed from the numerous hides scattered throughout the park.

Northern hunting grounds: In the Maka Diama hunting reserve there is a specially designed lodge from which guides conduct visits into the reserve. Well equipped accommodation includes 16 bungalows, a bar and restaurant with panoramic views across the low-lying Djoudj basin. Expeditions can be pre-booked in Dakar at most travel agents' offices or through the hotel receptions in most of St Louis' hotels.

To obtain one of the three categories of hunting permits, three passport photos are needed, together with a valid firearm certificate and regulation insurance and dues. On both the Maka Diama and the Keur Massene reserves, only a small game hunting permit is required unless the applicant is intending to hunt wart-hog or gazelle.

Official lists record a variety of game which includes francolins, guinea fowl, partridge, pheasant, bustard, rail, snipe and a variety of species of duck. The larger game consists of jackals, hyenas, African wild cats, hares, wart-hogs, white-fronted or dorcas gazelles and monkeys, although many of these are protected species. In the creeks and marshlands snakes, crocodiles and hippopotami are not uncommon and visitors to the reserve are advised to keep to the tracks and paths outlined between the hides.

The nearest accommodation for visitors is either at Richard Toll to the east, or St Louis on the coast. Not far from the Maka Diama hunting lodge there's a recently-constructed dam built to expand the rice fields which, paradoxically, attract many of the migrating species of wildfowl from the National Park of Djoudj across the Gorom Stream. At the southernmost point of the hunting reserve the river widens as it nears St Louis and the sea.

The delta region of the Senegal River, as it flows between the long spits of land before the island city of St Louis, is

Getting to the other side.

wide and fertile. Downstream from Rosso the river delta has silted up over many years, which has made even the port of St Louis ineffectual as a major ocean-going port. (This was one reason why the capital of Senegal had to be transferred to Dakar, further down the coast.)

Rice and some vegetables are grown on the low, marshy stretches of land alongside the river which, at this point, runs parallel to the coastline just a short distance across a sandy spit. From the river mouth the tidal waters run almost 300 miles (500km) upstream as the land is so low and flat.

About 15 miles (25km) up-river lies the city of St Louis, most of it concentrated on a long, narrow island running alongside the spit dividing the river from the sea.

Borders and gardens: After Rosso the scenery changes as the presence of the Sahel begins to make the northern bank look parched. Palms edge the sandy banks and red rock cliffs. From Rosso it is 120 miles (200km) to **Nouakchott**,

the Mauritanian capital and a small ferry links the bitumen road on the Senegalese side of the river with a sand track on the Mauritanian side.

This highway is most important as it is Nouakchott's only land link with St Louis, Dakar and the rest of the West African coast. Many Mauritanian traders made use of this route in search of work in the richer country of Senegal until 1989's inter-racial bloodletting temporarily closed the border and many Mauritanians migrated back to their home country. The little settlement of Rosso is a crossroads and it is also used as a base from which to visit the hunting park of Keur Massene. Although no accommodation is available at Rosso itself, there is a hunting lodge with 17 rooms at Richard Toll, situated a little further upstream.

Richard Toll is a pretty, medium-sized township lying on the south bank of the Senegal River, about halfway between Podor and the Atlantic coast. The name of the settlement derives from a French horticulturist called Richard, who founded an agricultural irrigation project there in 1830, and the word *toll* which means "garden" in the local Wolof language.

The irrigation scheme grew progressively over the years and, by 1957, around 14,000 acres (5,700 hectares) of land were under irrigation. The project was soon helping to produce a wide variety of products, including cotton textiles, paint, liquid gas, refined sugar, chocolate, biscuits, chemicals, rope and sacking.

The expanded irrigation programme at Richard Toll is evident in the patchwork of rice fields in the surrounding countryside – like little squares of bright green carpet when the rice is young. Rice is grown throughout the year but the main harvest, when the grain is picked by hand, takes place in November. The main sugar-growing area is to the east of the town and the farmers produce more than 12,000 tonnes of sugar a year.

Richard Toll is an excellent base from which to visit hunting areas and make **Taking** fishing trips either on the river or the **cover.**

nearby lakes. There are two hotels; the Hôtel de la Poste, a well-maintained hotel with a fine, clean restaurant and a nightclub, and the Hôtel Massaada which also has a restaurant and nightclub but only two air-conditioned rooms to let. Although it is the opportunity to hunt and fish that mainly attracts visitors to stay in Richard Toll, the town has an interesting historical background and is worth exploring.

A baron's folly: Set on the high riverbank, overlooking the river, stands a building which looks every bit as incongruous in this part of Africa as an African compound would in the Bois de Boulogne. A huge colonial mansion set in beautiful botanical gardens is a breathtaking sight after a long river trip with little to break the landscape but the bulbous baobab tree.

This magnificent building was constructed by the eccentric Baron Roger, Governor of Senegal from 1822 to 1827. Roger was an avid horticulturalist who imported a great variety of trees and plants from France, cultivating them in a setting of cocoa palms and date groves. As a consequence of Roger's work European flowers and shrubs now flourish alongside tropical trees and exotic African blossoms.

Today the gardens are overgrown and untended. The great house itself, with its monumental façade, columns, grandiose stairway and numerous terracotta statues, has been the subject of several rescue plans, in particular for conversion into a hotel. So far no such scheme has come to fruition.

The parklands around the folly extend as far as **Taouey**, a weir on the river above the **Lac de Guiers**. At Taouey, a cleverly designed dam divides the saline river water from the sweet water of the lake and once provided irrigation for 2,800 acres (7,000 hectares) of surrounding land. Today only a few of the remaining dykes and canals are in operation and only half the area is now farmed for rice and sugar cane. A recent project is now reviving the original water system here and in the future production is expected to increase.

Mauritanians and camels crossing at Rosso.

The "frontier" settlement of **Dagana** is 15 miles (24 km) further upstream from Richard Toll and marks the division of the territory of the Wolof from that of the Tukulors. An ancient rivalry over land between two half-brothers established Dagana as the acceptable dividing point and the town's name derives from the Wolof word *deugna*, meaning "it is truly".

From Dagana, one can detour down to the Lac de Guiers, crossing to the fishing centre of **Mbane** by ferry. Many visitors stop off at Dagana simply because it is near the lake. The town itself has little of special interest except the ancient French fort awaiting restoration, the jetty where pleasure boats tie up and the old part of town with its typical houses. The region's main attraction is the lake and the fishing settlements around it.

Around Lac de Guiers: The Lac de Guiers, formed by the waters of the Ferlo River running towards Richard Toll, attracts visitors for its wealth of birdlife. There is also a hunting reserve to the east of the lake which is popular with weekenders from St Louis. A particular attraction is the fishing season during the rise of the Ferlo and Senegal Rivers from November to January each year, when the lake's waters are teeming with fish. Huge nets are cast from the banks of the lake and drawn in by fishermen in *pirogues*.

However, since the recurrent droughts that have affected the area in recent years, the catches have diminished and fishing is often insufficient to support the population of the lakeside.

To the south of the lake is the small settlement of **Merinaghen**, reached over 50 miles (80 km) of practically impassable road. This is a pastoral region and the people here concentrate mainly on rice production.

Tour companies offer several circuits of the countryside from Richard Toll. The lakeside trip follows a route through **Ndiago**, Mbane and **Syer**, deep into the Ferlo Valley, terminating at Merinaghen. Around the area of Mbane many small lakes stretch out along the Ferlo River, **An alley in Rosso.**

230

surrounded by numerous tiny fishing villages. Two notable settlements where fishing co-operatives can be observed are the villages of **Mal** and Syer.

Many of these lakes and villages can be easily reached as the main **Gnith** to **Louga** tarmac road follows the line of the Ferlo Valley and the region is criss-crossed by small tracks. Tours can be booked in Dakar or in St Louis and groups of birdwatchers and hunters regularly visit the more easily reached lakes. Few visitors venture far up the Ferlo River but one could follow its wide course as far as **Linguère**.

Much of the countryside on both banks of the river is desert. One difficult circuit, trekking into arid regions, is that which follows a trail to **Diagle**, east to the oasis of **Niassante**, to isolated **Tatki** and thence back to Richard Toll via Dagana. This tour is sometimes made by weekend hunters from St Louis or those arriving by air from Dakar at nearby Podor. The region east of Lac de Guiers is an officially designated hunting region.

Although the native population are Peul, there are a number of Chinese here on a technical assistance programme experimenting with new varieties of rice. The Chinese have also contributed to the recent development of irrigation schemes at Meringhen.

Driving is not recommended in the desert or in terrain where no proper tracks have been established. Even on those routes already described in this chapter, the road surface can vary from deep pot-holes to mini-ravines, from axle-high dust to wheel-deep mud. Four-wheel drive vehicles are therefore advisable. Bush taxis, converted from an assortment of pick-up trucks, negotiate the roads frequently but their arrival is never guaranteed and breakdowns are common.

100-Mile Island: About 110 miles (185 km) up the Senegal River the wide stream divides into channels forming one of the largest inland islands in West Africa. The **Ile à Morphyl** is a marshy, low-lying, narrow island which extends to 50 miles (80 km) in length. At the is-

Riverside life near Podor.

land's northernmost tip, **Podor**, which has a population of around 6,000, is one of Senegal's oldest cities. Historians claim that the region of Podor has been inhabited since the third century AD. Both the Kingdom of Tekrour and the great Ghana Empire left their mark on the area.

By the time the Fouta Toro Kingdom converted to Islam in 1776, the English had already reached that part of the country and, in 1745, had constructed a fort at Podor. The regular confrontations with the Peul tribes eventually destroyed the British fort but, in the mid-19th century Louis Faidherbe rebuilt the battlements, which can still be visited today.

It is well worth spending some time looking around Podor as, apart from the old fort, the architecture of the houses and ancient warehouses which line the riverside is of particular interest. The housing in this area is constructed of dry earth in the style of Mali, known locally as *banco*.

Industry in Podor is restricted to river transport, the movement of fertilisers and the recovery of aggregates from the bed of the river. In the town's Dieri region, there is a little port with a jetty where rivercraft moor.

The Ile à Morphyl has an interesting history. Legend has it that many hundreds of elephants once used to live on the long island and became isolated by the deep arms of the Senegal River. Cut off, the elephant eventually died out and the island became known as the site of the mysterious "elephants' graveyard". Mud-bricked mosques are among the scenic attractions of the region and ptrips can be arranged to see some fine examples at the surrounding villages, such as **Guede**, **Ndioum**, **Kaskas**, **Salde** and **Tielao**.

A small *gite* is located on the edge of Podor. Adventurous hunters use this as a base from which to hunt the crocodiles which are prevalent in the marshy areas surrounding the island.

Access is from the main highway which follows the course of the Senegal River. A branch of the road leads to a **Podor post office.**

232

small jetty where the ferry boat will take you across to the island for a small charge. There is an airfield at Podor, served by the River Airline.

The main road to the next large town, **Matam**, is reached either by the bridge or the ferry. Before leaving Podor, most visitors like to browse in the town's small market where beautiful and inexpensive pottery, a speciality of the town, can be purchased. This town also used to be a centre for the gold trade – the name Podor is thought to derive from *pot d'or*, "golden jar" – and some exquisitely fashioned jewellery can still be bought at the market.

The road from Podor continues on the south bank of the river, almost 140 miles (220 km) to **Matam**, a large town of some 9,000 inhabitants. Matam is known throughout the region for its crafts, in particular metalwork, jewellery and pottery, but its name originates in tribal history.

According to this, during the regular skirmishes between the rival tribes of the area, a small town known as Tiade

developed as a staging post along the slave routes. The Peul drove their captured slaves through the town, stopping to make the most of the Tukulor hospitality and paying for their needs in the currency of their trade: slaves.

The story goes that, having bartered away their slaves, the Peul then came back at nightfall and reclaimed them whilst the Tukulor slept. Other stories relate that the Tukolor themselves collected slaves to trade with the Peul but found the Peul were not credit worthy. Whatever the true background, the Tukulor of Tiade began demanding cash from the Peul tribesmen for any service which they afforded the merchants. *Matama* in the Tukolor language, means "pay cash" – hence the name for Tiade became **Matam**.

Forts and dams: The oldest colonial remains of Faidherbe's fort, in Matam are to be seen on the banks of the river where a flood carried the battlements away early this century. Louis Faidherbe built the original structure as one of his defending chain of forts in 1857. Down-

Cowherd by the river.

stream from the town is another crumbling structure, again on the riverbank, known as the Residence de Djourbivol. Both this colonial mansion and the fort are in dire need of restoration but little has been done to save these relics from the ravages of time, weather and the indiscriminate removal of stones and bricks from the sites by locals in need of building materials .

The only other building of any significance in Matam is its attractive mud-bricked mosque which is topped by two tall minarets. A dam, similar to the one on the river delta north of St Louis, has been constructed at Matam in order to develop the rice-growing potential of the area. This region is also known as the "granary of millet" as a result of the many acres of millet fields surrounding the town.

Accommodation in Matam is limited and the Hôtel Fadel, or Hôtel du Fleuve, is the only reasonable place to stay. The hotel has five rooms with showers but no air-conditioning and is run by a Lebanese proprietor, Mohammed Fadel. Al-though the hotel is in a sorry state of repair, the restaurant has a surprisingly good selection of local and Lebanese dishes and M. Fadel runs the only cinema in the region.

Matam, which is just over 300 miles (500 km) from St Louis, has its own airfield, served by the River Airline. The main Podor to Bakel road is reached by an unmade track which crosses the bitumen highway and continues on to the town of Linguère on the Ferlo River. Joining the main highway and continuing upstream, the road follows the course of the Senegal River for another 100 miles (160 km) before reaching the town of **Bakel**.

The far east: Bakel is an historic town and lies near the junction of the borders of Senegal, Mauritania and Mali in the far east. Originally the inhabitants formed part of the vast Ghana Empire which spread across a vast section of West Africa. Later, the invasions of Malinké tribes into the southern Casamance region originated in the area of Bakel. These migrations left the town-

River Region mosque.

ship rather depopulated until its re-occupation by a mixture of Sarakholé and Bambara peoples.

From 1690 the entire region came under the rule of the Boundou branch of Islam. University towns were set up throughout the area linked to the Kairouyine Mosque in Fez, Morocco, and the Grand Mosque city of Tlemcen in Algeria. These included Bakel and towns in what is now western Mali. Despite the great military strength of the Islamic rulers, the French were able to take the town of Bakel in 1819 and establish an outpost under a treaty with the local chief.

The French forces began to organise a system of commercial traffic with barges on the river, building a fort overlooking the waterway in 1847. Louis Faidherbe, who became Governor of the French West African territories in 1854, visited the town three years later and organised the construction of much more substantial fortifications. Faidherbe's defences also included installation of a gunboat just offshore to protect shipping and

Two generations on the river.

ward off an attack by Omar Saidou. The great *marabout* of the Sarakholé ethnic group, Mamadou Lamin, laid siege to Bakel in 1885 but was shot outside the fort. Retreating to Kayes, in Mali, Lamin died of his wounds and the town returned to rule under the French for another five years.

Strategically located at the head of the Senegal River, not far from its confluence with the Falémé, Bakel represents the terminus for commerical river traffic. This historic town has a number of colonial houses worth a visit and several attractive mosques. Still well-preserved after Faidherbe expanded the original structure, the fortress is an impressive building on the bluffs overlooking the river.

Bakel's fort is the country's third most important fortress. It is not, however, open to the public, as it is now occupied by the Prefect of Bakel.

One splendid relic which can be viewed is the grand pavilion built by the explorer René Caillé. Constructed on a spur of rock dominating the river simi-

lar to the location of the fort, the 1819 pavilion became a stop-over point for the military commanders Dupont and Dusseault.

The major expedition through Bakel was the first attempt by Caillé to reach legendary Timbuktu. Today, the sight of the fort and pavilion outlined against a Saharan sunset is one of Senegal's unforgettable images and worth hanging around for. However, overnight visitors will have to make do with the very basic accommodation provided by the administration. If the nearby *campement* is full, you should enquire about temporary accommodation from the Préfecture at the fort.

Before leaving the town, drivers should be sure to fill up with petrol at the station near the marketplace as the next town, **Kidira**, lies 40 miles (64 km) away on a rough unsurfaced road. There is an airport at Bakel, served by the River Airline.

Kidira, around 400 miles (640 km) upstream from St Louis, is a crossroads which few travellers reach. Adventurous travellers drive up the bitumen highway from St Louis only as far as Bakel where the tarmac road ends. The condition of the road from Bakel to Kidira is unpredictable and varies at different times of the year. It is certainly not recommended in the rainy season, when heavy mud makes it impassable even for four-wheel drive vehicles.

The only reason that Kidira survives is that it is built on the Dakar to Bamako railway. It is therefore the easternmost railway station in Senegal and the first stop for traders and visitors entering the country from Kayes, in Mali, or from further east.

Although Kidira is an important crossroads it offers no accommodation to travellers. The nearest hotel is almost 120 miles (200 km) west, in **Tambacounda**. Kidira and **Naye** are about 400 miles (640 km) east of Dakar and there are two trains a week. For faster access to the capital, it is easier to take the train from Kidira to Tambacounda and fly on the weekly plane to Dakar.

<u>Right:</u> *pirogue* in front of Bakel fort.

DJOURBEL AND FERLO REGIONS

This area lies between the Atlantic coast and the northern section of the Senegal River. Mainly arid with sparse vegetation, the **Djourbel** region forms the heart of Senegal's groundnut producing zone. The **Ferlo**, named after the **Ferlo River**, a tributary of the Senegal, is a belt of desert bisected by the river which runs through its valley and links with the string of lakes which include the Lac de Guiers.

The district known as the Djourbel includes part of the Ferlo desert and extends to within 45 miles (70 km) of both Dakar to the west and St Louis in the north. Locals call the western part of the Djourbel region **Baol**, as the area was once an ancient kingdom of that name. Today Baol, on the edge of the Sahel, is the country's richest source of peanuts and its flat, sandy plains support a variety of wildlife – hyena, gazelle, pheasant and partridge – and sev-

eral towns, including the region's capital, **Djourbel**.

The Ferlo desert covers one-third of the total area of Senegal, around 27,000 sq. miles (70,000 sq km). The more productive parts of the Ferlo are around the lakes and along the River Ferlo, which is dry along half of its 300-mile (500-km) length during the dry winter season. The surrounding desert consists of a vast plain covered in dunes, scattered rocky outcrops and occasional small depressions of clay where waterholes form.

Between the Atlantic shores and the Ferlo Valley is the district of **Louga**, named after its main town. It is from Louga that most visitors travel into the Ferlo region, as an important highway and a railway links St Louis to **Linguère**, the Ferlo's main township, through Louga. Another major road and rail route links the town with Dakar. Louga is also a major producer of groundnuts, generating 10 percent of the nation's total income from the crop. Apart from the Grande Côte area of the region, Djourbel and the Ferlo are completely land-locked.

Senegal's peanut capital: The major town of Djourbel has a population of 50,000, of mainly Wolof origin, and is located 90 miles (145 km) east of Dakar on the northern banks of the **Siné River**. An important crossroads, Djourbel is located on the main railway and highway which links Dakar with Tambacounda in eastern Senegal and ultimately with Bamako in the Republic of Mali.

Apart from being the hub of the peanut production district, the town is a major marketplace. Food production and processing are supplementary industries to groundnut collection while the local craftsmen attract customers from as far away as Dakar.

Outstanding among the craft workers is the local celebrity Sheikh Diop, a master of the art of bronze sculpting. Diop's favourite subjects, the ancient kings of Senegal, are among the most sought-after souvenirs of the country. They are created by the old method of "lost wax" moulding and the resulting casts are hand-finished, producing a unique artefact each time.

The wood carving booths lining Djourbel's marketplace and its Centre Artisanale are favourite attractions with visitors, as are the many stalls selling exquisite local embroidery. Leatherwork and gold and silver jewellery are also produced in the market and paintings with the common theme of the exploits of the national hero Lat Dyor make decorative, if bulky, reminders of a visit to Senegal.

As Djourbel is an important religious centre, the main mosque is one of the town's most spectacular structures. Its pinkish dome makes an impressive sight set in groves of deep green palm trees and from the balcony which surrounds the minaret one can get a fine view of the town and its surroundings.

Pilgrims converge on Djourbel during the annual pilgrimage to nearby **Touba**, when the town's population doubles. The date of the pilgrimage, or *Grand Magal*, is around the 10th day of the 11th month of the Islamic calendar

and devotees of the Mouride sect cling to every form of transport possible in order to travel to Djourbel and thence to the sacred town of Touba.

In the months apart from *Grand Magal*, accommodation can be found at the Hotel Le Baobab. Set in parkland and boasting its own swimming pool, the hotel and its spacious, traditionally decorated restaurant, is a haven from the bustling streets. Sixteen rooms with air-conditioning, five without, a discothèque and shops make this a welcome stopover for the visitor who has experienced the twice-a-week train ride from Dakar.

The trip takes around three hours and leaves Dakar mid-morning. Traders carrying market wares can cram the train hours before it departs. The journey, once a seat has been secured, is comfortable, with a dining car – provided the train is Senegalese. As the railway connects Dakar with Bamako, Malian trains, which are much less comfortable, also use the line. The Senegalese train generally leaves Dakar on Wednes-

Groundnut sorting by hand.

242

days, but nothing is guaranteed and it is always best to check with station staff a day in advance.

The best way to reach Djourbel is by train as the route from Dakar, although a bitumen road, is busy, dusty and a tiring six-hour drive. A regular bush-taxi service links Djourbel with the capital, but there is no air service.

There is little to visit in the immediate vicinity of Djourbel. One possibility is the agricultural research establishment at **Banbey**, 14 miles (23 km) west, on the Dakar highway. Experiments are conducted here to develop hardier species of vegetables and fruit suitable for the increasingly arid conditions. The encroachment of the sands of the Sahel has demanded technical advances in irrigation and crop management, which the centre is also researching.

Touba, desert shrine: In the centre of the ancient kingdom of Baol and just 30 miles (50km) north of Djourbel, **Touba** can be reached by road or rail. Both routes run through the town of M'Backé which has the only accommodation

along the way. Touba has a large campsite, run by the Mourides, which is only opened during the period of the pilgrimage. Also during the religious celebration one may find that the local people open their houses to visitors. In M'Backé, 3 miles (5 km) before Touba on the main highway, there is a permanent campsite.

During the pilgrimage, both towns celebrate through the night. In Touba the ceremonies are more reserved and religious in character, so most strangers tend to stay in M'Backé, making the short trip to Touba during the day. Touba is also an important crossroads and a rail terminal, around which a large marketplace has grown. Touba's most important role, however, is as the Mourides' religious centre. The Great Mosque's towering minaret is the tallest in the country – 87 metres high.

If you want to visit the town during pilgrimage, you are strongly advised to seek the permission of the Grand Caliph. A small gift is customary when introduced to the Caliph; once his bless-

Northern cattle traders.

DESERT DRIVING

More than a third of Senegal is desert and a good part of the rest of the terrain is laterite rock and sandstone through which tracks have been carved. At times these routes can be impassable. Rain creates gorges and pot-holes – and sometimes landslides which obliterate tracks completely.

Not all of Senegal is so daunting to the motorist. In fact, the country has an excellent network of good, surfaced roadways between its major urban centres. Nearly 2,000 miles (3,200 km) of asphalt roads link all the main towns and more than 10,000 laterite roads support the network. However, it is in the outlying regions of open desert and the sandy central plateau where one is likely to run into some difficulties.

This is not to discourage drivers from touring Senegal by car, merely to remind them that care and planning are necessary.

When choosing a vehicle to hire, opt for the most rugged. Peugeots are very popular in Africa and so spares are relatively easily obtained, but a number of Japanese marques are well established. Hot climate specifications – which usually comprise extra air filters, reinforced suspension and steering, and sump guards for the engine – are desirable, as is four-wheel drive, though the latter is not vital.

The list of equipment needed for desert driving is a long one: an oil temperature gauge, towing cable, lock on the petrol cap. laminated windscreen and replacement kit, car compass, jump leads, a full set of tools, an extra spare wheel, corrugated metal track lengths for sand-driving, a powerful hand lamp for night-driving, footpump, first-aid kit, a jack (particularly one with a wide base plate), puncture repair kit and tyre levers, replacement spark plugs, fan belt and extra filters.

Petrol, water and oil are life-savers in desert driving. Make sure all petrol tanks, plus a reserve, are topped up at every available opportunity. Petrol may not be available even if the map indicates so; garages and petrol stations listed may have gone out of business or even have run out of stock. Water will be needed both for the radiator and for human consumption. In desert conditions the human body consumes eight to nine pints (five litres) of water a day, without any strenuous activity.

A larger than normal quantity of oil should be carried and, because of the climatic conditions, regular cooling-off stops should be taken. Identify the locations of all water and petrol stops by means of a good map and try to confirm this information by asking along the road. The best maps are those produced by the Institut Géographique National, Michelin, or Esso.

On the road, the heat of the day should be taken into account, as should the fact that darkness falls quickly. Dehydration is a common hazard and can occur stealthily. The head and neck should be protected from the direct rays of the sun. Large quantities of fluid and increased salt intake is the best way to avoid, or to cure, heat exhaustion. Rest is also important and therefore it is best to judge distances and driving stamina carefully. A second driver is desirable when covering long distances. Most people prefer to travel in a convoy of at least two vehicles.

If possible, it is wise to take a local guide. In the event of a breakdown, stay with the vehicle, flag down passing assistance but be watchful over possessions when it is being rendered. Sound your horn when approaching an oncoming vehicle, or flash your lights repeatedly in night conditions to warn other drivers.

When driving in sand, the trick is to maintain sufficient speed to get through loose patches without becoming bogged down. If you do, however, either reduce the air pressure in the tyres to increase traction or, better still, lay metal sand tracks (which you should include in your equipment list) in front of the driven wheels, having first dug the sand away from around them. ∎

THE LITTLE COAST

Lying just an hour's drive from Dakar in the shelter of Cap Vert, the scenic beaches of the **Petite Côte** stretch southwards for 75 miles (120 km). With a stunning coastline, idyllic climate and a number of good modern hotels, the "Little Coast" has become a magnet for European sun lovers who have little hankering for the more adventurous side of Senegal.

With calmer waters than its counterpart, the "Grande Côte", to the north of Dakar, the Petite Côte draws thousands of visitors. Shimmering white beaches along the foam-edged Atlantic coastline are cooled by constant tradewinds and shaded by towering cocoa palms and lofty kapok trees. And if the attractions of the beach begin to pall after a while, active holidaymakers can make excursions into typically African forest or take a boat trip. The deep blue waters of the coast teem with a bewildering variety of fish.

Most of the Petite Côte's inhabitants are fisherfolk who live along the shore – as the hundreds of *pirogues* which line the wide sandy beaches testify. The majority of the population lives in the coast's five main towns, **La Somone**, **Saly Portudal**, **M'Bour**, **Nianing** and **Joal**. The people are mainly from the Serer or Lébou tribes and this area is predominantly Christian. Portuguese and French influences can be seen everywhere, in Catholic churches, missions and schools. Ex-president Léopold Senghor, who was born on the Petite Côte, is a Catholic, a member of the Serer tribe. He was educated at the Catholic mission school in Joal.

Crags and beach clubs: Access to the beaches is via the N1 road south through **Rufisque**. A regular coach service operates to most of the townships along the coast. The N1 is a major highway as it connects the capital with both the Transgambia Highway and the main route east to Mali. Just over 25 miles (40 km) from Dakar, at Bounga, there is easy access to the cliff-encircled beaches of **Yenne**, **Niangol** and **Nougouna**. For a day's excursion these beaches make a welcome escape from the bustle of Dakar; unfortunately at the weekends most of the capital's inhabitants seem to be of the same mind.

There are a couple of villages nearby, approached by separate roads. The first, **Toubab Dialao**, is noted for its spectacular setting. In contrast to the rest of the Petite Côte, Toubab Dialao's beaches are bounded by steep cliffs of red rock. At sunset these craggy backdrops reflect a range of colours from bright orange to deep crimson and bathe the little fishing beach in gorgeous shades of red.

One has to return to the highway to reach **Popenguine**, just a few kilometres along the coast, though it is possible to walk along the beach from Toubab Dialao to Popenguine for a visit of a few hours. There is little to see in this village of around 1,000 people, but it does contain the first big hotel on the coast after Dakar, the Pelican.

Popenguine is the centre of a religious

Preceding pages: Layène Muslims worshipping at Yoff. Left, the bridge of Fadiouth. Right, empty beaches can still be found.

pilgrimage and has also been chosen as the site of one of the President's residences. Each Whit Monday, a procession sets out from the little church and makes its way towards a cleft in a nearby cliff. This is the site of the "Miraculous Grotto" where devotees pray to a statue of the Black Virgin. It is believed that, at this spot, the image of the Virgin Mary appeared to a group of fishermen.

The road from Popenguine joins the N1 at **Sindia**. Continue to **Nguekokh** to visit the beaches and villages of La Somone, Ngaparou and Saly Portudal.

The next permanent holiday establishment along this coastline is the **Village-Hotel of Hippocampe** at La Somone about 46 miles (75 km) south of Dakar. Somone is also a popular weekend destination for the capital's workers. The Hippocampe has a traditionally decorated restaurant and bar and offers excursions in *pirogues* and horse riding treks along the beach or in the countryside.

Pirogue trips can be taken on the little river which runs through Somone and comes down from the hills between the coast and Thiès. Where the river joins the sea, a blanket of mangroves around its mouth harbours a variety of wildlife from flamingos to pelicans. On a cruise upstream, the scenery changes to high-galleried forest and the river narrows as the vegetation shades its slow-moving waters.

Birds and baobabs: For ornithologists, there is an extensive bird sanctuary at Somone. Water sports enthusiasts can hire nautical equipment from the **Village du Baobab**. This 200-bed bungalow village also offers fishing excursions, rents out *pirogues* and has its own nightclub. Le Baobab has an elegant restaurant decorated to suit the traditional fishing ambience and the menu is suitably fish-oriented.

Saly Portudal, often shortened to Saly, linked to Somone by a coastal road, was one of the earliest Portuguese slave trading posts in the country. The 17th-century site is now a small town. The **Palm Beach** hotel is rated one of the most luxurious on the coast. Brilliant flower-

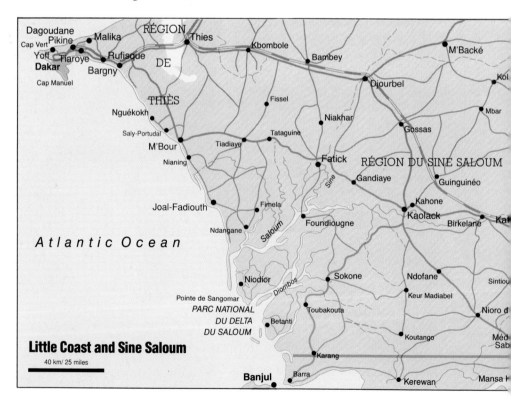

Little Coast and Sine Saloum

40 km/ 25 miles

ing hibiscus and oleander add splashes of colour at every corner, while cocoa palms tower over a large pool and fringe the tennis courts.

The four main hotels on the Saly Portudal beach provide horses, buggys, diving equipment and all manner of watersports. The **Novotel Club**, typical of the modern facilities, has video rooms, a theatre and a night club. The **Savana Koumba**, the second largest hotel on this beach, has an almost Olympic-size swimming pool. All the hotels organise excursions to places of interest such as the market at M'Bour a few kilometres away, or to the **Siné-Saloum** delta region in the south.

Located in the heart of the "Little Coast", **M'Bour** is the main port. This town of around 4,000 people lies just over 50 miles (80 km) south of Dakar. The township dates from the period when the French settlers began to push the Serer tribes south towards the Siné-Saloum district. The colonial leader, Pinet-Laprade, finally gained control of the entire area in 1859 and established a military zone around M'Bour which quickly evolved into the thriving fishing port you see today.

All around the port region, which is the life and soul of the town, fish-drying sheds and smoke houses for preserving the catches endow the dockside with a powerful aroma to which one slowly becomes accustomed. This odour is common around all the villages along the coast as the bulk of the Serer people's livelihood comes from the sale of dried and smoked fish.

Fishing opportunities: Deep-sea fishing trips can be arranged through agents in Dakar or directly through most of the hotels on the coast. A day's trip usually commences at 8 am and returns at 4 pm. Where the warm Guinea current meets the cold current of the Canaries, migrating fish can be caught in large numbers. Twenty-two of the larger fish to be caught in these waters are now recognised by the Game Fishing Association of Florida and at least 30 other game fish are prevalent. Swordfish, blue marlin, tunny, sea bass, wahoo, capitaine,

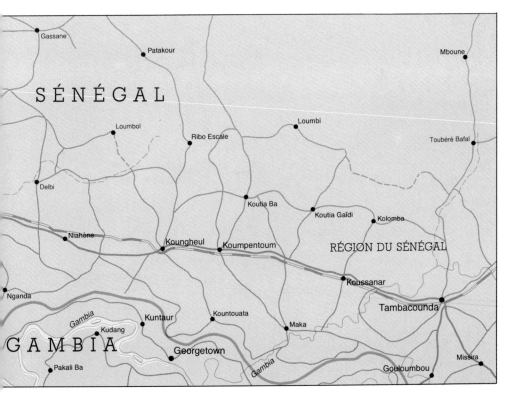

yellowfin, sailfish, bigeye, squalus, dolphin, barracuda, sawfish, blackfin, skipjack, a number of shark including hammerhead, and rays of all sorts – even the massive sunfish – have all been caught off this coast.

The boats available carry four to six passengers and provide meals and refreshments on board. Most are well equipped with VHF radio, outriggers, downriggers, electronic depth sounders and even fish finders. With all this sophisticated equipment on board, it is an interesting comparison to meet up with a fishing *pirogue* several miles out into the Atlantic Ocean which has no more advanced technology than 20 strong oarsmen.

If you fancy an adventure during your stay on the Petite Côte, it is possible to hire a place in the *pirogues* of the local fishermen or to charter a *pirogue* with crew for a private expedition. But remember that this is not an option for anyone who is easily made sea-sick – the waves can be pretty high.

Tourism is now having its effect on the traditional occupations of M'Bour's inhabitants and many craft stalls have been introduced. From the hotels of Saly Portudal, holidaymakers come on day excursions to M'Bour port and beaches and organised tours can regularly be seen wandering through the lines of fishing craft on the beach or photographing the wooden racks used for curing fish.

There are two hotels in M'Bour. The **Relais 82** has only six rooms but maintains a delightful restaurant specialising in local dishes. The **Centre Touristique de la Petite Côte** is located near the Prefecture and runs to 90 rooms, most with air-conditioning. It has a friendly, family atmosphere and is situated in a prime spot on the beach with simple bungalows located in a park-like area. At M'Bour the N1 highway branches away from the coast towards **Fatick**; the road that continues along the beaches is the N2.

Six miles (10 km) south of M'Bour is the delightfully isolated beach resort of Nianing, the location of a large holiday **Fish-smoking by the sea.**

village, the **Club Aldiana**, which has 300 bungalow-style rooms – all air-conditioned and with lovely, picture-book views across the beach or over the swimming pool. Between the Atlantic Ocean and the **Marigot de Nianing**, Club Aldiana is situated on the edge of an impressive forest where an amazing variety of birdlife can be observed. Set in parkland and surrounded by tall baobab trees, coconut and other palms, the **Domaine de Nianing** has 100 rooms in bungalows.

A delightful alternative to the beach is browsing in the village craft markets or those set up on the roadside near resort hotels. One can find exquisite carvings from a variety of African hardwoods, ebony, mahogany, sapele, afromosia or iroko. Basketwork from local bamboo and reeds, raffia work-woven baskets and hats made from the fibres of the raffia palm, fish baskets and even woven armchairs all make excellent purchases which are light to carry home.

Crocodile, snake or monitor skin belts and handbags should be purchased with caution as these skins come under strict regulations both for exportation and importation (into your own country). Ivory, tortoise and turtle shell items also come under strict control, but objects made from bone or horn are exempt. Pottery objects are also easily transported home, as are the delicately-wrought items of gold and silver. Cast bronze objects may also be found in the specialist markets.

The joy of Joal: South of M'Bour, about 70 miles (115 km) from Dakar, is the small town of **Joal**. The tarmac road ends here and if one travels further it is on a new road constructed from the shells of oysters, mussels and cockles. Joal has a history which goes back to the Portuguese occupation of the 15th century. The port was one of several which Portuguese traders used after acquiring them from the Dutch. A wide main street dominates the town with its population of around 5,000 and its rows of mouldering colonial houses which date from the middle of the 19th century. A house of particular interest is the one in

One-humped beach buggies.

which Léopold Sédar Senghor was born in 1906.

The setting of Joal, across the water from **Fadiouth Island**, is picturesque and there are also interesting sights in the surrounding countryside. Around Joal the great mounds of dry earth known as *tanns* are used as defences against the sea, bolstered by huge banks of sun-bleached shells some eight metres wide. Giving the scene a somewhat desolate look, hundreds of ancient gaunt baobabs are the only life to survive on the heaped shells and arid soil. These barren areas give the region a ghostly atmosphere which is even more pronounced around the fishermen's graveyards.

Accommodation is limited in Joal but **Le Finio**, which is thought to be an Africanisation of the French word for "the end", has 10 rooms, and its traditional restaurant serves high quality Senegalese dishes. Specialities include grilled mutton, lobster, giant shrimps, spicy chicken and the region's famous oysters – available from November to June. On the outskirts of Joal, where the bridge links the mainland with Fadiouth Island, there is a tiny Catholic mission run by nuns.

The village of **Fadiouth** is of considerable interest and most visitors cross the narrow stretch of water to it via the footbridge, although one can take a little *pirogue*. Constructed on an island made entirely of sea shells accumulated over many centuries Fadiouth is unusual for the lifestyle of its inhabitants and the isolation of the settlement. Held together by the roots of mangroves, reeds and the giant baobabs, Fadiouth Island is a strange mixture of the picturesque and the grotesque. The houses are made of the same discarded shells and pounded shells make a kind of cement from which the fishermen have constructed their small round huts.

The *pirogues* which ply the narrow channel between Joal and the settlement are the same as those which take the fishermen out to sea, while smaller canoes are used by the shellfish collectors who paddle through the creeks. On the gangling roots of the mangrove the oys-

View of the cemetery, Fadiouth.

ters can be seen hanging in black festoons like giant barnacles and it is these that the women gather, standing almost waist-deep in the muddy waters with wicker baskets in one hand, holding their canoes by a short line. The ancient island is partly surrounded by mangrove and on the other side there are coconut palms and shallows where the settlements have been built.

Six thousand people live and work on the island. Whitened heaps of empty shells lie everywhere. And there are blackened patches on the earth where the women have burned the shells in order to make them into a powder for use as paint for daubing the palm wood beams inside their conical huts. On the side of the island where the coconuts grow, the clusters of huts which are set over the water on coco-wood piles, with pointed roofs ending in top-knots, are used as grain stores for the staple diet, millet. The reason for these millet and groundnut stores being built in such a way is to protect the crops from vermin and to economise on land use. There is

All hands to the nets.

an acute lack of building space anywhere on the island.

From Fadiouth, the shoreline extends south for 25 miles (40 km) to the **Pointe de Sangomar**, a long, thin spit of sand and dunes without any road access. The Pointe de Sangomar acts as a barrage which protects the **Siné** and **Saloum** river deltas from the Atlantic Ocean.

Instead of trying to continue south from Joal-Fadiouth, where the N2 road terminates, some visitors prefer to make a round trip to M'Bour by following the shell road on to Ndangane, turning north by **Fumela**, **Séssène** and **Tiadaiye** to the Dakar road at M'Bour. This route cuts across the western edge of the Siné-Saloum delta and offers an interesting change of scenery from the white sandy stretches of the Little Coast.

The entire circuit is more than 180 miles (300 km) and can be comfortably explored in two or three days by making stops at M'Bour, Joal, or even at **Ndangane** where basic accommodation is provided in 10 cabins at the **Campement de Djiffer**.

THE SINÉ-SALOUM

North of the Gambia and almost twice its size, the Siné-Saloum region is named after the two major rivers which cross this extensive area. The extreme southern part of the region, near the Gambian border, can be reached from an unreliable track inside the Gambia . Roads do run south from the Kaolack-Tambacounda Highway, but, due to the prolonged dry season and short, sharp, heavy rains which quickly wreck their surface, parts of these trails can double as river gorges in places. Of the most frequented region around the estuaries of the two rivers, it is the more southerly Saloum delta which is best supplied with tourist accommodation.

North of the Saloum: Arriving by *pirogue* on the **Pointe de Sangomar** at **Djiffer**, one can't help regretting the presence of a sand-processing factory in such a pleasant location. To screen the **Hôtel de Thiès** from the scenes of industry, a large number of trees – cocoa palms, eucalyptus and others – have been planted nearby.

Among the many little villages which can be visited in the area are **Diakhanor** and **Palarin**. This area is most picturesque, both for the way the villages are constructed – often on ancient banks of shells – and for the pointed-topped rice stores built on stilts away from the rising waters.

The Siné-Saloum is rich in bird and animal life. Meandering over flat areas, doubling back in creeks and bolongs and widening into lake-like estuaries, the two waterways, plus the expansive Gambia River, form one enormous delta. Hundreds of mudflats, sandbars and vast areas of mangrove swamps have provided an ideal habitat for a rich variety of birdlife.

In the mangroves, osprey can be seen wheeling over the fish-stocked waters while, in the northern, more desert region, buzzards search for reptiles. The two areas are in complete contrast, but it is the delta region which attracts the ornithologist and wildlife enthusiast.

This coast has been the subject of much ecological study as it is feared that the coastal defences of naturally formed mud banks and the vegetation which binds the banks together are slowly being eroded both by the forces of nature and by man, who has cut down many trees for firewood.

Among the gangling roots of mangroves white storks wade in shallows, searching out frogs and swimming snakes. On higher land, further up-river, shrikes ("butcher birds") impale their catches – from grasshoppers to small rodents – on the sharp prongs of thornbush.

Sometimes dolphins can be seen surfacing in the estuarine waters of the Saloum and flocks of great white egrets vie with solitary black cormorants for small river bass, eel and gobis. Palm plantations provide perfect cover for a colourful assortment of brilliant birds such as the violet starling, golden bishop, orange-cheeked waxbill and a variety of bee-eaters.

The opportunity to sight some of the

giants of the air is also available to visiting ornithologists: the palm nut vulture, a large black-and-white bird, the West African harrier hawk, Verreaux's eagle owl, the shikra, or, the greatest coup of all, the huge long-crested hawk eagle. Many visitors come across the border from the Gambia or down from Dakar specially to witness the flights of enormous flocks of rosy spoonbills on the wide estuaries or to photograph hordes of migrating storks and pelicans.

This is one place where a good field guide to West African birdlife, a pair of binoculars and a camera are essential. Local villagers may also be able to direct the enthusiast to some of the region's interesting bird and animal life.

No very large creatures inhabit the Siné-Saloum, apart from the three varieties of crocodile – the pygmy, the bottle-nose and, largest of all, the Nile crocodile. There are said to be several families of rarely sighted hippopotami and a number of dugongs, or manatees, in the saline waters. Journeying by boat through the maze of waterways, one can sometimes see a school of dolphins join the wake of the craft or dive across the *pirogue's* bows.

On land, the largest animals are the river (or bush) hogs, which should be treated with great respect. Python here often grow to considerable size, although the forest deer which sometimes venture into the mangroves are rarely bigger than a small dog. Monkeys – green, vervet, colobus, patas, or red – are among the largest mammals. Occasionally, tribes of baboons can be seen holding council under roadside trees – a rare excitement.

The dark, pod-like appendages festooning the exposed roots of the mangroves are a variety of oyster, a delicacy in this region. Walkways constructed between settlements across shallows are usually built of mud surfaced and strengthened with the shells of oysters. On the black mudbanks, the thousands of small holes are the burrows of sand and fiddler crabs which will emerge in their hundreds if one keeps still. Mud **Sidewater of the Saloum.**

skippers, with adapted front fins, walk across the banks from pool to pool and may even be seen climbing the mangrove roots.

Foundiougne and further: At **Foundiougne** the holiday village of **Les Piroguiers** offers good, basic accommodation and tours on the river and through its creeks, reed beds and waterways. The complex has 60 rooms in a setting on the banks of the Saloum. From here, one can visit the little fishing villages of **Dionevar** and **Niodior**, where very simple tourist accommodation is available. These villages are built on islands in the winding estuary waters facing the long sand spit of **Sangomar**.

Regular ferries, four a day, leave from Foundiougne to link with the main road into Dakar. The boat also takes in stops at the villages of Dionevar, Nio-dior and **Ndangane**, terminating at the town of **Kaolack**.

Opposite Foundiougne, across the wide arm of the Siné River delta, is the village of Ndangane. Not easily reached, Ndangane lies on a remote bolong towards the north built on a peninsula with good fishing grounds on both sides. Fishing craft of all sizes congregate here. Apart from making a tour of the small village and its surroundings, there is the opportunity to trek south along a spit of land inhabited by large numbers of waders, ducks and other kinds of wildfowl.

At Ndangane, the **Pelican Hotel** provides 60 comfortable rooms in comparatively basic conditions, although the wildlife here more than compensates for the lack of luxury accommodation and one has no doubt as to why the lodge is named "Le Pélican".

South from Foundiougne is the town of **Sokone**, a petrol stop for traffic from Kaolack to Banjul. Few visitors spend long here, as there is little to see, though it is possible to take a *pirogue* trip out to the offshore islands of **Betanti**. Most travellers journey on to the town of **Toubakouta**, another major centre for wildlife enthusiasts, served by the Keur-Saloum village-hotel. A pool, restaurant, bar, air-conditioning in all the bun-

Salt-flats near Kaolack.

galows, and fishing trips for barracuda give the place extra attractions. *Pirogue* excursions and hunting trips to **Sangako** and **Medine Djicoye** can be arranged at the lodge.

Another lodge, **Les Palétuviers**, has 40 beds in 20 bungalow-style cabins, a pool and similar diversions to the Keur-Saloum. Les Palétuviers was once known as the Jardin d'Allah hotel but has since been renovated. As the town is located on the **Diombos River**, Toubakouta's 300 inhabitants earn a living ferrying tourists and hunters in their *pirogues* and organising events such as Sunday afternoon wrestling matches and evening dance performances.

Both Toubakouta and Missirah are important locations in the **Parc National du Delta du Saloum** and the region has become a favourite with hunters. The variety of game includes duck, francolin, pheasant and wood pigeon in the large National Hunting Zone, which contains all types of terrain from mangrove to scrub. River transport is available for bird watchers and hunters and there are regular shuttle trips between Toubakouta and Ndangane, via Djiffer and Niodior.

Enquiries about the availability of these trips should be made through the main hotels in Toubakouta or Kaolack, where the cruises can be joined. Fishing trips on the river, walking treks into the swamplands of the delta region and tours into the inland park regions for birdwatching or hunting can be booked at the Keur-Saloum Hotel or the Hotel Les Palétuviers.

Kaolack and Kaffrine: With a population of around 150,000, **Kaolack** is the largest town of the Siné-Saloum region, and an important centre for the export of groundnuts, which are grown throughout the area. In addition, it is is also an outlet for salt, a valuable commodity, which is produced on the outskirts of the town and along the water margins of the Saloum River.

Kaolack stands on the northern bank of the river, just over 110 miles (180 km) south of Dakar. A road runs east from here to Tambacounda and the **Timber-cutting in the Siné-Saloum.**

Casamance area, including beautiful Diola sculptures.

Ziguinchor takes its name from the Izguinchors, the indigenous tribe which occupied the region in ancient times. The dominant ethnicities today are the Diola, Mandingo and Tukulor. Woodland tribesmen, such as the shy Balanté, Mandjack and Mankagné from the forests of Bayottes in the south, can also be seen in the markets.

The **Hotel Le Diola**, on the Avenue R. Delmas, offers 50 air-conditioned rooms, set in a square facing the swimming pool, with a good locally-decorated restaurant and bar. The less luxurious **Aubert** has 34 air-conditioned rooms, a pool, which is one of the best in West Africa, and features traditional French bourgeois cuisine and African dishes expertly rendered and modified to French culinary practice. The Aubert bar is especially pleasant, making good use of tropical plants and flowers to brighten the whitewashed walls and marble-tiled floors.

The **Nema Kadior**, the third top-class hotel, has 48 air-conditioned rooms, its own pool, and no restaurant, although food can be ordered at the bar or from the reception. **L'Escale**, a much smaller and less expensive hotel, is the only establishment in town with a nightclub. It is bright, clean, well-serviced and has 14 air-conditioned rooms and a restaurant where typical Diola dishes can be ordered. Another good eating place is the restaurant in the **Hotel de Tourisme** in the town centre, which has 10 air-conditioned, basically-furnished rooms.

Further out of town, on **Pointe St Georges**, is the **Hôtel-village de la Pointe St Georges**, with a fine restaurant in a rustic setting, excellent pool, tennis courts and 28 chalet-style rooms. Tours of both the northern and southern sectors of Casamance can be organised at the larger hotels and the Pointe St Georges offers it own treks and *pirogue* excursions.

Other tours can be made east up the Casamance River as far as **Kolda**, to coastal resorts such as **Cap Skirring**, in the jungle area to the southwest of

Palm wine collector up tree, Casamance.

Ziguinchor before the Atlantic coast.

South and west: South Casamance can be reached conveniently by bus from Ziguinchor's centre. From **Elinkine**, where the bus terminates, there are several well-trodden excursion tracks. The management at the economical camp at Elinkine will direct you to the estuary of the wide Casamance River where palm and sandy soil give way to thick mangrove, winding bolongs, or creeks, and narrow waterways alive with an extraordinary variety of sea and river birds.

A good trek from Elinkine is the island of **Karabane**, mangrove encircled and reached by small *pirogue* or dugout canoe. On Karabane, near the traditional hut village, is the site of an ancient, long-deserted colonial settlement. The ruins of an old Breton church can be seen just a short walk from the crumbling remains of the early houses. Karabane has its own campement, giving one time to explore the interesting surroundings of this river village.

There are many tourist circuits through this richly wooded region and the basic lodgings – known as *gîtes* – are located at Pointe St Georges, **Oussouye** and **Enamporé**.

One very interesting trip, which can be accomplished quite easily in a day, is via the lovely tree-lined rice field track to the famous *impluvia* or reservoirs of Enamporé. Great circular double roofs form funnel shapes over reservoirs where rain water is collected and kept for the dry season. The water system here is unique in Africa, as is the construction of the huts whose main compounds can shelter 50 people as well as their cattle, goats, chicken and grainstore.

On the bend in the Casamance River where the estuary is at its widest is the hôtel-village of Pointe St Georges. Here visitors can take boat rides out to the numerous islands in the estuary. Both the largest island, Karabane, and the 2,000-strong community of **Niomoune**, have Catholic missions and the four villages on the island of **Hillol – Kanoun**, **Kaoui**, **Kouba** and **Mantat**, are worth visiting in their delightful setting of high forest.

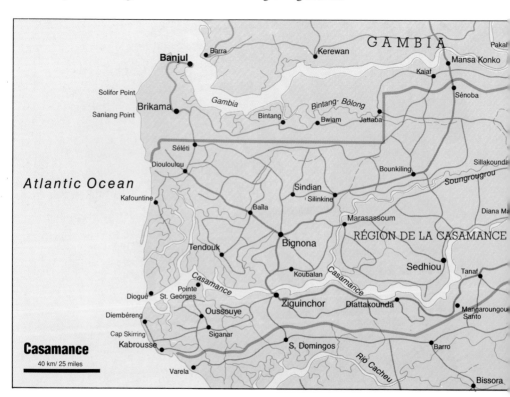

Cap Skirring and the coast: After the exertions of bush or forest, *pirogue* trips and visits to the islands, the fresh sea breezes of the coast are a delight. Cap Skirring is one of Senegal's most famous resorts. One hour's flight from Dakar and 45 miles (70 km) by road from Ziguinchor, the Cape lies almost on the border with Guinea Bissau.

The beautiful coastline is punctuated by sandy bays and rocky outcrops. Fishing villages are dotted from Cap Skirring north to **Diembering** and the Casamance estuary. Coconut palms fringe the white sandy beaches and behind the shoreline little tracks lead through palm forest rice fields to palm-thatched villages. Exploitation of these natural attributes by tourism has been carefully monitored by the Senegalese Government. Nonetheless, the hotel complexes cannot help being the dominant feature of the coastline.

Club Méditerranée runs a 300-bed village-hotel on a prime site at Cap Skirring. It has 266 bungalows, a pool, restaurants, a night club and facilities for tennis and watersports and numerous excursions. **Kabrousse Mossor** is smaller – 132 air-conditioned rooms with pool, restaurants, and the usual activities. **La Paillote**, managed by the Hotel Aubert in Ziguinchor, has 34 rooms in small bungalows, and the **Emitai** has just 27 rooms. The smaller hotels, as well as the Kabrousse Mossor, close from mid-May until the end of October.

Other tourist hotels on the Cap Skirring strip range from the 100-room **Savana**, and the luxurious **Kassoumay**, to a number of *gîtes* and campsites. Seven miles (10 km) north of Cap Skirring at **Diembering** is a less-developed beach, with palms fringing white sand and Atlantic surf. A 40-bed safari-type hotel offering basic accommodation, the **Aten-Elou**, occupies the prime site here and shares the beach with a campsite called **Delmas**.

Most of the activity along this coast is beach-oriented but there is the opportunity to visit local villages or the fishing town of **Kabrousse**, south from Cap

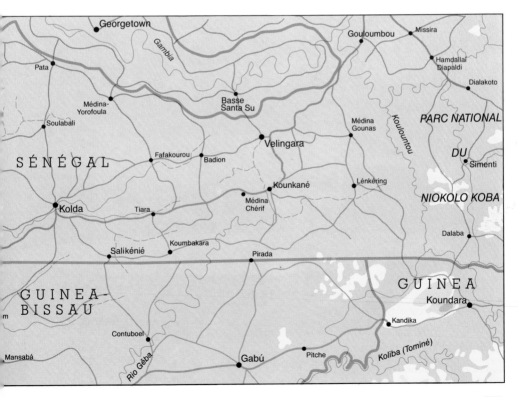

Skirring, where the Diola king in 1942 declared war against the French.

The great **National Park of Basse Casamance** is a favourite day's excursion. Thirteen miles (20 km) from Cap Skirring, on the road to Ziguinchor, the Park covers 12,000 acres (5,000 hectares) but has only one overnight base, with 10 rooms and a restaurant, located near the park entrance. If you arrive by dawn you will have time to make a full tour of the park in one day. The authorities insist on groups of 10 visitors at a time entering the park and prices have been known to vary. At the exit from the park, there is a Diola settlement where one can purchase souvenirs.

Up-river exploration: As one travels up the Casamance River from Ziguinchor, the waters widen dramatically, becoming almost an inland lake. Wide areas of mangrove swamp and marsh each side of the river become less deep after the junction with the **Soungrougrou**. The banks, however, still clad with almost impenetrable mangrove, become higher in places and one passes the small river villages of **Goudomp** on the south bank and **Tintinkomé** opposite. The river narrows after **Diatakound** and, after a bend in the river, the area administrative centre and town of **Sedhiou** comes into sight on the north bank.

Sedhiou can be reached faster by road from **Bignona** or even Ziguinchor, via the villages of **Diéba** and **Marasassoum**. This route cuts across the Soungrougrou tributary and some quite barren, rocky terrain, with only a few hills and palm groves to break the monotony of the scenery. Because of this, the opportunity to travel by *pirogue* really opens up the landscape and certainly the most interesting route is by river.

Although Sedhiou is more of a village than a town, it is one of the most impressive river settlements after Ziguinchor. Colourful *pirogues* line the banks of reddish soil and nets show that the inhabitants depend on the river for a livelihood. The river is still wide, around a mile across at this point. **Sandinière** fishing hamlet can be made out on the southern bank. Wildfowl are fewer but

Central well of a rain-gathering house.

the inevitable cormorants and heron stab at fish from branches and roots caught in the stream.

Back from the river bank a little further on to the right is the French experimental agricultural station and, after several twists and bends, the north bank village of **Mankono** can be seen. The river narrows considerably as it winds east towards **Kolda** which is a main crossroads town for trans-west African trade and has its own airstrip. Above Kolda, the river begins to disappear into the hard rock and sandy desert on the fringes of the great mountains to the southeast. Furthest east of all the settlements on the Casamance is the village of **Fafacourou**, which is on the main Kolda-Tambacounda Highway.

After this outpost, the real desert encroaches until one reaches the hilly region near **Velingara** where the River Gambia etches its way through deeply incised banks. From one of the most spectacular estuaries on the West African coastline, with vast carpets of lush mangrove swamps brimming with life, the scenery has changed to barren, rocky outcrops jutting from arid desert sand, supporting only the hardiest of elephant grass or palm.

Northward bound: If one takes the shortest road from Dakar to Ziguinchor, via Banjul, **Sélét** is the first village inside the Casamance region. Driving south from , one gets a good idea of the varied landscape of this region. Desert, sparse vegetation and thorn scrub precede areas of marsh, small creeks and bolongs. **Diouloulou** is located on a *bolong* of the same name and at this point the road heads east to Baila, Bignona and Ziguinchor.

From Diouloulou, one can visit a typical Diola village compound, or take the track to the coast at **Abané** where a tourist encampment has been established. If one prefers the African *rondavel* to the chalets at Abané, such accommodation can be found further south at **Kafountine**, 20 miles (32 km) from Diouloulou.

Apart from the attraction of the Atlantic coastline, the region is a magnet for

Casamance rice fields.

ornithologists. A 13-mile (20-km) hike from Kafountine, the **Peninsula of Birds** (Presqu'île des Oiseaux) indicates the importance of this area. The nearest accommodation is the overnight lodge at **Sitokoto**. There are also camping grounds at Sitokoto and Kafountine.

Around the Forest of Tendouk there are a number of other villages offering accommodation in *gîtes* or basic lodging-houses. **Thionk-Essyl**, a village just north of the forest has such a facility, with two or four-bedroomed huts.

A *pirogue* service from Ziguinchor to **Diatok** stops at **Afiniam**, 20 miles (32 km) on from Thionk-Essyl. There are 40 beds in the Afiniam *gîte*, which is served by local villagers. Continuing along the road from Afiniam, the track returns to the main road at Bignona. This is an important stop-over, being half-way between the border with Gambia and Ziguinchor. The most substantial of the small hotels at Bignona are the **Relais Fleuri** and the **Palmier**.

In the Bignona region, there are several circuits of interest into the **Forest of Kalounayes**, or up to the fishing settlement of **Marasassoum** on the Sougrougou River. From Marasassoum or nearby **Dieba**, one can head off into virgin countryside, a 30-mile (50-km) trek to Sedhiou on the Casamance River.

South of the Forest of Kalounayes, there is a rest house at **Koubalan**. The circuit from Bignona and along the creek of the same name includes an interesting variety of terrain and wildlife.

From Bignona, the short distance to Ziguinchor is especially picturesque with high roadside forest alternating with rice fields and village huts topped with the conical roofs typical of this part of Senegal.

Harvest time is cause for celebration everywhere and in Casamance the two-day festival of *Beweng* is extremely colourful. Sheaves of rice are offered to the gods in the hope that permission will be granted to store the crop. Feathered costumes, beaded and tassel-decked arm and leg-bands, flamboyant headdresses and flowing garments whirl in organised chaos to the pulsating beat of drums and gourds.

The ceremonies of the Ziguinchor area vary considerably from those celebrated 30 miles (50 km) away in the area of Oussouye nearer the coast. Fire is a part of the dance of initiation occuring during the last week in April, in which the initiate's old personality is ritually burned, releasing a new, more responsible character. In May, the feast of initiation, or *Nity*, is followed by *Zulane* – the feast of the King of Oussouye.

Dances feature prominently in all celebration rituals. *Zumebel*, one of Senegal's most popular spectacles, involves a wrestling contest between young girls. It is held in July. At *Ekonkon*, a festival celebrating fertility and productivity, men and women leap about like acrobats in a spectacular display of their agility. *O Lumata,* which involves trance-inducing drugs and rhythms, occurs at the end of the year, again in the Oussouye region. The ritual dances of *O Lumata* are designed to induce acolytes to communicate with the dead and with gods related to the "great dead" and the "eternal living".

Left, spearfishing in the river. **Right**, explosive dance from an initiation ceremony.

little more than a large village but it does provide accommodation. The river after which the park is named runs through the town. One of the reserve's two hotels is located nearby, as is the town's service station and garage.

The **Campement-Hôtel Niokolo Koba** has 18 rooms, six of which are air-conditioned, but otherwise the level of comfort of the hotel is fairly rudimentary. The park's other hotel is more sophisticated and much larger and more popular. Easily reached by forest roads from the N7 at Dar Salam or Tali N'de Boulou, the Simenti safari lodge is exquisitely situated in the depths of the wildlife reservation and has 40 air-conditioned rooms, all modern facilities, a pool and an excellent restaurant – usually the first place the visitor will taste real African game.

From the hotel's bar, situated beside one of the most beautiful lakes in the park, guests congregate in the evenings to watch hippopotamus, elephant and antelope come for their nightly drink. Simenti readily conforms to most people's image of the classic safari lodge.

All other accommodation in the Niokolo Koba reserve consists of campsites where conditions are primitive, though enjoyable.

At **Camp de L'Eland**, located on the ford of **Vorouli**, a great bank has been constructed to contain the frequent floods of the River Gambia. Most of the forest camps are located at river crossings and some consist of little more than clearings, such as those at **Damantan** and **Fourou**. Also located on the banks of the Gambia, the "haltes" of **Malapa** and **Badoye** are free camping places but with no water or electricity. The traveller must carry everything with him and it should be remembered therefore that an adult needs at least five litres of liquid a day in this climate.

Other official camping sites on the itineraries of guided tours include the **Camp du Lion** on the **Ba Foula Be** ford, one of the prettiest camping locations in the entire park, and **Camp du Koba**, alongside the Niokolo Koba River. A little more sophisticated than

The biggest of Senegal's big game.

the basic safari camps is the **Campement de Badi**, located off the N7 road about 60 miles (100 km) west of **Tali N'de Boulou**. Equipped with showers and WCs but with no electricity, the accommodation consists of 20 *rondavels* in local style on the ford at **Koba**.

No food or drink is provided at the Campement de Badi, so one must bring supplies. Generally, organised tours supply all the group's needs for the duration of the one or two-day safaris. One particularly popular day trip runs from Niokolo Koba, along the winding course of the Gambia River, through the ford settlements at **Vorouli**, **Banharé**, **Malapa**, **Bafoulabé** and on to the lodge at Simenti.

High forest gallery follows the river and this route allows for a stop-over at the campsite at **Malapa**. This trip can be made in half a day, although the circuit can also be extended to take in the river loop at **Badi**, the clearing of **Bafoulabé**, the beauty spot known as **Goose Foot** (Patte d'Oie) and the ford at **Fourou** camp, before reaching **Wassa Don** and turning back on to the main highway to Niokolo Koba.

Much shorter treks can be made on well-signposted paths like those to the ponds of **Diamouel** and **Mansa-Farak** – an afternoon's jaunt from Niokolo Koba. Such routes are well-organised; visitors are issued with a track plan and signs clearly mark the paths and the wildlife which can be seen at the different points.

The park is overlooked in the south by the Futa Djalon range of mountains, where individual peaks rise to more than 1,200 feet (400 metres). In the park itself, the highest mountain is **Assirik**, which is located along the Niokolo Koba-Vorouli road.

Bassari Country: At the southern end of the N7 highway is the crossroads township of **Kédougou**, near the border of Guinea Bissau. The town has 6,500 people, and is located on the banks of the Gambia River, south of the Niokolo Koba Park. The region around Kédougou is known as **Pays Bassari** after the local tribe. Developed into its current

Bassari village dwelling.

size in order to service the iron mines of the Falémé district at **Nafadji**, the original settlement dates back to the gold trade of the Mali Empire.

About 5 miles (8 km) from Kédougou, through a range of picturesque hills, are the quarries of **Ibel**. It is from these quarries that the marble is taken to build the houses of the town. In striking contrast to the usual straw-roofed huts, these marble houses bear the multiple hues of the stone. Although Kédougou contains little to delay a visitor for very long, it is an interesting fact that the town was used as a base by many early explorers into the headwater regions of the Gambia River.

There is no accommodation in Kédougou apart from a small camping site on the outskirts of town. Situated in the mountainous region of the Futa Djalon range, the roads are almost impassable by ordinary car and even four-wheel drive vehicles can find the going quite difficult.

The countryside around Kédougou is more of an attraction than the town as the Bassari people maintain a number of traditional ceremonies worthy of the attention of anthropologists and exciting to photographers. In addition, experts are studying the merits of the traditional remedies and medications evolved by the Bassari, who are now mainly employed in growing cotton, fishing, hunting and, of course, making souvenirs. A favourite local souvenir is the woven rice winnower.

During April visitors might have the opportunity to take photographs of initiation ceremonies marking the rites of passage of young men in the tribes.

In this region there are also branches of the Peul tribe and another local tribe, the Boin, inhabit the region west of Kédougou, especially around the villages of **Ebarak**, **Salemata** and **Etiolo**.

Etiolo, about 50 miles (80 km) west of Kédougou, is reached from the main road at **Salemata**. This village, which is set within a circle of mountains providing a stunning backdrop, has become a popular tourist attraction. Located in the heart of the Bassari country Etiolo is

Below, boy at circumcision ceremony. **Right**, young Bassari man.

one of the best places to view an initiation ceremony.

The tribes of the Bassari region are less dispersed than those in the rest of the country. There are a number of smaller groups in addition to the majority Bassari. In the hills around **Bandafassi**, just west of Kédougou, there are some 1,500 members of the Badik tribe, known more commonly by the Peul name "Tandanké".

Further south, in the **Fougolembi** area of the Futa Djalon mountains, live the Diallonké. These and the other tribes of the area also overspill the border into Guinea Bissau. Generally, the tribes of Guinean origin inhabit the hilly regions and those of Peul descent cultivate the low-lying areas.

East of Kédougou, it is possible to meet gold prospectors in the foothills and to visit local villages such as **Binbou**, **Saraya** and **Ilimalo**. A few kilometres from Ilimalo there is an important site for pilgrimages and a centre for traditional religious ceremonies. Called **Kourouniengouniengou**, this sacred place

is overlooked by a massive rock balancing on a cliff edge high above the valley floor. It is considered to be one of the most spectacular geological formations in Senegal.

Around 15 miles (24 km) from Kédougou, across the Futa-Djalon hills, is the settlement of **Fougolembi**, which makes an interesting excursion into the Senegal/Guinea Bissau border region. This is the country of the Diallonké tribe and there are several villages such as **Sintiou**, **Wallan**, **Toumanéa** and **Niagalankomé** where the traditional way of life of this tribe persists almost unmodified by the 20th century.

One of the curiosities of the region is a village named **Iwol**, near Bandafassi, which is noted for a baobab tree on its outskirts. This spectacular tree is said to be the largest baobab in the country. Other picturesque villages include **Ibel**, **Etchouar**, **Sangola** and **Landiéni**, all within a short distance of each other along tiny forest tracks.

The Futa Djalon mountains are the homelands of the Fulani tribe and are deeply scoured by numerous gorges and fertile valleys. Bananas and fonio (a tiny form of millet) are grown in the valleys and livestock is reared on the hillsides. Between the Niokolo Koba National Park and the Bambouk mountains is the Falémé River valley with its rolling savannah. This region is a well-loved hunting area.

To the east of Niokolo Koba lies one of the country's seven officially designated hunting grounds. It is open from December to April. For details of times and permits, contact the Direction des Eaux et Forêts in Dakar. Hunting, however, is severely restricted because the Senegalese are concerned about the preservation of wildlife.

The Parc National du Niokolo Koba represents one of the last enclaves for big game in the whole of West Africa. The terrain of southeast Senegal, the enclosing Futa Djalon mountains and the arid areas to the north and east ensure that the wildlife is contained in its natural surroundings for the enjoyment and education of the park's thousands of visitors.

Left, full moon over Niokolo Koba. Right, Bassari bark, leaf and palm mask. Overpage: dreaming by the Atlantic.

INSIGHT GUIDES
TRAVEL TIPS

Simply travelling safely

American Express Travellers Cheques

- ▪ are recognised as one of the safest and most convenient ways to protect your money when travelling abroad

- ▪ are more widely accepted than any other travellers cheque brand

- ▪ are available in eleven currencies

- ▪ are supported by a 24 hour worldwide refund service and

- ▪ a 24 hour Express Helpline service provides assistance and information when travelling abroad

- ▪ are accepted in millions of shops, hotels and restaurants throughout the world

Travellers Cheques

CONTENTS

Getting Acquainted

The Place

The region of Senegal and the Gambia occupies the most western part of the African continent. Senegal is bordered to the north by Mauritania, to the east by Mali, to the south by Guinea and Guinea-Bissau and to the west by the Atlantic Ocean.

The Gambia, the smallest country in Africa, is a narrow strip of land, not more than 30 miles (48 km) at its widest, running east-west for about 300 miles (500 km) along both sides of the River Gambia into the centre of Senegal. It is bounded on the west by the Atlantic Ocean and on all other sides by Senegal. Except for a few rocky outcrops at the eastern end of the river, the country is very flat. To the north, it gives way to scrub and eventually desert in Senegal. The south gradually becomes more tropical, with oil and coconut palms, silk cotton trees, bamboo, mahogany and tropical fruit trees in abundance. The river, which divides these two distinct regions, is tidal for about 60 miles (100 km) and is navigable as far as Basse for the groundnut-collecting lighters. Mangroves line the river banks and rice is cultivated in small fields irrigated by river flooding. In the drier, sandier areas, millet and sorghum are grown. Citrus fruits do well in this climate, grapefruit, oranges and limes particularly. Beautiful sandy beaches stretch along the Gambia's 30 miles (48 km) of coast attracting both visitors and fishermen.

The topography of Senegal follows the directions indicated by the division of terrain within its own central dividing belt, which is the Gambia.

Time Zone

Both the Gambia and Senegal stick to Greenwich Mean Time all year round.

The north, which forms part of the Sahel, is dry and sandy with patches of scrub, and has faced increasingly grave threats from drought and locusts in recent years. The terrain is generally flat; the only substantial mountains in the country are in the extreme southeast, where the Futo-Djalon range extends deep into Guinea and adjoining territories. The interior of Senegal north of the River Gambia is arid and semi-desert. The great River Senegal curves round the top of the country, irrigating a long arc of land and forming the country's effective northern border. The rivers Siné and Saloum and their many tributaries irrigate a large delta between Dakar and the Gambian border. South of the Gambia, Senegal's Casamance region is green, forested and rice-growing, while the Casamance River provides another wide area of mangrove-clogged waterways.

Climate

The entire region has an agreeable sub-tropical climate. The dry season runs from November to April/May with sunshine, an average temperature of 72–74°F (24–26°C) and a cool breeze blowing off the sea. In the eastern interior of Senegal, however, temperatures can reach considerably higher, into the 30 or even 40 degrees Centigrade. Nonetheless, it can be chilly enough in the evenings for a light jacket or cardigan, or a blanket on the bed, especially inland. It will not rain, except for a freak storm. The dry Harmattan wind, coming from the desert, often blows in January and February, bringing with it thick red dust that settles everywhere very suddenly and can even prevent planes landing and taking off. Throat lozenges are a relief at this time.

The dust will disappear as suddenly as it arrived. Up-river, the cool season is shorter, ending in February/March.

During the wet season (June to September), humidity rises drastically (80 percent or more) which makes the temperature (average 84°F or 28°C) seem even hotter. Rain falls in torrential downpours with high winds, lasting a few hours at most, giving way to clear skies and a brief cool respite before the sun and humidity take over again.

The hottest months are between the two seasons: May/June and October on the coast, March/June and October inland.

The People

Gambia

The population of the Gambia is about 800,000, set to rise to just over 1 million by 2000. The most densely populated town is Serrekunda. The Mandinkas are the largest ethnic unit (40 percent) and are spread throughout the country. The Wolofs (15 percent) are found mainly in Banjul. The Akus are descendants of freed Africans and formed the pillar of the Establishment in the first half of the 20th century. The Fulas (19 percent) are wanderers, the Sarakholés (8 percent) traders and the Diolas (10 percent) a closely-knit, hard-working group in the south extending towards Senegal.

Other residents include Christian Lebanese, Europeans, Indians and expatriate Africans from Ghana, Nigeria and Sierra Leone. Until recently, Mauritanians ran small stalls selling everything useful at street corners.

Senegal

The population of Senegal is around 6 million. All of the same ethnicities as are found in the Gambia are present, with the exception of the Aku, whose numbers are insignificant. The large Peul population (Senegal equivalent of the Gambian Fula) are mainly found in the north, and the interior and east of the country. A substantial Tukulor population is mainly in the north. Dakar lies in a primarily Wolof area, while the Cap Vert region around the capital is also the traditional home of substantial numbers of Lébou. The south is the preserve of Diolas and Mandinkas. The same non-African residents are found in Senegal as in the Gambia, although the former colonial English presence in the latter is replaced in Senegal by a French community.

The Economy

Gambia
The economy of the Gambia is mainly agricultural, depending on groundnuts which account for nearly 90 percent of exports. Fishing has great potential and is being encouraged by the United Nations Development Fund. Drought has played havoc with crops in recent years so that the country cannot rely on being self-sufficient in rice, millet and sorghum and has to import rice from Thailand and the USA. Tourism is a dynamic sector of the economy and brings seasonal work to many Gambians. General policy is to try to broaden the economic base of the Gambia and many initiatives are being funded by international aid. The majority of the people make their living from agriculture, fishing and forestry.

Languages

In both countries, the predominant indigenous language of the major population areas is Wolof. However, each ethnic grouping has its own language, which dominates regions where the grouping is particularly concentrated.

In the Gambia, English is widely used as an official, business and social language, while in Senegal a similar role is played by French.

For useful phrases, see also Language page 325.

Senegal
Senegal's economy is largely agricultural, depending on subsistence crops, millet, sorghum, rice, maize, vegetables and pulses, and cash crops, groundnuts (the most important, used mainly for pressing into oil), cotton and sugar. In addition, Senegal's long Atlantic coastline means that fishing is of great importance, both for home consumption and for a substantial source of export revenue.

Tourism accounts for a smaller percentage of the country's income than in the Gambia, but is nonetheless an important and growing industry. A limited quantity of mineral resources exists, mainly phosphates and iron ore.

The Government

Gambia
Until the military coup of 1994 the Gambia had been a remarkably stable country since independence from Britain in 1965 (it remains a member of the Commonwealth). An independent sovereign state, it was headed by President Sir Dawda Jawara of the People's Progressive Party (PPP), and became a Republic in 1975. In July 1994 a bloodless military coup (on the grounds of corruption) led to a military government, led by the youthful Lieutenant Yaya Jammeh, with the promise of elections in July 1996.

Senegal
Senegal became independent in its own right in 1960. Its constitution remains modelled broadly on that of France, with a President and national assembly elected by universal suffrage. It has proved stable and relatively peaceful in spite of occasional student-led civic unrest. The current president, Abdou Diouf, took over peacefully according to constitutional procedures from his predecessor, the country's founding father Léopold Sédar Senghar, and has since won two reasonably fair elections. There are more than a dozen opposition parties which are legally tolerated. The short-lived

Confederation of Senegambia, which attempted to co-ordinate policy in certain fields between the two countries, was dissolved in 1989.

Religion

Although the great majority of both Gambians and Senegalese are Muslim, there is complete religious freedom, and Islam does not dictate the official days of business, which instead follow the Sunday-based weekend of the former colonial mother-countries, Britain and France.

Friday is, however, the Muslim holy day and working hours are modified slightly to allow for the times of prayer and mosque attendance.

Practising Muslims, in any event, pray five times a day. These are the names in Arabic (first) and Wolof (second) of the five daily prayers: *Subh* or *Fajar* (6am); *Suhr* or *Tisbar* (2pm); *Asr* or *Takusan* (5pm); *Maghrib* or *Timis* (7pm); and *Isha* or *Gewe* (8pm).

Planning the Trip

What to Bring

It is best to bring everything you think you will need with you and not to rely on buying it in the region. The only town in either of the two countries with a reasonably extensive selection of consumer goods is Dakar. Even if it is available, it will be more expensive than at home.

From the chemist: high-protection suntan lotion, plenty of insect repellent; antihistamine or sting relief cream; anti-stomach upset medicine; indigestion tablets; water-sterilising tablets if you are travelling up-country; throat lozenges; anti-malaria prophylactics

(see *Health*) and cures (ask your doctor); basic First Aid equipment including sticking plaster, antiseptic cream, cotton wool; headache tablets; tampons; deodorants; etc. A small selection of such items is available in supermarkets and hotel shops, but they tend to be expensive.

Miscellaneous: a beach towel (hotels don't like you using theirs), a torch (in case of power cuts), a knife for dissecting mangoes, etc., binoculars for bird watching.

For tips, presents, children: items which in the developed world might be considered too petty to give are often much prized, particularly in the country. Literally nothing is too small to make at the least a very welcome present for a child. Disposable ball point pens and notebooks are especially useful.

Electricity

Gambia

The country's mains power can be erratic, with frequent power cuts. Hotels, supermarkets, banks and restaurants usually have their own

generators so food and drink are kept fresh and cold and air-conditioners working. The current is 220–230V but the constant fluctuation of power can damage hi-tech equipment, freezers etc. Private citizens often bring stabilisers. Street lighting is minimal.

Up-country towns (Basse, Mansa Konko, Farafenni, Bansang and the larger villages) normally have electricity in the evening and for some period during the day but power should not be relied on. Battery-operated radios, shavers and torches are essential and cold drinks will often be unobtainable.

Senegal

The major towns are all well supplied with reliable mains electricity. The voltage is 220V. In remote parts of the interior, generators, private supplies and battery-operated equipment may have to be relied on.

Weights & Measures

In the Gambia, both metric (metres, grammes, litres) and imperial (feet, ounces, pints) measures are used.

In Senegal, only metric measures are used.

Maps

Gambia

A small selection of maps for tourists can be found at the Methodist Bookshop, Buckle Street, Banjul, tel: 228179. Macmillan produces the most up-to-date and comprehensive map of the Gambia.

Senegal

The best maps of Senegal and Dakar are published by the Institut Géographique National de France (107, rue de la Boétie, 75008 Paris or PO Box 4016, Dakar). Michelin's sheet 953, Africa, North and West, is the best general map to the region with most important information for travellers shown.

Both are available from a number of bookshops in central Dakar.

A free Dakar city plan can be obtained from the Ministry of Tourism.

What to Wear

From November to May, the region has a very pleasant sub-tropical climate, warm, dry and sunny during the day but with an unexpectedly cool breeze in the evenings so bring a cardigan, jacket or sweatshirt as well as normal summer clothes. Trousers are necessary in the evenings (against mosquitoes and the chilly breeze) and on expeditions into the bush. From November to May it is not too hot to wear jeans. Jacket and tie are acceptable for businessmen. A hat is useful on the beach and on excursions (locally-made bush hats are cheap, cool and readily available). In the wet season, an umbrella, light-weight raincoat and shoes that can get wet without spoiling should be brought.

Both men and women need open sandals or flip-flops for

beach, hotel and street. Roads are exceptionally sandy so shoes should be strong enough to resist the pressure and open enough to be able to shake out the sand. Stouter shoes such as trainers (with socks) are recommended for excursions into the bush.

It is acceptable for women to go topless on the beach or by the hotel pool but beyond these areas it would give offence. Hotels usually request their guests to dress respectably but not formally in their indoor restaurants and bars, especially in the evenings.

In public, visitors should respect Islamic customs: women should try to wear knee-length skirts, trousers or a wrap-around piece of cloth and shirt; men are tolerated in shirt and shorts.

Hotels provide laundry service at very reasonable prices.

More colour
for the world.

HDCplus. New perspectives in colour photography.

AGFA

Probably the <u>most</u> <u>important</u> TRAVEL TIP you will ever receive

Before you travel abroad, make sure that you and your family are protected from diseases that can cause serious health problems.

For instance, you can pick up *hepatitis A* which infects 10 million people worldwide every year (it's not just a disease of poorer countries) simply through consuming contaminated food or water!

What's more, in many countries if you have an accident needing medical treatment, or even dental treatment, you could also be at risk of infection from *hepatitis B* which is 100 times more infectious than AIDS, and can lead to liver cancer.

The good news is, you can be protected by vaccination against these and other serious diseases, such as *typhoid*, *meningitis* and *yellow fever*.

Travel safely! Check with your doctor at least 8 weeks before you go, to discover whether or not you need protection.

Consult your doctor before you go... not when you return!

SB
SmithKline Beecham
V A C C I N E S

Produced as a service to public health

Entry Regulations

VISAS & PASSPORTS

Gambia

A full passport (valid for at least three months after your return from the Gambia) is required. Visas are not required by British or Commonwealth citizens, nor by nationals of Norway, Sweden, Finland, or Iceland. Other nationals should contact their nearest Gambian embassy.

In Britain: the High Commission of the Republic of Gambia, 57 Kensington Court, London W8 5DG. Tel: 0171 937 6316.

Transit visas for a period not exceeding five days are issued on condition that a visa to the continuation country has already been obtained by the applicant.

Visas for trips into Senegal can be arranged on the border.

Senegal

Full valid passports are required for anyone entering the country. Citizens of the following countries do not require visas: France, Germany, Italy, Morocco, Tunisia, Algeria and all West African states bordering on Senegal.

Nationals of all other countries need visas, which may be obtained from Senegalese missions abroad or on arrival in Senegal.

Multiple-entry visas valid for three months are normally granted.

Customs

Gambia

Personal belongings (including cameras, binoculars and video cameras which are not for resale) are admitted duty-free. Also duty-free are 200 cigarettes or 250 g tobacco, 1 litre spirits or 2 litres of fortified or sparkling wine, plus 2 litres of still table wine, 60 ml perfume or 250 ml eau de toilette, £32 (US$48) worth of gifts.

There is a small branch of the Gambia Commercial Development Bank at the airport for exchange of currency, also a Gamtel telephone office, which will make international calls and a kiosk.

Senegal

Senegalese duty-free allowance consists of: two cameras, a cine camera, a tape recorder, a portable radio receiver, a portable record player, a portable typewriter, personal jewellery (not more than 200g of gold), 200 cigarettes, 50 cigars, 250g of tobacco and your personal clothing.

Extension of Stay

Gambia

If you want to stay in the Gambia beyond the three weeks on your visitor's visa, you will have to apply to the Immigration Department, Ministry of the Interior, Banjul (on the corner of Dobson Street and Anglesea Street) giving a good reason why you want to stay on and proving you can support yourself financially.

Senegal

The same procedure applies for Senegal, where visa extensions are dealt with by the Ministry of the Interior, Dakar (Place de Washington office).

Health

Comprehensive medical insurance should be taken out before you leave your home country. Details from your travel agent, insurance company or bank.

Immunisations advisable for both the Gambia and Senegal:

Typhoid – a gastric fever caught from infected or dirty food. Valid three years.

Hepatitis A (jaundice) – caught from infected water or food and sometimes, regrettably, from local oysters. A new form of this vaccine is valid for 10 years providing you have a booster within six months.

Cholera – diarrhoea, vomiting, dehydration. Valid six months.

Polio – valid two years.

Meningitis – valid for 10 years.

These immunisations are all optional unless you are coming from an infected area but are to be recommended. Check with your doctor the best time to have them done – some can be given on the same day as the yellow fever – otherwise you may have to wait a week or two between injections and thus delay your departure.

Malaria: Anti-malarial drugs should be taken by visitors (and residents) in both countries as this disease, carried by the anopheles mosquito, is prevalent everywhere and can strike anyone at any time. The recommended prophylactic dose is 250 mg of Lariam (the most effective prevention) on the same day each week beginning one week before travel and continuing for as long as your doctor advises (dependent on the length of time spent in a malarial zone). Women should avoid getting pregnant within three months of taking Lariam. Anyone who suffers from epileptic fits or is subject to depression should take an alternative prophylactic such as Paludrine. If you get malaria, see a doctor immediately. Symptoms are a high temperature, wracking headache and alternate bouts of the shivers and hot fevers. There are fewer mosquitoes around in the dry (tourist) season (November to May) than in the wet season. Hotel rooms usually have mosquito-proofed windows and an air-conditioner and/or fan (if you have electricity) will help keep them away. Up-country, where there is little or no electricity, a mosquito

Compulsory Immunisation

Gambia

A certificate of vaccination against yellow fever is now only compulsory if you are travelling from an infected zone.

Senegal

There is no longer a requirement for visitors to present a yellow fever vaccination certificate, but vaccination is strongly recommended.

net or strong anti-mosquito spray is necessary or you can burn anti-mosquito coils which give off a scented smoke obnoxious to mosquitoes but tolerable for humans. One coil lasts about eight hours. Bring a good supply of insect repellent as a back-up.

AIDS: It is prevalent in the region, although figures are unreliable. Considering both Senegal and Gambia are mainly Muslim, the population is promiscuous with prostitution fairly common. Billboards warn of the dangers of unprotected sex. The virus is transmitted as much by heterosexual contact as by homosexual, and also by contaminated needles and blood transfusion equipment. Emergency medical packs containing sterilised needles and plasma are now available in the developed countries for visitors to take with them.

Although free emergency medical treatment is theoretically available in both countries, it is likely to be unreliable or non-existent (the latter obviously in remote areas) and full medical insurance to cover all eventualities is therefore necessary.

Drinking Water

Bottled water is widely available and should be used in both countries. The extent of other precautions to avoid stomach upsets will vary depending on how much restriction of food choice you are prepared to put up with. It is sensible to peel all fruit, whether washed or not, before eating. Some people will wish to avoid salads and other uncooked, washed foods, as well as ice-cream and ice in drinks. Others will resign themselves to the occasional bug and eat whatever is going. In general, standards of hygiene in both countries in most commercial establishments are well controlled.

Currency

Gambia

You can take as much money into the Gambia as you wish, either in travellers' cheques or in hard currency, but you may not take out more than you brought in. A currency declaration form sometimes needs to be completed on arrival.

The local currency is the Dalassi, made up of 100 Bututs. Notes are in denominations of D50 (purple), D25 (blue), D10 (green) and D5 (red). Coins are in denominations of D1 (heptagonal), 50, 25, 10 and 5 Bututs. Recent exchange rates have fluctuated around £1=D14.60; or US$1=D9.6.

Black Market

As you will soon discover, the easiest way to change money is on the black market (cigarette vendors often double as money changers). The rate is slightly better than the banks give (and certainly better than any hotel) and there are no commission charges. Money changers handle traveller's cheques as well as cash. However, it should be said that the black market is, in theory, illegal. It may be worth checking that no "clamp down" is in operation.

Banks will exchange both travellers' cheques and currency at the official rates posted up daily in the banks. Take your passport with you when you go to the bank. Sterling is frequently accepted, indeed preferred, by traders, and US dollars and CFA francs (from Senegal) will sometimes be accepted. Foreign currency from Algeria, Ghana, Guinea, Mali, Morocco, Nigeria, Sierra Leone and Tunisia is neither accepted nor exchanged.

All major hotels have foreign exchange facilities at their reception desks but commissions will be greater and rates will be poorer than at banks.

Credit Cards are accepted by the larger hotels and by some car

hire companies, but you may have to pay a surcharge. Check with your credit card company before leaving and with your bank and hotel on arrival. Main credit cards acceptable: Visa, MasterCard, Diners Club. American Express is rarely accepted, and when it is tends to work out expensive, as all credit card transactions are processed in London (Dalassi is converted into sterling which in turn is converted into dollars).

European Eurocheques supported by Eurocheque cards are accepted by some hotels.

BANKS

Banking Hours: Normally from 8am–1pm (Monday to Thursday) and 8am–11am (Friday and Saturday).

In addition, some banks in Bakau are open in the afternoons from 4–6.30pm (Monday to Friday only). **Standard Chartered:** Buckle Street, Banjul (Head Office); Serekunda, Kololi, Bakan and Basse Santa Su. This bank will forward up to £50 a day against Visa or Access. Branches in the tourist areas open on Saturdays. **International Bank for Commerce & Industry** (BICI): 11 Wellington Street, Banjul (Head Office); Bakau (behind CFAO); Serekunda. **Central Bank of the Gambia:** Buckle Street, Banjul. **Gambia Commercial & Development Bank:** Buckle Street, Banjul (Head Office); Bakau; Yundum Airport. **Gambia Commercial Development Bank:** Farafenni; Basse Santa Su. **Meridien:** Bakau and Kairaba Hotel.

Senegal

Similar currency regulations to those obtaining in the Gambia apply. In theory, you must declare the amounts of currency you bring into and take out of the country.

Senegal belongs to the CFA franc system which is common to all of France's former West African colonies. The CFA franc issued by any of these territories is accepted by all of them. The exchange rate of the CFA franc is tied to the French franc at French franc 1=CFA francs 100.

There are notes of CFA 10,000, 5,000, 1,000 and 500 and coins of CFA 100 and 50 (silver in colour) and CFA 25, 10 and 5 (copper in colour).

In addition, French francs are widely accepted as are, to a lesser extent, US dollars, but nothing else. Major hotels have foreign exchange facilities but charge commissions.

The main credit cards (American Express, Diners Club, Visa and MasterCard) are widely accepted, except in small businesses.

European Eurocheques supported by Eurocheque cards are accepted by an increasing number of hotels and some banks.

BANKS IN DAKAR

Banking Hours: Normally from 8am– 11.30am and 12.45–4pm (Monday to Friday).

In addition to the major hotels, the Chamber of Commerce on the Place de l'Indépendance offers a service outside banking hours for the exchange of travellers' cheques.

Al Manar Islamic Investment Bank: Avenue Sarraut.

BCEAO (Central Bank of West African States): Avenue Abdoulaye Fadiga (ex-Barachois).

Banque Internationale pour l'Afrique de L'Ouest (BAIO): Place de l'Indépendance.

Banque Internationale pour le Commerce International du Sénégal (BICIS): Avenue Roume.

Banque Nationale pour le Développement du Sénégal: Avenue Roume.

Banque Sénégalo-Koweitienne (BSK): Rue de Thann.

Banque Sénégalo-Tunisienne (BST): Avenue Georges Pompidou.

Bank of Credit and Commerce International: Place de l'Indépendance.

Caisse Nationale du Crédit Agricole: Rue Huart.

City Bank: Place de l'Indépendance.

Société Générale des Banques du Sénégal (SGBS): Avenue Roume.

Sonabanque: Place de l'Indépendance.

Union Sénégalaise de Banque (USB): Boulevard Pinet Laprade.

Public Holidays

Senegal and the **Gambia** both celebrate the feast days of the Muslim Calendar. These are moveable feasts that depend upon and sightings of the new moon and may not be known until very shortly beforehand.

- *Korité* (known in Arabic as Aid el Fitr, the end of the month-long fast of Ramadan).
- *Tabaski* (in Arabic, Aid el Kebir or Aid el Adha, the feast of Abraham's sacrifice of the sheep).
- *Tamharit* (the Islamic New Year)
- *Mouloud* (the Prophet Mohammed's birthday).

In addition, the Gambia has the following public holidays:
- **January 1:** New Year's Day
- **February 18:** Independence Day
- **March/April** (variable): Good Friday
- **May 1:** Labour Day
- **August 15:** Feast of the Assumption of St Mary
- **December 25:** Christmas Day

Senegal celebrates the following:
- **January 1:** New Year's Day
- **March** (variable): Easter Monday
- **April 4:** Independence Day
- **May 1:** Labour Day
- **May 4:** The Assumption
- **May 15:** Whitsuntide

Getting There

BY AIR

Gambia

Banjul's Yundum airport is 30 km (18 miles) outside the city (slightly less from the hotel strip). Flights take about six hours from London.

Since the 1994 coup, the number of flights to Banjul has dropped dramatically. Both Gambia Airways, the national carrier, and British Airways stopped running flights between London and the Gambia. Services may resume when the political situation settles. In the meantime the only direct flights between London and Banjul are charters. Flight-only tickets are available from Gambia Experience, Kingfisher House, Rownhams Lane, North Baddesley, Hampshire, England, Tel: 01703 730 888. The only European airlines flying to Banjul are Swissair and Sabena.

Ghana Airways and Nigeria Airways have several flights a week, coast-hopping and linking Lagos, Abidjan, Freetown, Conakry and Dakar to Banjul. Gambia Airways and Air Senegal run a service between Dakar and Banjul.

Visitors from the USA could take the direct Air Afrique flight from New York to Dakar and continue by Air Senegal. Similarly, visitors from Europe can take scheduled flights by Sabena, Swissair, Air France, Air Afrique, Royal Air Maroc, Aeroflot or Iberia to Dakar and continue in the same way.

Senegal

Yoff International Airport, 10 miles (15 km) north of Dakar, is one of the largest and best equipped airports in Africa. There is an average of two scheduled flights daily between Dakar and Paris. Airlines operating scheduled flights into Dakar include Sabena, Swiss Air, Air France, Air Afrique, Royal Air Maroc, Aeroflot, Iberia, Ghana Airways, Nigeria Airways.

Certain flights from European capitals stop at intermediate airports such as Marseilles and Bordeaux.

Several French tour operators run charter flights to Dakar. In addition, visitors from Britain could buy a charter flight into the Gambia and continue to Dakar via Gambia Airways, Air Senegal or Ghana Airways.

BY SEA

Passengers wishing to travel by sea must allow themselves plenty of time (8–10 days) for the journey which is unpredictable and rarely used but still theoretically possible. Accommodation is on cargo boats from Liverpool, London or certain European ports, which call at other ports en route and may even leave out a port if there is no reason to stop there for cargo. Not all ships allow passengers so make your enquiries in good time. It is even rarer for ships returning to Europe to take passengers, so you cannot count on obtaining a return ticket.

For details of European lines serving Dakar, which include Paquet, Socopao and Delmas-Vieiljeux, contact the nearest Senegalese diplomatic or tourist representative well in advance of your intended departure date.

BY RAIL

There is a train between Bamako (Mali) and Dakar which runs twice a week, stopping at Tambacounda and Kaolack. Travellers to the Gambia can get off at either Tambacounda or Kaolack and continue by taxi, minibus or public transport bus (there is no railway in the Gambia). For information, contact any travel agency in Bamako or Dakar. For comfort, travel on the express train (once a week only). You must take your own food and drink.

BY ROAD

It is possible to drive to Senegal (and therefore on to the Gambia) from North Africa and the Mediterranean, but the long and complex trip requires considerable equipment and planning and is dependent upon open borders. It should be attempted only by groups in rugged four-wheel drive vehicles. Currently, the shortest route, south from Morocco through Mauritania to the border at St Louis, is virtually closed by the twin problems of conflict between Morocco and the

Polisario in the Western Sahara and disputes between Senegal and Mauritania. Similarly, routes via Algeria and Mali crossing the Sahara are closed due to civil violence in Algeria.

Senegal is connected by a perfectly serviceable road with Guinea-Bissau in the south, crossing from Fatim, in Guinea-Bissau, into Tanaf (Senegal). It is also possible to enter from Guinea; the crossing point is from Koundara (Guinea) into Velingara (Senegal).

Road connections between Senegal and the Gambia are reasonably efficient. There are good roads from Dakar via Kaolack to Barra (4 hours drive) on the mouth of the River Gambia, directly opposite Banjul, or to Farafenni (five hours) by the Trans-Gambia Highway.

At Farafenni, a 15- to 20-minute car-ferry crossing takes you to Mansa Konko from where a tarmac road with a reasonable surface goes east to Basse, west to Banjul (three hours) or south on to Ziguinchor in Senegal by the Trans-Gambia Highway continuation. Be prepared for a longish wait in the queue to get on the ferry. Private cars often get preferential treatment but taxis can wait hours.

If you cross the River Gambia at Barra, the ferry delivers you straight to Banjul. The ferry runs approximately every hour, depending on tides (last one 6pm) and takes 45–50 minutes to cross and unload. Foreign registered cars have to pay in foreign currency (CFA francs if you are coming from Senegal) and the fare is double that for a Gambian vehicle. Gambian registered cars pay in dalassis (D50

for a normal saloon, D95 for a Land-Rover). Tickets are bought from an inconspicuous ticket shed on the left, about 15 minutes after the border and well before you reach Barra. Easy to miss.

Customs and Immigration controls are at Karang on the Senegalese side and at Amladai on the Gambia side. Verify that your car insurance covers you in the Gambia. Senegalese insured cars need extra cover for the Gambia.

To go to Barra from Kaolack, turn sharp right off the Transgambia Highway after crossing the mud/salt flats, at a tumble-down signpost marked to Les Palétuviers and Karang. No mention of Banjul and hence easy to overshoot and find yourself going to Ziguinchor.

Coming from the south, the Transgambia Highway goes from Ziguinchor to Mansa Konko. At Bignona, there is a left turn to the Gambia via Dioudoulou which takes you to Banjul (two hours). No ferry crossing necessary. Only Customs and Immigration on both Senegalese and Gambian borders.

Taxis and minibuses ply all these routes and the Gambia Public Transport Corporation runs a reasonably comfortable airy bus between Dakar and Barra, leaving Dakar at 9am and 11am from Place Leclerc just below the Novotel. (Five hours travelling time with a 10-minute stop at Kaolack.) At Barra you get out and cross to Banjul as a foot passenger.

Special Facilities

DOING BUSINESS

The general atmosphere of approaching a transaction in Africa is more leisurely, roundabout and personal than in Europe and America. Personal contacts are important and middlemen are common and may expect a commission even where no formal agreement exists.

Gambia

People wanting to set up businesses in the Gambia should apply to the Ministry of Economic Planning, 1/2 Buckle Street, Banjul, for work

Tour Operators

Gambia

Black and White Safaris Ltd. Tel: 393174/339306.
Discovery Tours, PO Box 2915, Serekunda. Tel: 495551.
The Gambia River Excursion Ltd. Tel: 495526.
Gambia Tours, PO Box 217, Banjul. Tel: 391041.

Gamtours (Gambia National Tours Company), Kanifing Industrial Estate, PO Box 101, Banjul. Tel: 392505/391497.
West Africa Tours, Bakau New Town, PO Box 222, Serekunda. Tel: 495258.

Roman Catholic
Cathedral of Our Lady of the
Assumption, Hagan Street, Banjul.
Church of the Holy Spirit, Box Bar
Road, Banjul.
Star of the Sea Church, Bakau.
Methodist
Wesley Church, Dobson Street,
Banjul.
Methodist Church, Atlantic Road.
Trinity Church, Serekunda.
New Apostolic Church of the Gambia, Serekunda.
Glory Baptist Fellowship, Kanifing
Road, Old Jeshwang.

Senegal
The following is a selection of the
places of worship of the major religions in Dakar. In addition, Catholic
churches will be found in all
sizeable towns throughout the
country.
Protestant
St Paul's Church, Rue Carnet.
Roman Catholic
Cathédrale du Souvenir Africain, Avenue de la République.
Evangelical
Evangelic Church, Rue 11, Sicap
Amitié 2, Dakar.
Assembly of God
Chapel, Boulevard de Général de
Gaulle.

Media

NEWSPAPERS & MAGAZINES

Gambia
The Gambia had a free press in theory until the coup in 1994, though
due to scarcity of resources not
much was made of this liberty. The
main paper is the *Daily Observer*,
published on Monday, Tuesday,
Wednesday and Friday, which is a
lively if idiosyncratic read, offering
insights into the culture. Other
papers include *The Citizen*, a weekly
published on Mondays, and *The
Point*, published on Mondays and
Thursdays. Very few foreign
publications are available.

Senegal
Senegal also has a free press and
in this larger, more sophisticated
country a reasonable selection of

papers and magazines gets
published.
The only national daily is *Le
Soleil* which is widely available in
the main towns in the morning.
Other publications include: *Sud
Hebdo*, a weekly devoted to politics,
current affairs and business;
Walfadjiri, a current affairs weekly;
Le Devoir, a bimonthly also devoted
to current affairs; *Le Cafard Libéré*,
a satirical weekly modelled on the
celebrated French magazine *Le Canard Enchaîné*.
Le Dakarois is a free monthly information pamphlet which also
carries small features, recipes,
many advertisements of interest to
visitors and good up-to-date
information on leisure activities and
culture. A small English-language
equivalent named *This Month in
Dakar* also exists. The news kiosks
of Dakar offer quite a good selection of international publications.
Obviously, the French press is best
represented, but British and American papers also are available,
usually not many days late.

RADIO & TELEVISION

Gambia
The government controls two radio
stations which both follow official
government policy, but run their own
programmes.
Radio Gambia is a government–
controlled station with programmes
in all the main Gambian languages
and in English, with regular news
bulletins, schools' broadcasts and
general programmes on education,
culture, religion and music.
Transmission is on 648 kHz.
Radio Syd was started in 1970 by a
Swedish woman, Britt Wadner, who
moved to the Gambia via Radio
Caroline and the Canary Islands,
when her pirate radio station, Radio
Mercury, operating off the Danish
coast, was threatened by the
Danish authorities. The present
station is on dry land at Mile 2, on
the way out of Banjul. Programmes
range from European and African
music to local news bulletins in
English and, in the tourist season,
Swedish (regularly listened to by
Swedish tourists). Local information

is advertised and requests can also
be broadcast for a small fee. Transmission is on 329 m medium wave.
Radio Senegal (1300 kHz), with
programmes in Wolof, Diola, Fula
and French is also regularly listened
to in the Gambia.
BBC World Service is easily picked
up on several short wave frequencies, depending on the time of day.
During the day, 16-, 13- and 19-
metre bands are best, with 25-, 31-
and 49-metre bands for the early
morning and in the evening. The BBC
Africa Service (African News, Focus
on Africa, Arts and Africa) is
available between 6.30am and
8.45am and again at intervals
between 4.15pm and 10pm.
London Calling, their overseas
programme journal, is available by
post from BBC World Service
(African Section), PO Box 76, Bush
House, Strand, London WC2.
Television: Gambian television does
not yet exist, though there are
plans for a station in the future.
Senegalese TV can be picked up in
the Gambia by those who don't
mind programmes in French.

Senegal
The ORTS (Office de Radiodiffusion
Télévision du Sénégal) is the
national government-controlled
radio and TV network, which
operates a monopoly on
broadcasting in the country. Its radio broadcasts take place in Wolof,
Diola and Fula but French is the official and most used language.
There are news programmes in
English on Radio Senegal
(1300kHz) on Mondays to Fridays
between 6.40pm–7.05pm and on
Saturdays between 6.45pm–7pm.
In addition, it is possible in Senegal to pick up Radio Syd, Radio
Gambia, BBC World Service (see
above under the Gambia for details
of all three) as well as a wide range
of far-flung stations if you have
good short-wave equipment.
Senegalese Television broadcasts a
mixture of current affairs, cultural
and sporting programmes and films
from 6.15–11.15pm daily. There is
News in English on Thursdays and
Sundays from 7.50–8pm.

Postal Services

Gambia

Mail to and from UK and the Gambia is quick and cheap. Letters or post cards usually take four or five days to reach Europe.

The main post office is in Russell Street, Banjul, next to the Albert Market and there are branches in Bakau (set back off the road opposite the African Village Hotel), Kairaba Avenue (just opposite Mrs Ndow's school), Serekunda and in all of the larger up-country towns. Opening hours are generally 8.30am– 12.15pm and 2pm–4pm (Monday to Friday) and 8.30am–noon (Saturday).

Most hotels will sell you stamps provided you buy the postcards there as well. They also have their own postboxes which are regularly emptied in time to catch the flights out of the region.

Senegal

Mail between Europe and Senegal is reasonably efficient. A letter should not take longer than a week and can take as little as four days.

Dakar's main post office is on the Boulevard Pinet Laprade and is open 8am–4pm Monday to Thursday and 8am–1pm Friday.

All major towns have post offices and most medium-sized and large hotels will sell stamps and accept letters for posting.

Telecommunications

Gambia

Telephone: GAMTEL, Gambia's telecommunications service, is excellent. You can call internationally as easily as you would from home. Phonecard booths are the best means of making a call – buy your phone card (D45) from the GAMTEL office (make sure the cellophane is sealed and the red band intact). There are GAMTEL offices in: Bakau (Atlantic Road, opposite African Village Hotel), open 8am–11pm; Kotu Beach Complex (next to Novotel), 8am –10pm; Serekunda (junction Kairaba Avenue/ Serekunda Avenue), 8am– 11pm;

Banjul (Russell Street, next to Post Office), open 24 hours; Banjul (Telegraph Road, near Atlantic Hotel), open 24 hours; Yundum Airport, 8am–10pm. Calls are slightly cheaper between 6pm and 11pm and on weekends, and cheaper still (up to 50 percent) 11pm–7 am.

For international calls, dial 00 then the country code followed by the number you want, omitting 0 from the area code – for example, central London 00-44-171-number; for New York 00-1-212-number. See under Senegal for a list of some common country codes.

Telexes and telegrams can be sent from any of the public international exchanges listed above.

Fax machines are at Russell Street and Telegraph Road branches in Banjul, as well as at a number of the large hotels.

Senegal

Telephone: Senegal has an efficient French-system telephone network, operated by the national company SONATEL. International calls, using coins or pre-paid cards, may be made at the two main SONATEL offices in Dakar – Boulevard de la Republique and Rue Wagane Diouf – which are open until 1am. There is a small number of less reliable public telephone booths in the street, but they are often in a state of disrepair.

For international calls, dial 00 followed by the country code, area

Dialling Codes

The following is a list of some of the most popular country codes:

Austria	43
Belgium	32
Denmark	45
France	33
Germany	49
Ireland	353
Netherlands	31
Norway	47
Sweden	46
Switzerland	41
UK	44
USA and Canada	1

code omitting the 0, and number e.g. for London 00-44-1-937-6316. The ringing tone is a single longish bleep, repeated; engaged is a rapidly repeated series of short bleeps.

Telexes and telegrams may be sent from the SONATEL offices mentioned above.

Fax machines are found in all of the major hotels.

Tourist Information

Gambia

National Tourist Office, Ministry of Information and Tourism, The Quadrangle, Banjul. Tel: 223186/ 227881.

Outside the Gambia

Gambia National Tourist Office, 57 Kensington Court, London W8 5DG, England. Tel: 0171 937 6316. Fax: 0171 937 9095.

Senegal

Ministère de Tourisme, 5 Avenue André Peytavin, BP 4049, Dakar. Tel: 22 22 26/22 53 71/22 13 80.

Outside Senegal

Bureau National Senegalais de Tourisme at 15 Rue de Rémusat, 75016 Paris, France. Tel: 40 50 07 90.

Sremdewerkchramt, Münchenertrasse 7, D-6000 Frankfurt-M, West Germany. Tel: 23 26 91/92.

Centre de Cooperation Internationale, Largo Africa, 20145 Milan, Italy. Tel: 46 44 21.

In other countries, contact nearest Senegalese diplomatic representation or tour operator.

Embassies

Gambian Diplomatic Representation Abroad
The Gambia High Commission, 57 Kensington Court, London W8 5DG, England. Tel: 0171 937 6316/8, fax: 0171 937 90095.
The Gambia Embassy, 126 Avenue Franklin Roosevelt, Brussels 1050, Belgium. Tel: (02) 640 10 49.

Private Transport

A valid national driving licence or an International Driving Licence is required. Driving is on the right, and French traffic rules are followed (e.g. priority to the right).

In the interior, the same warnings about lack of availability of breakdown assistance apply as to the Gambia. In Dakar, garage facilities are not too bad.

The following is a list of car hire facilities in Dakar:

Hertz, 26 rue Jules Ferry. Tel: 22 52 87. Self-drive and chauffeur-driven, selection of vehicles. Hertz also have offices at Dakar Airport. Tel: 20 11 74.

Avis, Dakar Airport. Tel: 23 63 40. Car Afrique, 100 rue J. Gomis. Tel: 21 88 67.

Dakar Auto, 7 rue Marclary. Tel: 21 55 58.

Eurocar, Boulevard de la Libération. Tel: 22 18 99.

Locatour, Avenue Lamine Gueye. Tel: 22 71 44.

Soatour, 29 rue A. A. Ndoye. Tel: 21 38 45.

Transacauto, 61 rue Felix Faure. Tel: 22 20 16.

On Departure

Gambia

Confirmation of return flight: this is not necessary for visitors on full package tours, but flight-only charter travellers should confirm 48 hours in advance with the representatives of their tour companies.

Travellers on scheduled flights should confirm.

An airport tax is levied on everyone leaving the country: D7 for foreigners, payable in hard currency; D35 for residents of the Gambia.

After registering luggage in the normal way and passing through passport control, you will then have to identify your baggage again before it is loaded into the aircraft.

There is a cafeteria, ice-cream and coffee bar and duty free shop (items are actually dearer than in Banjul or Bakau supermarkets). The Gambia Commercial Development Bank will change a certain amount of dalassis for you as they are useless outside the Gambia, as will many individuals.

Senegal

Confirmation of return flights: for scheduled flights, this should be done if possible 72 hours in advance with the airline in question or a travel agent.

There is no airport tax. It is advisable to keep ready the declaration of currencies form, which arriving visitors will have filled in, in case it is requested on departure.

Although Yoff Airport is reasonably well run and modern, it is advisable to allow double the amount of time you would calculate on at a European airport to check in luggage, complete customs formalities, etc.

Unless the flight is very late at night or early in the morning, the normal range of shops (including duty-free), cafeterias and a bureau de change should be available.

Where to Stay

Hotels

Gambia

Since the Gambia has become such a popular destination for winter holidays, hotels have sprung up at a rapid pace. Some are open all year round and others only during the tourist season (November–April). Tour operators from several European countries organise package tours at very advantageous prices. Even so, there is always room somewhere for the business person and the independent traveller. Only the larger hotels take credit cards.

Hotels catering for tourists on a large scale are little worlds on their own, set in landscaped gardens of colourful tropical trees and flowers with their own swimming pools, bars, restaurants, shops, sports facilities, entertainment and access to the beach. Numerous smaller hotels also exist at lower prices but without the same facilities. During the tourist season it is necessary to book early. Air-conditioning is not essential during the dry (tourist) season but is recommended for comfort at other times of the year. Most hotel bedrooms have their own shower and toilet en suite.

Where to Stay

With the exception of the **Atlantic Hotel** in Banjul, almost all the recommended hotels are between Cape St Mary and Kololi, either beside the beach or just a short walk away. They are all unobtrusively low-rise and engirdled by lush tropical gardens which attract colourful bird-life. Most have a Gamtel office, supermarket, taxi rank and craft market nearby. The

Kairaba and the **Senegambia** (along with **Kololi Beach Club**) have the best range of restaurants within walking distance and are also close to Bijilo Forest with its nature walks; **Kombo Beach** and **Bunglaow Beach** enjoy the best stretch of Kotu Beach and are close to the **Fajara Golf Club; Sunwing** and **Amies** benefit from the amenities and colour of Bakau and a beach that is relatively hassle-free.

With the possible exceeption of the **Kairaba**, standards are lower than comparable star-rated hotels in Europe. All the big hotels have their own generators. Independent travellers should book in advance, as all hotel accommodation tends to get fully booked during high season.

Banjul
Atlantic Hotel (4-star)
Banjul, tel: 228601. This was the first hotel in the Gambia. Situated near Senate House in Banjul, it is probably more suited to business people than tourists, though it is noted for its watersports on account of its position just inside the estuary of the River Gambia. Some signs of lack of maintenance.

The Coast
Kairaba (5-star)
Kololi, tel: 462940. The only truly luxurious hotel in the Gambia. Rooms are well-furnished, with terraces overlooking the garden, and comforts include a hair-drier, mini-bar and television. Superior rooms and suites also available. A little more formal than the other hotels (shorts are not permitted in the bar and restaurant) and it eschews organised "entertainment". Lovely Somerset Maugham-style cocktail bar, where one can also take breakfast. Own observatory for stargazing, and shares Senegambia's sport facilities.
Senegambia (4-star)
Kololi, tel: 462717. Large hotel (325 rooms) next door to the Kairaba. Stylish entrance is not matched by the rest of the public areas and rooms. However, the Senegambia has recently benefited from refurbishments. Some rooms

have air-conditioning, and studio rooms also have a separate lounge and kitchenette, making the hotel popular for families. Wide range of sports activities, including open-air gym. Belly-boards available on the beach.
Kombo Beach (4-star/Novotel)
Kotu, tel: 465467. Comfortable and friendly hotel on the best stretch of beach. Super-clean swimming pool and well-tended gardens. Some kind of entertainment is staged every evening in the open-air bar area (usually for no more than half-an-hour) and an excellent sports team organises games through the day (volley-ball, water polo, tennis, etc). Kombo Beach doesn't have as many restaurants on its doorstep as the Kairaba and Senegambia, but is well served by taxis. Rooms are air-conditioned and comfortable and the en suite bathrooms have a bath tub with overhead shower. Good breakfasts.
Sunwing (4-star)
Cape St Mary, tel: 495435. The Sunwing's fortunes declined during the slump that followed the 1994 coup. However, as tourism picks up it should recover its good reputation. Well laid-out, with restaurant overlooking the ocean. Convenient for the town of Bakau.
African Village (3-star)
Bakau, tel: 495307. Well-run small hotel with swimming pool and gardens. Attractive rooms, relaxing ambience.
Bungalow Beach (4-star)
Kotu, tel: 465288. Self-catering style accommodation, next door to Kombo Beach Hotel alongside Kotu beach. Swimming pool, mini-market and quite good restaurants.
Badala Park Hotel (3-star)
Kotu Stream, tel: 460400. Most amenities, including pool. A walk through rice fields to the beach. Signs of lack of maintenance.
Palma Rima (3-star)
Badala Parkway, tel: 463380. Worth opting for a bungalow room (with air-conditioning and fridges) rather than one of the standard rooms (which are poky and a bit depressing). Offers many of the facilities offered by the big 4-star

hotels (for example, nightclub, entertainment, sports facilities, etc.), but with the exception of its swimming pool (which is the biggest in the Gambia) to a noticeably poorer standard. Disabled access. 150 metres to the beach.
Bakotu Hotel (3-star)
Kotu, tel: 465555. Small, well-run hotel with pool and gardens, opposite Kombo Beach and Bungalow Beach hotels. Kotu Beach is a short walk away. Monkeys inhabit the area behind the hotel.
Amies Beach Hotel (2-star)
Badala Parkway, tel: 495035. Offers many of the facilities of the other hotels, albeit to 2-star standard. Rooms are basically furnished but with private facilities. Air-conditioning available at extra cost. Cape St Mary area.
Francisco's
Fajara, tel: 495332. Eight double rooms in garden setting, all with en suite facilities and ceiling fans. Notable restaurant, in which residents can benefit from a 10 percent discount. No swimming pool but use of the one at Fajara Golf Club nearby. Situated on the corner of Atlantic Road and Kairaba Avenue.
Safari Gardens
Fajara, tel: 495887. Agreeable small hotel (18 rooms) in garden setting. Rates include continental breakfast. Swimming pool.
Bunkoyo Hotel
Badala Parkway, tel: 463199. Eleven rooms with bathrooms, ceiling fans and garden setting. English breakfast. A 400-metre (437-yard) walk to the beach. Opposite Palma Rima hotel.
Fajara Guest House
Fajara, tel: 496122. En-suite facilities. English-run.
Malawi Guest House
Tel: 393012. Basic but clean, behind the US Embassy. English-run. Shared facilities, with one or two superior rooms with en suite. Pleasant garden. Restaurant, which offers good-value buffet on Friday evenings.
Bakadaji
Kotu Point, tel: 462307. This bar-restaurant also offers some self-catering bungalows and rooms. En

suite showers and toilets. Restaurant is one of the best for Gambian food.

Madiyana Bush Camp
Jinek Island, tel: 991994. Accessible by four-wheel drive from Barra or by boat, this offers perfect tranquillity in simple beach-hut accommodation. Advisable to ring ahead. Bar-restaurant. No generator.

Upriver

Tendaba Camp
Kemoto Hotel. Tel: 460608. On the banks of the Gambia River, 56 km (35 miles) upstream, 145 km (90 miles) by road. Simple but comfortable rooms (ceiling fans), swimming pool and own generator. Good base for taking canoe trips into the creeks or for taking safaris.

Mansa Konko Rest House
Two rooms offer simple accommodation. Electricity is regular until 2am.

Jangjang-Bureh Camp
Tel: 676182.
On the north bank of the river, just opposite Georgetown (320 km/200 miles upriver), this is the most comfortable base for exploring eastern Gambia. Mud-brick huts with thatched roofs offer twin-bedded accommodation with toilet and shower. No generator, so hurricane lamps light the way at night. Restaurant and bar. Boat trips organised.

Basse Rest House
Tel: 668240
Four beds; self-catering kitchenette.

Jem Hotel
Basse, tel: 668356. Eight simple rooms, all with private facilities. Restaurant. English or continental breakfast. The best option in town.

SENEGAL

As a much larger and more varied country than the Gambia, Senegal has a wide range of accommodation, from the most basic of overnight facilities to luxurious modern 300-room hotels exactly as you would expect to find in Europe or the United States. Unlike the Gambia, where the vast majority of hotels are recently built and designed for tourism, Senegal

also contains many small hotels in towns built at any time over the past century to cater for travellers of all descriptions. The general cultural background of the hotel industry in Senegal is French and a number of small establishments run by French proprietors offer a service not dissimilar to French country inns.

It is impossible to list all hotels, hostels and travel lodges and campsites here, but a selection of the more prominent places follows. See also the text in the *Places* section for hints on accommodation. Note that, in some cases, a telephone number is unavailable; in others, a complete address is not given where a town is too small to warrant it.

The Senegalese Ministry of Tourism grades hotels on a scale of 0 to 4 stars, although the actual top category is 4 stars plus the letter L for luxury. This category would be occupied by large modern air-conditioned hotels with sizeable, well-decorated rooms with bath and toilet en suite. The lowest category would be a campsite or extremely basic small hotel without any of these facilities.

Dakar

Teranga Sofitel (4-star L)
Place de l'Independence, tel: 23 10 44.

Novotel (4-star L)
Avenue Albert Sarraut, tel: 23 78 72.

Savana (4-star L)
Pointe Bernard, tel: 22 60 23.

Indépendance (4-star L)
Place de l'Indépendance, tel: 23 10 19.

Al Afifa (4-star)
46 rue Jules Ferry, tel: 21 85 43.

La Croix du Sud (4-star)
20 Avenue Albert Sarraut, tel: 23 24 10.

Le Lagon 2 (4-star)
Route de la Corniche Est, tel: 23 58 31.

Al Baraka (4-star)
35 Avenue A. K. Bourgi, tel: 22 55 32.

Afritel (4-star)
Avenue Faidherbe, tel: 23 16 41.

Nina (4-star)
43 rue du Dr. Thèze, tel: 23 22 30.

Pacha (4-star)
40 Avenue Lamine Gueye, tel: 23 10 18.

Le Plateau (3-star)
62 Jules Ferry, tel: 21 04 22.

Ganale (3-star)
38 rue A. A. Ndoye, tel: 31 55 70.

Atlantic (3-star)
52 Rue du Dr. Thèze, tel: 21 63 80.

Central (2-star)
16 Avenue Georges Pompidou, tel: 21 72 17.

Continental (2-star)
10 rue Galandou Diouf, tel: 22 03 71.

Gorée

L'Hostellerie du Chevalier de Boufflers. Tel: 22 53 64.

Ngor

Les Almadies (4-star L, Club Mediterranée)
Pointe des Almadies, tel: 21 38 41.

Complexe Meridien (4-star L)
Route de Ngor, tel: 20 21 22.

Diarrama
BP 8092, tel: 23 10 05.

Massata Samb (4-star)
Route de Ngor, tel: 20 05 12.

Le Sunugal (4-star)
Route de Ngor, tel: 20 03 30.

Le Village Club Calao (3-star)
Route de Ngor, tel: 20 05 40.

Hotel de l'Aérogare
Aérogare de Dakar Yoff, tel: 20 07 35.

Hotel Darkassé (1-star)
Route de Ngor, tel: 23 03 53.

Thiès

Hotel de Thiès (2-star)
Rue Faidherbe, tel: 51 15 26.

Hotel Rex (1-star)
Rue Douaumont, tel: 81081.

Petite Cote

Village/Club du Baobab (3-star)
La Somone, tel: 57 74 06.

Le Club Aldiana (4-star)
Nianing, tel: 57 10 84.

Domaine de Nianing (3-star)
Nianing, tel: 57 10 85.

Le Finio (1-star)
Joal, tel: 57 61 12.

Centre Touristique de la Petit Côte
M'Bour, tel: 57 10 04.

Savana Koumba (4-star)
M'Bour, tel: 57 11 12.
Saly Hotel (4-star)
M'Bour, tel: 57 11 31/57 11 25.
Royam (4-star)
M'Bour, tel: 57 10 79.
Fram Hotel (4-star)
Saly Portudal, tel: 57 11 37.
Novotel Saly (4-star)
Saly Portudal, tel: 57 11 91.
Savana Saly (4-star)
Saly Portudal, tel: 57 11 13.
Le Dior (3-star)
Rue de la Gare
Kaolack, tel: 41 15 13/41 18 45.
Le Paris (2-star)
Kaolack, tel: 41 10 19.
Keur Saloum (2-star)
Toubakouta, tel: 41 10 10.
Les Palétuviers
Toubakouta, tel: 21 87 73.
Les Piroguiers (3-star)
Foundiougne, tel: 45 11 34.
Le Pelican du Saloum (3-star)
Ndangane, tel: 23 54 46.
Centre Touristique (2-star)
Kahone, tel: 57 10 04.
Campement Hotel Djiffer
Tel: 51 15 26.

St Louis, Senegal River, Djourbel and Ferlo
Mame Coumba Bang (3-star)
Route Nationale 2, St Louis, tel: 61 18 50.
La Residence (3-star)
Rue Blaise Diagne, St Louis, tel: 61 12 60.
Hotel de la Poste (3-star)
St Louis, tel: 61 11 18.
Gite d'étape du Fleuve
Richard Toll, tel: 63 32 40.
Hotel de la Poste Rest House
At Richard Toll (contact Hotel in St Louis).
Campement Hotel
Maka Diama, tel: 21 97 68.
Le Baobab (3-star)
Djourbel, tel: 71 10 07.

Casamance and Southeast Senegal
Club Mediterranée (4-star L)
Cap Skirring, tel: 93 51 04
Savana (4-star)
Cap Skirring, tel: 91 15 52.
Kabrousse Mossor (4-star)
Cap Skirring, tel: 93 51 52.

La Paillote (3-star)
Cap Skirring, tel: 93 51 51.
Emitaï (3-star)
Cap Skirring, tel: 94 11 26.
Hotel-Village de la Pointe Saint Georges (2-star)
Tel: 93 36 39.
Le Diola (4-star)
Route de Kandé, Ziguinchor, tel: 91 12 62.
Le Nema Kadior (4-star)
Route de Kandé
Ziguinchor, tel: 91 10 52.
Aubert (3-star)
Ziguinchor, tel: 91 13 79.
Le Tourisme (2-star)
Ziguinchor, tel: 91 12 27.
Le Relais Fleuri (2-star)
Bignona, tel: 94 12 02.
Campement Hotel "Le Hobe"
Kolda, tel: 96 11 70.
Asta Kebe (3-star)
Tambacounda, tel: 81 10 28.
Niji Hotel (1-star)
Tambacounda, tel: 81 12 50.
Hotel de la Gare
Tambacounda, tel: 98 015.
Relais de Simenti (2-star)
Niokolo Koba, tel: 32 804.
Campement-Hotel du Niokolo Koba
Tel: 23 10 55.

In addition, the Casamance Region is the centre for the project of village *campements*, a way of offering low-rent accommodation to travellers who are interested in experiencing village life at close quarters. The *campements* are run cooperatively by villagers and consist of huts exactly like the others in the village, furnished with between two and four simple beds equipped with foam mattresses and mosquito nets. Lighting is usually by paraffin lamp and there will be simple separate WCs and showers. Basic meals will be offered, as well as the chance to participate in any activities, ceremonies, etc. that may be scheduled. *Campements* are situated in the following villages in the region: Elinkine, Enamporé, Baila, Koubalan, Thionck Essyl, Affiniam, Abané, Oussouye, Palmarin.

Where to Eat

What to Eat

The general gastronomic background of the region of Senegambia is fairly simple. The staples are millet in the north and rice in the south, with rice making inroads generally. A great deal of fish is eaten – from the sea all along the Atlantic coast, and from the rivers throughout their hinterlands. There is less meat, although it is freely available everywhere.

In many cases, meat could do with more expert butchering before it reaches the kitchen. Steaks, stews, minced meat balls and kebabs are the most popular ways of serving meat dishes in almost every restaurant. Chicken, freshly grilled or roasted, can be tender and tasty.

A wide range of vegetables is available, and a typical cooked dish might consist of a meat or fish and vegetable braise served with rice or millet. Peppercorns and chillis often add a touch of heat to the recipe.

Visitors should take advantage of the abundance of fresh fruit available: mangoes, pineapples, bananas, oranges (local ones are green, not orange, when ripe), water melons, pawpaws. All are sold outside tourist hotels, along roadsides and on the beaches, and supply ready-made refreshing desserts at all times of the day. Wash them well, peel, eat and enjoy.

Try also the cashew and groundnuts, dry-roasted in their skins and sold by the market women. Although most groundnuts (aka peanuts) are crushed into oil, they are also available everywhere at negligible cost, and find their way into tasty sauces and soups.

Onto this African background has been grafted, in the case of the Gambia, the English culinary practices of the country's former colonisers, while Senegal has local adaptations of French cuisine. This can be extremely good.

Both Senegal and the Gambia share a taste for Arab-style tea, sometimes with mint, served after meals according to an immutable ritual. Three little glasses – the first strong, bitter and frothy, the second sweeter and a little weaker, the last very sweet and quite pale.

Where to Eat

Gambia

Most hotels and restaurants serve both European and Gambian food but there are ample opportunities to try a wide range of other cuisines: Chinese, Malaysian, Vietnamese, Swedish, Lebanese and "international". Fast food snack bars are springing up everywhere too, especially Lebanese shawarmas – grilled meat slices served in pitta bread.

Fish is the obvious food to ask for in a country which lies along both sea coast and river. There is a disappointing lack of variety in the methods of serving fish dishes but garlic prawns, prawns Gambian-style and freshly fried or grilled ladyfish, barracuda, mullet, butterfish or sole are excellent. Local lobsters are fortunately quite safe to eat (whereas local oysters from the creeks, with their risk of hepatitis, are not) and are delicious served either as soup (bisque) or grilled with herbs over an open fire.

Gambian specialities which should definitely be tried include: benachin (fish stewed with a variety of vegetables and served with rice), domoda (groundnut stew with meat and vegetable, chicken yassa/sissay yassa (chicken smothered in fried onions), sissay nyebe (chicken with black-eyed beans), akara bean fritters (ground black-eyed bean fritters), oleleh (steamed bean cakes with palm oil). At all markets, women sit with large bowls of different types of cooked

dishes which they serve to you in a piece of fresh bread, should you wish to be a bit more adventurous: D5, or less, for a palm oil and nyebe sandwich which is very satisfying.

The following is a list of interesting restaurants in the country. Except in the big hotels, the Gambia entirely lacks any very up-market restaurants, so do not expect haute cuisine in any of these establishments. A pleasant meal in quite jolly surroundings may be had, however. In addition to the restaurants listed below, there are countless makeshift beach bars which tout for custom. These can be surprisingly good – it is usual practice to place your order early in the day, together with a deposit, and then return at a pre-arranged time to find you meal ready.

Al Basha
Tel: 463300. The best Lebanese restaurant in the Gambia. Pleasant ambience, air-conditioning, wide range of dishes. Situated outside the Senegambia and Kairaba hotels.

African Heritage Gallery
Wellington Street, Banjul. Light lunches, Danish-style. Good selection of meat and fish main dishes. Overlooking harbour.

Bakadaji
Tel: 462307. Inexpensive, authentic Gambian cuisine, plus additions from North Africa and the Middle East. Come for the buffet on Thursday and Saturday evenings, when there is also a strolling kora player. On the road to the Senegambia hotel, not far from the Palma Rima hotel. Accommodation is also available.

Bamboo
Tel: 495764. Reasonable Chinese restaurant with standard range of dishes. In the Fajara area, signposted off the road. Amex the only credit card accepted.

The Brasserie
Tel: 460813. Restaurant in the Kololi Beach Club (but open to non-residents), serving usual range of meat and fish. Great crêpes Suzette for pudding. Worth coming when the

reggae band is playing in the adjacent courtyard. Credit cards accepted, including American Express.

Braustuble
Leman Street, Banjul, tel: 28371. Indoor or outdoor seating. German-Lebanese run. Snacks, freshly grilled barbecued fish, good main dishes.

Calypso Cape
Tel: 496292. Pleasant beach bar near the Sunwing Hotel on Cape Hope, serving good food. The Irish/Egyptian partnership behind Calypso attracts an interesting regular ex-pat clientele.

Clay Oven
Tel: 496600. Reputed to be the best Indian restaurant in West Africa, the Clay Oven (Bakau area) is worth the taxi fare. Sensible to book. Air-conditioning. Credit cards.

Dolphin
Tel: 460929. Popular British-run bar and restaurant near Senegambia hotel. Traditional English food, plus some Gambian specialities.

Dublin
Irish bar, with food (steaks, seafood, Irish coffees). Next to the Tropic Garden Hotel, in Bakau area.

Francisco's
Tel: 495332. Stylish garden setting. Menu offers good range of fish and meat, with a number of Gambian specialities. Good steak au poivre rubs shoulders with more imaginative options such as butterfish with bananas and peanuts. Best to book unless dining early. Guests staying in Francisco's get a 10 percent discount. At the junction of Atlantic and Pipeline roads. Credit cards accepted.

Il Mondo
Tel: 466573. Beach bar/restaurant which is a useful standby for guests in the Kombo Beach and Bungalow Beach hotels. Usual range of fish and meat, plus home-made desserts and good liqueur coffees. The English owner also runs fishing trips and will cook what you catch.

Lamin Lodge
Tel: 996903. German-run, this attractive, higgledy-piggledy stilt lodge enjoys an idyllic setting on the edge of the Abuko National Park.

Springboard for canoe trips into the creeks for bird-watching. Great breakfasts (features in the Birds and Breakfast excursions offered by tour companies) and a good option for lunch. If tourism is quiet, telephone ahead to let them know you are coming.

Lou-Lou's
Tel: 460177. Charming Gambian restaurant near the junction of the road to Badala Park and Kombo Beach hotels. Excellent, inexpensive food (Gambian and international), but slow service (which may be its downfall). Ask for your table to be moved outside to escape the heat of the kitchen.

Malawi Guest House
Tel: 393012. Simple, plentiful food. Good value buffet on Friday nights. Fajara area.

Neptune
Tel: 460434. Justly popular, well-run newcomer with nautical motif running round its walls. Especially noted for its steaks and seafood. Opposite Palma Rima Hotel. Advisable to book as it gets very busy.

Siam Garden
Tel: 496141. Recommended Thai restaurant in Fajara area, noted for its seafood specialities. Buffet on Friday and Monday.

Snr Williams
Next to Bokatu Hotel. Good international fare. May be closed in the wet season.

Valbonne
Tel: 460224. Upmarket Italian restaurant, with adjacent casino. Kololi area, near Senegambia and Kairaba hotels.

Senegal

A greater range of dishes is available in Senegal, the Gambia being, in effect, a small sub-region of its larger neighbour from a gastronomic point of view. In addition, the French influence has been beneficial, providing much superior non-indigenous cuisine as well as a range of French-African compromise dishes, which are excellent.

Fish is a very important feature. The big white sea-bream known as a *thiof* is a superb fish simply grilled, stuffed à la St Louisienne or as part of a stew. Senegal's most famous dish, *thie-bou-dienne*, is known throughout West Africa. It consists of rice cooked with fish and vegetables. Other well known dishes are *mafé* (peanut stew with meat) and *yassa* (onion and lemon stew with chicken, fish or meat).

Shellfish are also excellent. Oysters, which are farmed as well as gathered in Siné-Saloum and Casamance, are excellent and pose less of a health risk than Gambian ones. Huge prawns are caught off most of the coast, as well as clams, mussels and superb lobsters and crayfish.

Unlike the Gambia, Senegal contains a variety of restaurants from the little *dibiteries* which serve grilled meat, through French-style brasseries (though do not expect a full-scale Alsace-style establishment under this name), up to quite classy and therefore pricey restaurants.

The following is a list of establishments in and around Dakar. Elsewhere in the country, the best restaurants belong to the hotels already listed. Outside the capital, it is rare to find high-quality restaurants existing independently of hotels, although there are always plenty of little *dibiteries* and cafés.

Chez Loutcha
Rue Blanchot, tel: 21 03 02. Reasonably priced Euro-African menu.

Terrou Bi
Corniche Ouest, tel: 22 02 47. Luxurious fish specialities including live lobsters from tank.

Le Ramatou
Route de N'Gor, Dakar-Yoff. Medium-priced French and Senegalese dishes.

Le Bilboquet
Avenue Roume, tel: 22 17 42. Good French traditional cuisine in mock Normand setting.

Le Virage
Route de N'Gor, tel: 20 06 57. Panoramic view of sea, good fish and seafood specialities.

Le Lagon
Route de la Petite Corniche, tel: 21 53 22. Excellent fish with view over ocean in smart modern setting.

Brasserie Sarraut
Avenue Sarraut, tel: 22 55 23. Good Parisian-style family restaurant with terrace.

Le Kermel
Place du Marché Kermel. French café-restaurant.

Le Rustic
Avenue Georges Pompidou, tel: 22 18 76. Standard and quite well-run French café-restaurant.

Le Ponty
Avenue Georges Pompidou. Busy café/restaurant with terrace on main shopping street.

La Dagorne
Rue de Dagorne, tel: 22 20 80. Good moderately priced French fish dishes.

Chez Charli
Route de Rufisque, Thiaroye sur Mer, tel: 34 07 42. Tables under straw roofs, fish specialities.

Le Rond-Point
Place de l'Indépendance, tel: 22 10 29. Fish and shellfish.

Maitre Boeuf
Centre Nautique Pehoa-N'Gor, tel: 20 03 64. French-style meats grilled on wood fire, plus fish.

Le Forum
Avenue Lamine Gueye, tel: 21 93 88. Café/restaurant/tea-room. Popular with journalists from ORTS nearby.

La Voile D'Or
Copacabana Beach, Bel-Air, tel: 21 86 48. Fish restaurant in beach setting with palm-trees.

Le Coq Gaulois
Boulevard Dial Diop, tel: 22 19 11. French and Senegalese specialities.

La Marmite
Rue Felix-Faure, tel: 21 41 98.
Senegalese and other West African
dishes.
Le Wallame
Avenue Bourguiba, tel: 22 78 24.
Good African specialities.
Café de Paris
Avenue Georges Pompidou, tel: 21
56 20. Another reliable French
establishment.
La Croix du Sud
Avenue Albert Sarraut, tel: 23 29
47. Elegant old-style hotel
restaurant serving excellent and
expensive French-Senegalese cui-
sine.
Le Chevalier de Boufflers
Gorée Island, tel: 22 53 64. Small
restaurant in pretty Gorée hotel
serving excellent French seafood.
L'Auberge Rouge
Rue Blanchot, tel: 21 72 56. Pretty
old hotel courtyard with good
French food.
Safari 2000
Rue Parent, tel: 21 27 19.
Expensive, classy French cuisine.
Hotel de la Paix
Rue N'Doye, tel: 22 29 78. Well-run
traditional French country
restaurant, with pleasant bar
adjoining.
Hotel-Restaurant Saint Louis
Rue Félix-Faure, tel: 22 54 23.
Lovely old courtyard with plants,
reasonably priced tasty cooking.
Le Cauri
Rue Bourgi, tel: 22 55 59. Good
Senegalese cooking, including thie-
bou-dienne.
M'Baye Barik
off Avenue Bourguiba.
Senegalese dishes served in a
Sahelian ambience.
Le Djolof
Marché Soumbédiounne.
Good Senegalese cooking.
Le Trastevere
Rue Mohamed V, tel: 21 49 20.
Pizzas and home-made pasta.
La Pizzeria
Rue Bourgi, tel: 21 09 26. Pizzas
and Italian and French dishes.
Restaurant Farid
Rue Vincens, tel: 21 61 27.
Lebanese specialities.
La Tonkinoise
Rue Dagorne, tel: 21 60 80.

International menu including
Chinese specialities.
Hanoi
Rue Carnet, tel: 21 32 69.
Chinese and Vietnamese dishes.

Drinking Notes

Both the Gambia and Senegal are
predominantly Muslim, but, though
Islam disapproves of alcohol consumption, neither country imposes
restrictions on its sale.

Gambia
Beer is very much the favourite
Gambian drink. Gambia has its own
brewery, producing a refreshing
light lager "Joyful" Julbrew, which
can be served bottled or draught
(the same brewery also makes soft
drinks). Imported beers also
feature. At some point on your trip,
you will probably taste palm wine
fresh from the tree. This has a low
alcohol content but the longer it is
allowed to ferment the higher this
becomes. White and slightly frothy,
it has a sourish taste. The local
firewater is sorrel gin.
    There are no opening hours in
the Gambia. A cool beer or other
drink can be taken at any time of
the day (electricity and fridge
permitting). Pubs and bars are open
most of the day and evening, many
serving snacks as well as drinks.
    Many restaurants which have re-
stricted eating hours will, however,
serve drinks throughout the day.
    There are innumerable local
bars in Serekunda and Banjul,
some more, some less appealing.
One of the more notorious venues
is Eddie's, Mama Koto Street,
Serekunda, with its girls, back
rooms and pool tables. If you want
to experience it, go with a Gambian.

Senegal
The Senegalese also drink a good
deal of light, continental-style beer
to quench thirst. The most popular
local brand is Flag; imported beers
are readily available but more
expensive.
    In addition, wine is imported
from France, Spain and North
Africa, but is reasonably expensive

because of the cost of importing
and storing it. Moroccan wines are
often worth considering as a good
compromise between quality and
expense.
    There are no set drinking hours.
Many restaurants double as
café/bars in the French manner.
    Here is a selection of some bars
in Dakar where the prices are reasonable and the atmosphere is
pleasant. Conversation is easy if
you say "hello" to anyone there.
Senegalese people are very
responsive to greetings and they
will open up if you show them you
are ready to enter into a discussion.
Auberge Rouge, rue Moussé Diop.
Bar Yang Yang, Avenue Blaise
Diagne.
Bar le Mama Guedj, Avenue Lamine
Gueye.
Bar Odeon, Sicap Liberte 6.
Le Fouquets, Avenue Lamine
Guèye.
    In addition, particularly in the
suburbs, there exist little unofficial
back-room or back-yard bars known
as clandos (short for clandestine).
If you are adventurous and
persistent (they are not advertised),
a visit to a clando will give you real
insights into the lives of ordinary
working Senegalese.

Attractions

Things to Do

The pleasures of Senegambia are relatively simple ones. Dakar is not Rome or Paris, and Banjul is scarcely a suburb of either. Most of the holiday attractions of the region are described in the sections dealing with beaches, hunting and fishing, sports and so on. Many visitors do little more than lie on the beach in the sun.

Another large area of activity concerns excursions, from half a day to a week, to visit other parts of the country. Many people on a two-week holiday in Cap Vert or the Little Coast visit Casamance briefly, for example, to get an idea of the very different type of terrain in the south. Visitors to the Gambia often take a day's return flight to Dakar for big city thrills, while French holiday makers in Senegal frequently hire a car and check out little Anglophone Gambia. Vacationers in either country might go overnight to Guinea-Bissau in the south, or the Cape Verde Islands out in the Atlantic. The possible variations are numerous. A list of the principal tour operators in both the Gambia and Senegal is printed below; between them, they cover the whole range of excursions available. In addition, the Places section describes the main features of interest across the region.

Culture

Gambia

You wouldn't expect such a little country to be rich in museums, opera houses and so on, and the Gambia isn't. In Banjul, the National Museum, Independence Drive, is a pleasant little museum with clean, well-kept exhibits of local jewellery, clothes, utensils, housing, customs and rituals, supported with photos, maps and other clear explanations. A full-size groundnut sailing boat, formerly used to carry the groundnuts down river to Banjul but now replaced by motorised lighters, is being built in the grounds outside, commissioned by President Jawara.

The African Heritage Gallery, Wellington Street, is the only art gallery in the accepted tourist sense of the word. Local carvings, paintings, clothes and jewellery are tastefully displayed and all for sale as well. Set in lofty, cool rooms with a balcony overlooking the river.

In addition, artists display their paintings and sculptures in their own local galleries. Several will be found in Bakau, at Cape St Mary near Sambou's restaurant, along Atlantic Road, off New Town Road – each with their own signboard pointing the way.

Otherwise, one can simply wander and observe Banjul's architecture. Disregard the potholes, the dusty buildings, the open drains and walk, if it is not too hot, round the streets, not forgetting the back streets behind Independence Drive. (Or take a taxi drive.) Notice the style of architecture, the two-storeyed houses with shady courtyards through open gateways, and balconies overlooking the road, pastel-coloured walls of pink, blue or cream (needing a coat of paint maybe, but possibly all the more attractive in their run down mellowness), the corrugated iron pagoda-style roofs.

For concerts, film screenings and other cultural events, you will either be obliged to use the tourist hotels or watch local posters and the media for the occasional public event.

Senegal

This bigger, more sophisticated country is better equipped with cultural infrastructure, much of which is described elsewhere in this book.

Senegal has few museums. In Dakar, visit the IFAN museum, Place Soweto, with its collection of rare masks.

Despite the government's genuine efforts to help the arts, the presence of art galleries is something of a miracle in the country.

In Dakar, visit the Galerie 39 (Avenue Georges Pompidou), a French-run gallery which manages to put on several exhibitions every year, and the National Art Gallery (Avenue Albert Sarraut).

Concerts are held fairly regularly in the main towns. The two stadiums (Iba Mar Diop and Demba Diop) and the Sorano National Theatre host most concerts in Dakar.

The Sorano National Theatre is the main venue for most plays. In the popular areas, actors use houses and government-sponsored youth and sports centres to perform.

Senegal gets, sooner or later, the latest movies produced in the west. The Senegalese are very fond of cinema, their country being the most important in Africa in film production. Names like Ousmane Sembène are world famous in the cinema industry.

In every major city, there is a cinema. Most films are in French, but there are many films from India in original Hindi with French subtitles.

National Parks/Reserves

Gambia

There is only one National Park open to the public in the Gambia: Abuko Nature Reserve, between Serekunda and Yundum Airport. Started by Eddie Brewer, a former forestry officer who was later made the first Director of Wildlife Conservation by ex-President Jawara, and his daughter, Stella, these 22 acres (9 hectares) of original Gambian forest have been preserved in their natural state for visitors to walk through at leisure. Pools hide crocodiles and attract colourful birds to their banks which can be watched from carefully constructed hides. Monkeys, squirrels, the occasional iguana and, if you are lucky, the shy sitatunga antelope, can be seen among the trees.

Abuko's sister project, Baboon Island, is not open to the public so as to protect the chimpanzees from intrusive visitors while they learn to survive on their own in their natural habitat. It was started as a conservation island by Stella Brewer for this purpose.

Senegal

Senegal is well equipped with National Parks, which are particularly rich in bird life. For details of all parks, contact Direction des Parcs Nationaux, Point E, Dakar BP 5135. Tel: 21 06 28.

The following is a list of the parks. For further details, see the relevant section of *Places*.

Parc National du Niokolo Koba: One of the largest big mammalian reserves in West Africa, this park occupies a total area of 180,000 acres (73,000 hectares) in the southeast of Senegal. You will find elephants, lions, gazelles. Accommodation is available in campsites and hotels (see Tambacounda Hotels).

Parc National des Oiseaux du Djoudj
In the north east, not far from the mouth of the River Senegal, 40 miles (60 km) from St Louis by good sand road. This is the gathering place for millions of migrating birds. The best time to visit is between October and April. Camping is possible, with excursions by canoe.

Parc National du Delta du Saloum
50 miles (80 km) west of Kaolack. The park is dotted with small islands made up of mangroves and sand dunes. You will find pink flamingoes, storks and many other birds. Tourist camps are available.

Parc National de la Langue de Barbarie
A refuge for birds and sea tortoises, this park is a narrow strip of sandy land between the Atlantic Ocean and the River Senegal. Easily reached from St Louis.

Parc de la Madeleine
Just by Dakar, on the Corniche, an archipelago used to protect the numerous colonies of sea birds. The park is accessible every day by canoe.

Parc National de la Basse Casamance
In the extreme south, 12,000 acres (5,000 hectares) of forests and mangroves. By road, seven miles (12 km) from Oussouye and 45 miles (75 km) from Ziguinchor. Camping possible, with excursions by canoe.

Nightlife

Nightlife

Gambia

Nightlife is rather limited in the Gambia, to the disappointment of both Gambians and some visitors. The larger tourist hotels have their own nightclubs, open to members of the public as well as to their own guests. Some are open every evening, some only at weekends. Some are free, some charge an entrance fee.

The larger hotels stage entertainments for their visitors. This is a good chance to see local dancers, drummers, fire-eaters, acrobats or fashion shows. Cabaret shows as in Europe are not common. Occasionally a hotel will put on its own cabaret, drawing talent from its visitors; sometimes an artiste is hired for the six-month season, doing a tour of these hotels. For performances by visiting African popular groups, watch out for posters and listen to the radio. Large concerts occasionally take place in the National Stadium.

These are some of the major nightclubs:

Dunda Nightclub
Atlantic Hotel
Tel: 28601
Disco music.
Bellengo Nightclub
Kombo Beach (Novotel)
Disco music. This is one of the liveliest places.
Senegambia Beach Hotel Nightclub
Tel: 92717/8/9
Live bands sometimes, e.g. during Monday night barbecue. Otherwise disco music.
Musu's Disco
Cape Point. No entrance fee.
Tropicana Nightclub and Disco on

the way to the Senegambia Hotel. In among the trees. Disco music.

Oasis
Clarkson Street, Banjul. Disco.

Tropic Garden Hotel Nightclub
Disco music. No entrance fee.

Senegal

Most towns have at least one disco or nightclub. As one would expect, Dakar has many to choose from.

In addition, live popular music is available both at large open-air concerts and in clubs reasonably regularly. Watch the press and listen to the radio for details.

Top Dakar artists and groups such as Youssou N'Dour and the Super Etoile de Dakar and Super Diamono de Dakar often have residencies for periods at a particular club, playing every night or two or three times a week. Both the clubs themselves and the resident groups change regularly, however. Check with your hotel for latest news.

Nightclubs open, and continue, late. At midnight they might still be three quarters empty and 4am is about the time of maximum activity. Usually you pay at the door (between CFA 1500 and 3500) and this price entitles you to your first drink free.
Some addresses are:

Harry's Club, Boulevard de la République, el: 21 90 88.

Miami, Rue de Rheims, tel: 21 39 69.

Kilimanjaro, Village Artisinale Soumbedioune, tel: 21 99 89.

Play Club, Rue Jules Ferry, tel: 21 24 84.

Sahel Night Club, Boulevard Gueule Tapée, tel: 21 21 18.

Gambling

Gambia

Kololi Casino, Kololi, for black jack, roulette, chemin de fer, etc. Saturday is the liveliest night to come and play.

Senegal
Casino du Cap-Vert, Ngor. Tel: 20 09 74.

Festivals

General

Gambia

Organised festivals in public for special occasions are rare in the Gambia. There are plenty of celebrations on feast days and for marriage or name-day ceremonies but they will be in private. You may be lucky enough to get to know a Gambian whose family will be celebrating something while you are on holiday and who will take you with him/her. Or you may happen to be passing a compound where dancing or drumming is taking place and be able to watch. On feast days, small groups of young people may dress up as birds, animals or magicians and dance in the road to the music of whistles and drums.

During the Christmas/New Year season, Fanal processions take place in Banjul, Bakau and Serekunda. Intricate ships made from split bamboo and cut-out paper patterns delicately glued together are constructed by clubs in honour of their patron. These are then paraded through the streets every evening in the dark, with candles lit inside them to illuminate the tracery, accompanied by drumming and dancing crowds, until they reach the patron's house. At the end of the season (just after New Year), the ship is given to the patron for him to display. Donations are accepted for the club. If you know where to go, you can watch the processions.

Good examples of the ships are in the National Museum in Banjul.

Senegal

The same remarks apply to Senegal as to the Gambia. The most noteworthy and famous Fanals are in St Louis, where the museum contains some examples of the construction.

There are in addition a number of regional tribal festivals and ceremonies. In the Thiès region, the month of May sees a series of dance rituals known as *syniaka*, while the Fil festival brings together another set of rituals and ceremonies in June and July. In the southeast, the Bassari peoples indulge in spectacularly-costumed initiation rituals for young boys in March. In Casamance, a number of ceremonies include the Zulane Festival in June, the Zumebel in July and harvest festivals in May.

Shopping

There are two sorts of buying transactions in Senegambia, which represent the modern, European, systematised method as against the traditional, African, informal one. The first is in the modern shops and supermarkets where prices are fixed and displayed by the goods and everything is very simple. The second, which still applies in many markets and small shops and stalls, involves bargaining and is therefore not simple.

How best to bargain? It would be seen as madness to pay the first price requested. The proper price is probably between a third and a half. To get to the correct price, however, you must play a leisurely game in which it is perfectly acceptable to feign impatience, walk off, pause, turn back, think, discuss details of the goods, etc. The vendor will not understand at all the idea that you might be in a hurry. The best method is probably to start at around one-third of the asking price, so that you can be seen to increase your offer at least once.

Shopping hours in the informal sector (markets, etc.) are very flexible, more or less from dawn to dusk. An African vendor will never turn away a visitor just because he has half-finished packing up his wares.

Gambia
Popular purchases include Gambian tie-dye or batik cloth, sold in lengths or made up into shirts, shorts, skirts, dresses, trousers, children's clothes, tablecloths plus napkins. Local cloth called *Lagos*, printed not tie-dyed, is brightly coloured with original designs. Dutch and English wax prints are also popular but slightly more expensive. There is also local indigo-dyed cloth (dark blue/light blue patterns) at certain stalls in the markets. For the ultimate choice in batik, and also to see it being made, visit Gena Bes in Bakau, Tel: 495068.

Tailors, machines whirring all day long, will run up anything from a pair of shorts to a man's suit in a matter of one or two days.

Wood carvings are also popular and these too can be custom made (simply put down a deposit for the wood, making sure you are dealing with a bona fide craftsman). Other souvenirs include filigree jewellery, bead necklaces and traditionally dressed dolls. Musical instruments are also for sale.

Books on Gambian history, myths and legends, flora and fauna, and novels by Gambian writers can be found in the Methodist Bookshop, Buckle Street, Banjul.

Senegal
All of the same items as in the Gambia are available in Senegal.

As far as cloth is concerned, it is worth remembering that in the Gambia it is considerably cheaper; indeed every bus from the Gambia into Senegal carries a number of women returning from an expedition to stock up on cheap materials.

As in the Gambia, markets throughout Senegal abound in tailors who will run up a costume – perhaps a magnificent flowing *boubou* gown – in 24 hours.

Gold and silver jewellery are both available, the latter particularly from Mauritanian silversmiths (though the 1989 exodus of Mauritanians has reduced this trade enormously).

Sport

Wrestling is the national sport, taking place on a Saturday or Sunday evening (except during Ramadan). The atmosphere and audience reaction are to be enjoyed as much as the wrestling itself. The wrestlers are usually draped in amulets to bring luck and often pour over their bodies and drink "magic" potions to protect themselves. Between bouts, followers of each wrestler dance, drum, blow whistles and flutes, playing to the crowd, whipping up excitement and spurring their hero to flaunt himself and show off his strength. The actual wrestling round lasts no time by comparison. First one down loses. Excursions to wrestling matches are organised from the hotels, but anyone can attend by simply turning up.

Canoe racing takes place irregularly (check with local hotels, tour operators, etc.) but can be quite spectacular, with up to 30 men propelling the large craft. The most active areas are Cap Vert and St Louis in Senegal.

Football is popular as a street game with improvised equipment but both countries have major stadiums where organised matches take place. Again, the events are irregular. Watch local press, talk to local people to get advance warning of a match.

Gambia
In such a small country, facilities are obviously limited. The major activities obviously relate to the beach and swimming pool, and these are available in abundance. Most beach hotels will have windsurfers, surf boards and perhaps small yachts available, usually with instructors.

Facilities are available at the Senegambia, Kombo Beach (Novotel), Fajara, Sunwing and Atlantic Hotels for tennis. Some of the above also have squash and badminton courts and facilities for volleyball and basketball. Short-term visitors can also join the Fajara Club and enjoy their 18-hole golf course (£15 a round), squash, tennis and badminton courts, snooker table and swimming pool. Tennis courts are also available at the Cedars Club, Serekunda and the Reform Club in Banjul.

HUNTING

The Gambia takes very seriously its duty to conserve wildlife and hunting in virtually all forms is heavily discouraged.

The only form of hunting permitted is a limited participation in the culls of wild pigs occasionally ordered by the police when the animals threaten the rice crops. Application to the police at such a time, which is entirely unpredictable, may result in permission to participate.

FISHING

Sea or river fishing with a line from the beach or bank is popular and needs no particular organisation. Up-river, piroques may be hired everywhere informally for short excursions. Game fishing for the wide variety of species which abound offshore is organised through the major hotels.

Also try: Il Monda, tel: 466573; and LA Creek Fishing, tel: 991313. Both of these offer a choice of deep sea fishing in the Atlantic or fishing in the bolongs and creeks of the Gambia river. You could also negotiate directly with fishermen themselves. If you do, you will probably want to stick to the Gambia river rather than risk the Atlantic seas.

Senegal

Since independence, Senegal has an active sports policy. At colleges, sport is a subject taught and included in the two main exams, that of BFEM (the equivalent of the British O-Level) and the Baccalauréate. So popular are the sports activities in Dakar that the authorities have made available a long stretch of running track on the Corniche Ouest, facing the University. Every day, from around 5pm, hundreds of people are to be seen along the Corniche doing push-ups, hurdling or simply having fun. Similarly, throughout the country groups of joggers in the morning and evening are a common sight.

As far as beach sports are concerned, all major centres of tourism supply the full range of windsurfers, etc. All of the big hotels in the most popular regions – Cap Vert, the Little Coast – have private beaches. Dakar is also surrounded by fine beaches.

The best beaches are Yoff, les Almadies and Anse Bernard. For the young, the beaches of Bel Air, Hann Plage are the most popular as waves are almost non-existent.

TENNIS

Although tennis courts are common in the tourist hotel complexes, public facilities are few. Tennis clubs in Dakar are: the Tennis Club Dakarois, tel: 21 16 07 and the Union or Olympique Club Corniche, tel: 22 21 98.

GOLF

Golf is similarly not a widespread game, being regarded as exclusive and a rich man's sport (which it is, of course, in Africa). Apart from the Cap Vert and Little Coast hotels, courses exist at: the golf club on the Route de Cambérène, tel: 22 40 69; the Lagon 1, Dakar, tel: 21 53 22; Les Marinas, Bel Air, tel: 22 25 77.

HORSE RIDING

Many major beach hotels offer horse riding facilities. Public riding stables are rare, however. Up-country, the Ranch de Doli hunting lodge in the Djourbel Region offers horse treks. In Dakar: the Centre de l'Etrier, tel: 32 52 63 and the Cercle Hippique Sportif, tel: 34 02 33 provide facilities.

DANCE SCHOOLS

After the closure of the Mudra Dance School, a ground-breaking institution engaged in the propagation of traditional African dance, several former teachers and students set up their own schools. All of them offer a full range of styles (jazz, classical, etc.), but they are particularly good in African dance. These are the best known:
Lorenzetti, 4 rue Mage, tel: 22 12 37
Manhattan Dance School, 127 rue Carnot
Marie Eve, Rue Victor Hugo, tel: 22 00 14
Atelier Sobo-Bade, 50 rue Mohamed V
Xarit Dance, 14 Avenue A. K. Bourgi, tel: 21 32 63.

HUNTING

The hunting season in Senegal is from 15 December until 30 April. Hunting is strictly controlled. The Water and Forests Bureau in Dakar issues hunting permits to those with insurance, firearm certificate, regulation permit papers and dues. Permits come in three categories: the Small Game permit is issued for one day's shoot, taking not more than 15 in total of stone-partridges, guinea-fowl, bustards, francolins or hare; the Medium permit includes the small game but also the shooting of one of each of the following – gazelle, oribi, waterbuck, cob, warthog or two great bustards; a Big Game licence is issued only through authorised hunting guides, and then rarely. It covers all of the large game. Rare species, such as lion, however, require the personal permission of the President to hunt. It is not often given.

In addition, there is a special permit covering water game-birds available.

Permission to bring firearms into the country must be obtained from the Ministry of the Interior. Authorised guides may obtain this permission on behalf of their clients, or, of course, provide guns for their use. It is forbidden to import ammunition, which must be bought in Senegal. Insurance is obligatory for all hunters.

All questions and applications should be addressed to: Direction Des Eaux, Forêts et Chasses, Parc Forestier de Hann, BP 1831 Dakar, tel: 23 76 14/23 06 28.

FISHING

Senegal is rich in fish of all descriptions, and a major centre for fishing of different categories. As in the Gambia, simple "surf casting" with a line or rod and line from the beaches or reefs will bring in a wide range of fish, even including sharks and rays on occasion.

From a boat in the bolongs off the rivers Casamance and Saloum and their substantial estuaries, a whole range of river and sea fish can be caught. Again, not only small specimens – barracuda may also be caught.

Underwater fishing, for which insurance is obligatory, takes place, particularly in the Cap Vert region, for large grouper and barracuda.

Finally, Senegal is a major centre for big game fishing, for the much prized sailfish, marlin, wahoo and sharks. Cap Vert and the Little Coast are the main regions for this activity.

The following is a list of centres can supply full equipment and arrange all possible details of a trip, from an afternoon in a pirogue to a full big game fishing holiday including stuffing and mounting of the catches. Enquire also with tour operators and the big hotels, particularly Club Mediterranée at NGor and at Cap Skirring.

Centre de Pêche Sportive de Dakar
(Air Afrique)
Embarcadère Dakar Gorée
BP 3132
Tel: 21 28 58
Centre de Pêche des Hotels Meridien
BP 8092 Dakar
Tel: 23 10 05
Centre de Pêche du Savana Frantel
BP 1015 Dakar
Tel: 22 60 23
Africa Safari
Dakar
Tel: 21 07 16/22 26 84

Centre de Pêche de la Petite Cote
BP 64 M'Bour
Tel: 51 10 75
Les Piroguiers
BP 22 à Foundiougne
Tel: 45 11 34
Line Fishing by Boat/Pirogue.
Les Barracudas
BP 14 Dakar
Tel: 21 94 38
Village Hotel Keur Salouma
Toubacouta
BP 334
Tel: 41 10 19
Hotel Kabrousse-Mossor
Cap Skirring
BP 236 Ziguinchor
Tel: 91 14 26
Hotel Savana
Cap Skirring
Tel: 91 15 52

DIVING

Diving facilities are available at a variety of places including:
Oceanium Diving Club
BP 3870 Dakar
Tel: 22 19 19

Language

General

English is the official language of the Gambia and is almost universally spoken. French occupies a similar position in Senegal. In addition, the region has more than 10 indigenous languages. The most widespread is Wolof.

USEFUL WORDS AND PHRASES

Hello *Sala maleikum* (this is, in fact, Arabic)
Good morning *Jamm ga fanan*
Good night *Fanan jamm*
How are you? *Nanga def?*
I am well *Magni fi rek; Jamba rek* (used in the Gambia)
How is your family? *Ana waa keur ge?*
They are well *Nyunge fe*
Are you well? *Ba dara metee wula?*
Thank you *Jerejef*
Yes *Waow*
No *Deedeet*
Come *Kai*
Come here *Kai fi*
I would like/I want *Dama buga*
I want to eat *Dama buga lek*
To eat *Lek*
To drink *Naan*
Breakfast *Ndeki*
Lunch *Agn*
Dinner *Rer*
To go *Dem*
To come *Nyo*
I am going (= Goodbye) *Mangi dem*
I shall come back
Dina nyo at; dina delussi at
The day *Betiek*
The night *Gudi*
Now *Leegi*
Today *Tey*
Yesterday *Demb*
Tomorrow *Elek; souba*

See you tomorrow *Be soube*
Till next time *Be beneen yon*
Bread *Mburu*
Water *Ndoh*
Meat *Yap*
Fish *Jen*
Just a little *Tutti rek*
I am hot *Dama tange*
I am cold *Dama sedde*
I am thirsty *Dama maar*
I am tired *Dama sonne*
It is hot *Dafa tange*
It is cold *Dafa tsedde*
Where? *Ana?*
Here *Fi la*
There *Fale la*
Here *Fi*
There *Fofu*
Where is the market/hotel?
Ana marsé/hotel?
Do you speak English?
Degg nge Anglais (English)?
I don't speak Wolof *Degguma Wolof*
I don't understand *Degguma*
How much? *Nyata?*
How much is this? *Bi, nyata le?*
It is too expensive *Dafa jafé*
Lower the price, please *Wanyi ko*
Good (it's good) *Baakhne*
It's bad (no good) *Baahul*
Wait! *Haaral!*
Go straight on *Talal*
Where is the restaurant?
Ana restaurant bi?
I want to get down here *Fi laay wach*
I have had enough to eat, thanks
Suur naa

Money

Slightly different from numbers
5 CFA francs (Senegal): *derem*

10 CFA	*nyar derem*
15 CFA	*nyet derem*
20 CFA	*nyent derem*
25 CFA	*juroom i derem*
30 CFA	*juroom benn derem* (=6 times 5 etc.)
50 CFA	*fouk*
100 CFA	*nyar fouk*
150 CFA	*fan wer*
500 CFA	*teemeer*
1000 CFA	*nyar teemeer*
5000 CFA	*jooni*

She (it) **is pretty** *Rafet ne*
It is good (of food) *Neehne*
My friend *Suma harit*
Give me *Joh me*
Sell me *Jai me*
Put it here *Bai ko fi*
Bring it *Indi ko*
Bring me a beer
Indi me beer (*bière* in French)
Take this *Amm*
Excuse me *Baal me*
I am going to rest *Damai dem nopelu*
My wife *Suma jigeen*
My husband *Suma jekeur*
Tea (Senegalese style) *Ataya*
Money *Halis*
I haven't any money *Anuma halis*
I have a headache *Suma bop dey meti*
I have a stomach ache *Sume biir dey meti*
Charity has already been made (a useful phrase to get rid of beggars)
Sarak be ague na

Numbers

1	*Benn*
2	*nyar*
3	*nyet*
4	*nyent*
5	*juroom*
6	*juroom (ak) benn*
7	*juroom (ak) nyar*
8	*juroom (ak) nyet*
9	*juroom (ak) nyent*
10	*Fouk*
20	*nyar four*
30	*fan wer*
40	*nyent fouk*
50	*juroom fouk*
100	*teemeer*

Further Reading

General

Gambia

Very little has been written specifically about the Gambia in English and virtually nothing modern is in print, apart from a number of guidebooks which include the country in a wider region, e.g. West Africa as a whole. This is a small selection, beginning with a good paperback edition of the 17th-century explorer Mungo Park's excellent account of his perilous journeys.

Park, Mungo. **Travels into the Interior of Africa**. Eland, London and Hippocrene. NY, 1983.

Rice, Berkeley. **Enter Gambia, the Birth of an Improbable Nation**. Angus and Robertson, London, 1986.

Sonko-Goodwin, Patience. **Ethnic Groups of the Senegambia**. Book Production Unit, Banjul, 1985.

Edberg, Etienne. **A Naturalist's Guide to the Gambia**. J.G. Sanders, Sweden, 1982.

Haley, Alex. **Roots**. Various editions, from 1976.

Other Insight Guides

There are almost 200 in the Insight Guides series which cover every continent. Titles focusing on Africa include: *South Africa, Namibia, Kenya, East African Wildlife, Morocco* and *Tunisia*.

ART & PHOTO CREDITS

Agence Hoa-Qui/Michel Renaudeau 14/15, 16/17, 18/19, 20/21, 22, 27, 34, 35, 37, 44/45, 46, 47, 49, 50, 51, 52/53, 54, 55, 57, 62/3, 66/7, 68, 69, 70, 71, 72, 73, 76, 77, 78L, 78R, 79L, 79R, 80, 81, 84, 86, 87, 88, 89, 90/91, 92, 94, 95, 96/97, 98/99, 100, 101, 102/103, 106, 107, 108, 109, 110, 111, 112/113, 114, 115, 117, 118/119, 120/121, 123, 124, 125, 127, 128/129, 130/131, 132/133, 138, 141, 142, 143R, 144/145, 147, 150L, 151, 154, 160, 161, 163, 164, 165, 170, 174/175, 176/177, 178/179, 180/181, 182, 184, 185, 188, 189, 190, 191, 192, 194, 195R, 196/197, 198, 200, 201, 202, 203,
204/205, 206, 207, 208, 209, 210, 211, 212, 213, 214/215, 216, 218, 219, 220, 221, 222/223, 224, 225, 226, 227, 228, 229, 230, 231, 232, 233, 234, 235, 236/237, 238/239, 240, 241, 242, 243, 245, 246, 247, 248/249, 250, 254, 255, 256, 257, 258/259, 260, 261, 262, 263, 264, 265, 266, 267, 268/269, 270/271, 272, 273, 274, 275, 278, 279, 280, 281, 282/283, 284, 285, 286, 287, 288, 289, 290, 291L, 291R, 292, 293, 294
Allsport Pictures 116
Associated Press 58/59
Andy G.Gravette 143L, 159, 251
Robert Harding 74/5, 150R
Louvre Museum 36

Mary Evans Picture Library 24, 26, 28/29, 30, 32, 33, 38/39, 40, 42, 43, 48
Kim Naylor 85
Susan Cunningham 8/9, 155
Susan Pierres 122, 126, 146, 152, 153, 156/157, 158, 165, 166, 168, 169, 171, 172, 173
Spectrum Colour Library 104/105, 244
Tony Stone Worldwide 64/5, 195L
Topham Picture Source 9, 56, 82/83, 136, 139, 162

Maps Berndtson & Berndtson
© 1999 Apa Publications GmbH & Co.
Verlag KG (Singapore branch)

Cartographic Editor **Zoë Goodwin**
Production **Stuart A Everitt**
Design Consultant **Carlotta Junger**
Picture Research **Hilary Genin**

Index

The Insight Approach

The book you are holding is part of the world's largest range of guidebooks. Its purpose is to help you have the most valuable travel experience possible, and we try to achieve this by providing not only information about countries, regions and cities but also genuine insight into their history, culture, institutions and people.

Since the first Insight Guide – to Bali – was published in 1970, the series has been dedicated to the proposition that, with insight into a country's people and culture, visitors can both enhance their own experience and be accepted more easily by their hosts. Now, in a world where ethnic hostilities and nationalist conflicts are all too common, such attempts to increase understanding between peoples are more important than ever.

Insight Guides:
Essentials for understanding

Because a nation's past holds the key to its present, each Insight Guide kicks off with lively history chapters. These are followed by magazine-style essays on culture and daily life. This essential background information gives readers the necessary context for using the main Places section, with its comprehensive run-down on things worth seeing and doing.

Finally, a listings section contains all the information you'll need on travel, hotels, restaurants and opening times.

As far as possible, we rely on local writers and specialists to ensure that information is authoritative. The pictures, for which Insight Guides have become so celebrated, are just as important. Our photojournalistic approach aims not only to illustrate a destination but also to communicate visually and directly to readers life as it is lived by the locals. The series has grown to almost 200 titles.

Compact Guides:
The "great little guides"

As invaluable as such background information is, it isn't always fun to carry an Insight Guide through a crowded souk or up a church tower. Could we, readers asked, distil the key reference material into a slim volume for on-the-spot use?

Our response was to design Compact Guides as an entirely new series, with original text carefully cross-referenced to detailed maps and more than 200 photographs. In essence, they're miniature encyclopedias, concise and comprehensive, displaying reliable and up-to-date information in an accessible way. There are almost 100 titles.

Pocket Guides:
A local host in book form

However wide-ranging the information in a book, human beings still value the personal touch. Our editors are often asked the same questions. Where do *you* go to eat? What do *you* think is the best beach? What would *you* recommend if I have only three days? We invited our local correspondents to act as "substitute hosts" by revealing their preferred walks and trips, listing restaurants they go to and structuring a visit into a series of timed itineraries.

The result: our Pocket Guides, complete with full-size fold-out maps. These 100-plus titles help readers plan a trip precisely, particularly if their time is short.

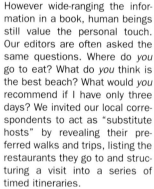

Exploring with Insight:
A valuable travel experience

In conjunction with co-publishers all over the world, we print in up to 10 languages, from German to Chinese, from Danish to Russian. But our aim remains simple: to enhance your travel experience by combining our expertise in guidebook publishing with the on-the-spot knowledge of our correspondents.

66 I was first drawn to the Insight Guides by the excellent "Nepal" volume. I can think of no book which so effectively captures the essence of a country. Out of these pages leaped the Nepal I know – the captivating charm of a people and their culture. I've since discovered and enjoyed the entire Insight Guide series. Each volume deals with a country in the same sensitive depth, which is nowhere more evident than in the superb photography. 99

Sir Edmund Hillary

Insight Guides

Alaska
Alsace
Amazon Wildlife
American Southwest
Amsterdam
Argentina
Atlanta
Athens
Australia
Austria
Bahamas
Bali
Baltic States
Bangkok
Barbados
Barcelona
Bay of Naples
Beijing
Belgium
Belize
Berlin
Bermuda
Boston
Brazil
Brittany
Brussels
Budapest
Buenos Aires
Burgundy
Burma (Myanmar)
Cairo
Calcutta
California
Canada
Caribbean
Catalonia
Channel Islands
Chicago
Chile
China
Cologne
Continental Europe
Corsica
Costa Rica
Crete
Crossing America
Cuba
Cyprus
Czech & Slovak Republics
Delhi, Jaipur, Agra
Denmark
Dresden
Dublin
Düsseldorf
East African Wildlife
East Asia
Eastern Europe
Ecuador
Edinburgh
Egypt
Finland
Florence
Florida
France
Frankfurt
French Riviera
Gambia & Senegal
Germany
Glasgow

Gran Canaria
Great Barrier Reef
Great Britain
Greece
Greek Islands
Hamburg
Hawaii
Hong Kong
Hungary
Iceland
India
India's Western Himalaya
Indian Wildlife
Indonesia
Ireland
Israel
Istanbul
Italy
Jamaica
Japan
Java
Jerusalem
Jordan
Kathmandu
Kenya
Korea
Lisbon
Loire Valley
London
Los Angeles
Madeira
Madrid
Malaysia
Mallorca & Ibiza
Malta
Marine Life in the South China Sea
Melbourne
Mexico
Mexico City
Miami
Montreal
Morocco
Moscow
Munich
Namibia
Native America
Nepal
Netherlands
New England
New Orleans
New York City
New York State
New Zealand
Nile
Normandy
Northern California
Northern Spain
Norway
Oman & the UAE
Oxford
Old South
Pacific Northwest
Pakistan
Paris
Peru
Philadelphia
Philippines
Poland
Portugal
Prague

Provence
Puerto Rico
Rajasthan
Rhine
Rio de Janeiro
Rockies
Rome
Russia
St Petersburg
San Francisco
Sardinia
Scotland
Seattle
Sicily
Singapore
South Africa
South America
South Asia
South India
South Tyrol
Southeast Asia
Southeast Asia Wildlife
Southern California
Southern Spain
Spain
Sri Lanka
Sweden
Switzerland
Sydney
Taiwan
Tenerife
Texas
Thailand
Tokyo
Trinidad & Tobago
Tunisia
Turkey
Turkish Coast
Tuscany
Umbria
US National Parks East
US National Parks West
Vancouver
Venezuela
Venice
Vienna
Vietnam
Wales
Washington DC
Waterways of Europe
Wild West
Yemen

Insight Pocket Guides

Aegean Islands★
Algarve★
Alsace
Amsterdam★
Athens★
Atlanta★
Bahamas★
Baja Peninsula★
Bali★
Bali Bird Walks
Bangkok★
Barbados★
Barcelona★
Bavaria★
Beijing★
Berlin★

Bermuda★
Bhutan★
Boston★
British Columbia★
Brittany★
Brussels★
Budapest & Surroundings★
Canton★
Chiang Mai★
Chicago★
Corsica★
Costa Blanca★
Costa Brava★
Costa del Sol/Marbella★
Costa Rica★
Crete★
Denmark★
Fiji★
Florence★
Florida★
Florida Keys★
French Riviera★
Gran Canaria★
Hawaii★
Hong Kong★
Hungary
Ibiza★
Ireland★
Ireland's Southwest★
Israel★
Istanbul★
Jakarta★
Jamaica★
Kathmandu Bikes & Hikes★
Kenya★
Kuala Lumpur★
Lisbon★
Loire Valley★
London★
Macau
Madrid★
Malacca
Maldives
Mallorca★
Malta★
Mexico City★
Miami★
Milan★
Montreal★
Morocco★
Moscow
Munich★
Nepal★
New Delhi
New Orleans★
New York City★
New Zealand★
Northern California★
Oslo/Bergen★
Paris★
Penang★
Phuket★
Prague★
Provence★
Puerto Rico★
Quebec★
Rhodes★
Rome★
Sabah★

St Petersburg★
San Francisco★
Sardinia
Scotland★
Seville★
Seychelles★
Sicily★
Sikkim
Singapore★
Southeast England
Southern California★
Southern Spain★
Sri Lanka★
Sydney★
Tenerife★
Thailand★
Tibet★
Toronto★
Tunisia★
Turkish Coast★
Tuscany★
Venice★
Vienna★
Vietnam★
Yogyakarta
Yucatan Peninsula★

★ = Insight Pocket Guides with Pull out Maps

Insight Compact Guides

Algarve
Amsterdam
Bahamas
Bali
Bangkok
Barbados
Barcelona
Beijing
Belgium
Berlin
Brittany
Brussels
Budapest
Burgundy
Copenhagen
Costa Brava
Costa Rica
Crete
Cyprus
Czech Republic
Denmark
Dominican Republic
Dublin
Egypt
Finland
Florence
Gran Canaria
Greece
Holland
Hong Kong
Ireland
Israel
Italian Lakes
Italian Riviera
Jamaica
Jerusalem
Lisbon
Madeira
Mallorca
Malta

Milan
Moscow
Munich
Normandy
Norway
Paris
Poland
Portugal
Prague
Provence
Rhodes
Rome
St Petersburg
Salzburg
Singapore
Switzerland
Sydney
Tenerife
Thailand
Turkey
Turkish Coast
Tuscany

UK regional titles:
Bath & Surroundings
Cambridge & East Anglia
Cornwall
Cotswolds
Devon & Exmoor
Edinburgh
Lake District
London
New Forest
North York Moors
Northumbria
Oxford
Peak District
Scotland
Scottish Highlands
Shakespeare Country
Snowdonia
South Downs
York
Yorkshire Dales

USA regional titles:
Boston
Cape Cod
Chicago
Florida
Florida Keys
Hawaii: Maui
Hawaii: Oahu
Las Vegas
Los Angeles
Martha's Vineyard & Nantucket
New York
San Francisco
Washington D.C.
Venice
Vienna
West of Ireland